The Basic Principles of the Business Rule A

- *Rules should be written and made explicit.*
- *Rules should be expressed in plain language.*
- *Rules should exist independent of procedures and workflows.*
- *Rules should build on facts, and facts should build on concepts as represented by terms.*
- *Rules should guide or influence behavior in desired ways.*

- *Rules should be motivated by identifiable and important business factors.*
- *Rules should be accessible to authorized parties.*
- *Rules should be single-sourced.*
- *Rules should be specified directly by those people who have relevant knowledge.*
- *Rules should be managed.*

Principles of
the Business
Rule Approach

Addison-Wesley Information Technology Series
Capers Jones and David S. Linthicum, Consulting Editors

The information technology (IT) industry is in the public eye now more than ever before because of a number of major issues in which software technology and national policies are closely related. As the use of software expands, there is a continuing need for business and software professionals to stay current with the state of the art in software methodologies and technologies. The goal of the Addison-Wesley Information Technology Series is to cover any and all topics that affect the IT community. These books illustrate and explore how information technology can be aligned with business practices to achieve business goals and support business imperatives. Addison-Wesley has created this innovative series to empower you with the benefits of the industry experts' experience.

For more information point your browser to http://www.awprofessional.com/itseries

Sid Adelman, Larissa Terpeluk Moss, *Data Warehouse Project Management.* ISBN: 0-201-61635-1

Sid Adelman, Joyce Bischoff, Jill Dyché, Douglas Hackney, Sean Ivoghli, Chuck Kelley, David Marco, Larissa Moss, and Clay Rehm, *Impossible Data Warehouse Situations: Solutions from the Experts.* ISBN: 0-201-76033-9

Wayne Applehans, Alden Globe, and Greg Laugero, *Managing Knowledge: A Practical Web-Based Approach.* ISBN: 0-201-43315-X

David Leon Clark, *Enterprise Security: The Manager's Defense Guide.* ISBN: 0-201-71972-X

Frank P. Coyle, *XML, Web Services, and the Data Revolution.* ISBN: 0-201-77641-3

Kevin Dick, *XML, Second Edition: A Manager's Guide.* ISBN: 0-201-77006-7

Jill Dyché, *e-Data: Turning Data into Information with Data Warehousing.* ISBN: 0-201-65780-5

Jill Dyché, *The CRM Handbook: A Business Guide to Customer Relationship Management.* ISBN: 0-201-73062-6

Patricia L. Ferdinandi, *A Requirements Pattern: Succeeding in the Internet Economy.* ISBN: 0-201-73826-0

Nick V. Flor, *Web Business Engineering: Using Offline Activites to Drive Internet Strategies.* ISBN: 0-201-60468-X

David Garmus and David Herron, *Function Point Analysis: Measurement Practices for Successful Software Projects.* ISBN: 0-201-69944-3

John Harney, *Application Service Providers (ASPs): A Manager's Guide.* ISBN: 0-201-72659-9

International Function Point Users Group, *IT Measurement: Practical Advice from the Experts.* ISBN: 0-201-74158-X

Capers Jones, *Software Assessments, Benchmarks, and Best Practices.* ISBN: 0-201-48542-7

Ravi Kalakota and Marcia Robinson, *e-Business 2.0: Roadmap for Success.* ISBN: 0-201-72165-1

Greg Laugero and Alden Globe, *Enterprise Content Services: Connecting Information and Profitability.* ISBN: 0-201-73016-2

David S. Linthicum, *Enterprise Application Integration.* ISBN: 0-201-61583-5

David S. Linthicum, *B2B Application Integration: e-Business-Enable Your Enterprise.* ISBN: 0-201-70936-8

Sergio Lozinsky, *Enterprise-Wide Software Solutions: Integration Strategies and Practices.* ISBN: 0-201-30971-8

Larissa T. Moss and Shaku Atre, *Business Intelligence Roadmap: The Complete Project Lifecycle for Decision-Support Applications.* ISBN: 0-201-78420-3

Bud Porter-Roth, *Request for Proposal: A Guide to Effective RFP Development.* ISBN: 0-201-77575-1

Ronald G. Ross, *Principles of the Business Rule Approach.* ISBN: 0-201-78893-4

Mai-lan Tomsen, *Killer Content: Strategies for Web Content and E-Commerce.* ISBN: 0-201-65786-4

Karl E. Wiegers, *Peer Reviews in Software: A Practical Guide.* ISBN: 0-201-73485-0

Ralph R. Young, *Effective Requirements Practices.* ISBN: 0-201-70912-0

Bill Zoellick, *CyberRegs: A Business Guide to Web Property, Privacy, and Patents.* ISBN: 0-201-72230-5

Principles of the Business Rule Approach

Ronald G. Ross

✦ Addison-Wesley

Boston • San Francisco • New York • Toronto • Montreal
London • Munich • Paris • Madrid
Capetown • Sydney • Tokyo • Singapore • Mexico City

The publisher offers discounts on this book when ordered in quantity for bulk purchases and special sales. For more information, please contact:

 U.S. Corporate and Government Sales
 (800) 382-3419
 corpsales@pearsontechgroup.com

For sales outside of the U.S., please contact:

 International Sales
 (317) 581-3793
 international@pearsontechgroup.com

Visit Addison-Wesley on the Web: www.awprofessional.com

Library of Congress Cataloging-in-Publication Data

Ross, Ronald G.
  Principles of the business rules approach / Ronald G. Ross.
    p. cm.
  Includes bibliographical references and index.
  ISBN 0-201-78893-4 (pbk. : alk. paper)
  1. Business—Databases—Management.   2. Database management.   3. Management information systems.   4. Information technology—Management.   I. Title: Business rules approach.   II. Title.

HD30.2 .R673 2003
658.4'013—dc21   2002151451

ISBN: 0-201-78893-4
Text printed on recycled paper
1 2 3 4 5 6 7 8 9 10—MA—0706050403
First printing, February 2003

To Gladys S.W. Lam, business colleague and friend,
and originator of many of the applied ideas in this book.

Contents

CHAPTER 10   **Functional Categories of Rules: The BRS Rule Classification Scheme 141**

CHAPTER 11   **Sentence Patterns for Rule Statements: The RuleSpeak Templates 145**

CHAPTER 12   **Expressing Business Logic by Using Decision Tables: The RuleSpeak Approach 161**

PART IV **WHAT IS THE BUSINESS RULE APPROACH?:
READINGS FOR IT PROFESSIONALS   177**

Preface

The driver for business systems should always be business need. Business workers should be involved in expressing this need in very direct, concrete ways. Applying these principles in practice means taking a fresh approach to business systems that will profoundly affect the roles of both business professionals and information technology (IT) professionals.

This fresh approach can be called *business analysis* and its basic deliverable a *business model*. Unfortunately, these terms are often used very loosely. Many system developers think their deliverables qualify as business models, but they do not. Rather than try to explain here (it does require some background), I will leave that topic for Part I. For now, let's simply call the fresh approach *business-driven* and move on.

A basic ingredient of the business-driven approach—a very exciting one—is *business rules*. Before continuing, let me clarify something. We could certainly talk about business rules without necessarily discussing everything else needed for a business-driven approach. In other words, we *could* discuss business rules separately.

But why would we want to? If business need is the driving factor for business systems, then both the business-driven approach and business rules should be put on the table and served together. That way the business can achieve the very best business solutions to the challenges it faces in the 21st century. In a nutshell, that describes the basic mind-set of this book.

That brings me to the audience, or more accurately the audiences, for this book. In general terms, there are three audiences: business professionals, IT professionals, and academics. In today's world, there are significant gaps between these three communities—and that in itself is part of the problem. To create the best business solutions possible, these three communities must come closer together in common purpose and approach. This book helps show the way.

About Technology

I will say a few words to each of these three communities in a moment, but first let me say a word about technology. Because I believe so strongly that business systems should be driven by business need, I have purposely avoided discussing technology (with some difficulty!) throughout the book. But the topic certainly does deserve comment, so let me talk about it briefly.

We are on the verge of a huge new wave of technological innovation focused on the knowledge capabilities of the business. Think of business rules (which I collectively call *business logic*) as a first—and in many respects relatively modest—step in that direction.

The plain truth is that such technology has never been a significant part of mainstream business IT. Expert systems made a minor foray into that realm in the 1980s but had very little impact. There were many reasons why, but perhaps the most important was technological. Computing architectures then (and since then until recently) were basically monolithic, and they provided no easy way to accommodate "outside" services.

Without going into detail, that fundamental barrier is now being eliminated, and plug-in services are becoming easier and easier to incorporate. And what better service to incorporate than direct knowledge support?

Knowledge support does sound a bit abstract. There are several terms in current usage for such a service, including *rule engine* and *decision management platform*. In Part V of this book, I suggest *business logic server*. By whatever name, I predict without hesitation that such services will be part of all major business software platforms within a mere matter of years.

To many, this technology will seem like a tidal wave from nowhere. But that's not really true. In fact, the theoretical foundations of this new technol-

ogy go back many, many years, again as discussed in Part V. Commercial offerings date to the mid-1980s; applied research goes back well before that.
Refer to the special boxed item for a brief review of where this technology
stands at present.

> **Business Logic Technology: Near-Term Directions**
>
> In the near future, commercial technology servicing business logic is likely to
> be offered in several different ways, including the following.
>
> - *Supported as a stand-alone component:* In this case, the business can
>   acquire a best-fit or best-of-breed package and incorporate it into its
>   computing architecture as appropriate.
> - *Coupled with a workflow engine:* This powerful combination features
>   automated process management with coordination and decision
>   making provided by the business logic technology. The result per-
>   mits not only more sophisticated workflow control but automation
>   of selected decision-making tasks as well.
> - *Bundled into other packaged software:* Many other kinds of software
>   capabilities, including customer relationship management (CRM)
>   and enterprise resource planning (ERP), provide natural niches for
>   business logic technology, which will undoubtedly be exploited to
>   the full extent their architectures permit.
>
> And the list goes on. A big question mark for the future concerns database
> management systems (DBMSs). In Part V, I argue that in the long run,
> database support should be integrated within a business logic server.

Again, our focus in this book is not technology, but rather where do the
business rules *come from?* That brings us to the business rule approach.

About the Business Rule Approach

Like the technology, the business rule approach did not suddenly appear
from nowhere. In fact, the core concepts (as described in Part II) date to the
early to mid-1990s, and many of the related techniques and methodologies
(including those in Part III) have been thoroughly battle-tested by pioneering

organizations during the late 1990s and early 2000s. (The same is true, incidentally, about business-driven approaches.) So what I talk about in this book is not unproven theory or academic conjecture but pragmatic, real-world stuff.

The interesting and perhaps unique thing about the business rule approach is that it did *not* arise as a response to any emerging new class of software tools—knowledge-oriented or otherwise. (Again, the same is true for business-driven approaches.)

Rather, the business rule approach is a real-world, grassroots movement whose driving force is business success, not technology. It arose from the vision of dedicated professionals with many years of experience in the trials and challenges of business software. Their goal: to offer companies the best possible approach to developing business solutions involving automated systems.

To Business Professionals

For that reason, it is appropriate that I address members of the business community first. To repeat, this is not a book about technology, but rather one about business opportunity. The key question should therefore be why knowing about business rules is important as a business proposition.

So exactly what is the value proposition of business rules? Part I provides the answer, but let me give you a short version here, then invite you to read on. Refer to the special boxed item.

> ### What Problems Does the Business Rule Approach Address?
>
> **Ad hoc rules:** Most businesses have no logical approach for defining their business rules. As a result, business workers often make up the rules as they go along. This leads to confusion, contradiction, and operational inefficiency. After-the-fact resolution of these problems wastes time and resources and causes frustration for customers and staff alike. The larger the organization, the bigger the problem. Also, since many business rules involve monetary

transactions (for example, whether a customer should be given a discount, and if so, how much), this problem can also directly affect the bottom line.

Business rule solution: A structured approach helps you think through rules before the fact.

Miscommunication: Misunderstanding of key business concepts inevitably results in miscommunication. Does *preferred customer discount* mean the same across all departments? If not, what are the differences? What rules apply? Do these rules differ for different areas of the business? Are the rules consistent?

Business rule solution: A clear set of concepts provides a foundation on which rules can be directly based.

Inaccessible rules: Finding out what rules apply to a given business situation often involves an open-ended search through multiple sources. It is not uncommon in the end to resort to the application source code. Pursuing rules in this fashion is time-consuming, inefficient, inaccurate, and frustrating.

Business rule solution: A way to manage business rules provides direct accessibility.

Massive differentiation: Many businesses seek to support highly individualized relationships with growing numbers of customers and other partners for ever more complex products or services. How can businesses massively differentiate between business parties and, at the very same time, conduct each business transaction faster, more accurately, and at ever lower costs?

Business rule solution: A rule-based approach featuring rapid development and deployment of rules supports differentiation.

The need to keep up to speed: Rapid change, at an ever faster pace, is a fact of life. In the Internet age, people expect almost instantaneous implementation of changes. How can line workers consumed with day-to-day activities ever hope to keep up?

Business rule solution: Real-time delivery of business logic to knowledge workers as errors actually occur creates a seamless, never-ending, self-training environment.

Knowledge walking out the door: By and large, baby boomers created much of the operational business capacity and operational systems we see in place in larger organizations today. Much of the related knowledge still sits in their heads—and nowhere else. What will happen when they retire? On a smaller scale, people with vital operational knowledge walk out the door almost every day.

> *Business rule solution:* A systematic way of capturing, documenting, and retaining the business rules prevents the loss of knowledge when people leave.

Part I also discusses what business-driven approaches are about. From a business perspective, the business rule approach fits hand-in-glove with them. Combined, they are potent indeed. I hope Part I will prove so compelling in this regard that you will read on. I have tried to use a readable, nontechnical style throughout the book, so there is much to be gained from going as deep into the book as you care to read.

Part II explains the basic ideas of the business rule approach using a broad analogy to the human body. Continuing from there (or skipping ahead if you choose), Part III provides a comprehensive language, called *BRS RuleSpeak*, to capture and express your business rules. You will find that material informative and in places perhaps entertaining.

Part IV is officially directed toward IT professionals, but it is actually a continuation of, or more accurately a different perspective on, the material in Part I. I believe it is very important for business professionals and IT professionals to speak with the same voice; this material should help your organization achieve it. By the way, the first chapter of Part IV is the only other place in the book where I talk about business-driven approaches directly.

To IT Professionals

Just a word about business-driven approaches first: I believe they are closely aligned with the architecture-based or model-based development strategies now emerging in the industry. In particular, a business-driven approach provides an excellent front end for these strategies in the form of the business model. A business model represents a top-down, multi-aspect blueprint of the business whose contents are driven by business professionals. That's a great starting point for system design and development of an application system (or deployment of an application package). These ideas are developed in Parts I and IV of the book.

If your interest centers specifically on business rules, you can concentrate on Parts II and III. You will also not want to miss important portions of Part IV devoted to rule management, rule capture, and data design.

The main objective for all this material is to help you gain a deep understanding of what business rules are about and to enable you to make them a comfortable part of your professional toolkit. I think you will be quite excited by the powerful ideas and techniques that await you.

To Academics

By *academics*, I do not mean only those readers who happen to be in universities or research labs. I mean any serious student of logical systems—*systems* here in the sense of theory, not applications. I also mean those who are just plain intellectually curious. Part V is aimed toward all such readers.

Part V provides answers to some of the big questions of business rules, such as their basis in formal theory—the predicate logic. You should not let that intimidate you. Part V is written as a tutorial so that the ideas are as accessible as possible to everyone. At the same time, I anticipate that this material will provide the basis for continuing research, some of which has already commenced.

The bottom line is this: You know you are on to something really powerful when good theory and successful practices converge. That convergence is exactly what has happened with business rules, and it is a very exciting time to be in the field!

PART I

The Business Problem: Why Business Rules?

Readings for Business Professionals

Overview

I will keep this Overview of Part I brief. If you have just finished reading the Preface, you already know where we are headed. If not, the content presented here will speak largely for itself.

The material in this part appears as a set of informal readings, each packaging a key insight about the business rule approach. These readings are organized into the following chapters.[1]

- Chapter 1 presents just enough information about the basic ideas of business rules so that we can move quickly into discussion of their business application in the chapters that follow.
- Chapter 2 discusses how business rules are key to many of the most exciting trends in business today. Indeed, I believe business rules make certain changes in the business landscape inevitable. This chapter identifies what these opportunities are and how you can stay on top of them.
- Chapter 3 revisits the idea presented in the Preface that automated knowledge (business logic) services will rapidly become part of mainstream information technology (IT) practices. This chapter provides a quick look at the role business rules will play in that change.

---

1. In some places in these chapters I describe practices and experiences shared by my colleagues and myself. In such instances, *we* refers to the Principals of Business Rule Solutions, LLC.

- Chapter 4 discusses the business-driven approach (mentioned in the Preface) for building better business solutions. Business rules are just one element of that approach. If you are interested in pragmatic yet innovative ways in which IT projects can be aligned more directly with business goals, be sure to have a look at Chapter 4.

CHAPTER ONE

What's This about Business Rules?

The Problem and the Fix in a Nutshell

A Telltale E-Mail Trail

The Case for Business Rules

The brief series of e-mails reproduced here illustrates some of the snarls in day-to-day tactical decision making that plague most organizations today. The overall problem is so pervasive—*so* big—that it can be difficult even to see at first. It is so much part of our everyday way of doing business that we tend to accept it as a given and simply work around it. (The exchange presented here is a real one, altered only to disguise the identities of those involved.)

As illustrated in the exchange, we often discover holes in operational policy only *after* it is too late to do much about them, at least without significant expense or loss of face. Is there a solution? Yes, there is—the business rule approach.

What are *business rules*? You probably have a pretty good intuitive sense of them already, at least from a business perspective. For now, let's simply characterize a business rule as follows.

 Business Rule

A directive intended to influence or guide business behavior.

3

Re: The GenTech Sale

The parties involved in the following e-mail exchange:

Tracy, accounting staff member
Ken, the product manager
Glenda, the sales manager

At 08:52 AM July 8 Ken wrote:

Tracy,

Yesterday we received the 2nd Qtr Sales Report and Income Statement. You listed the revenue from our 6/5 sale to GenTech as $14,358.00. How was this amount determined?

I know GenTech attended our annual conference, and since they initially saw the product there, they got the special 20% conference discount. Since they purchased two copies, shouldn't the total be $15,587.00 ($9,592 for the first copy under the special 20% discount, and $5,995 for the second copy)?

Ken

At 10:32 AM July 8 Tracy wrote:

Ken,

Since GenTech attended the conference, we extended them the special 20% conference discount on *both* copies. So the total was $14,358.00 ($9,592 for the first copy under the special 20% discount, and $4,796 for the second copy under the special 20% discount). Hope you don't have a problem with this(?).

Tracy

At 03:25 PM July 8 Ken wrote:

Tracy,

My understanding was that only the *first* copy of any sale was to be offered at the special conference discount. Subsequent copies are already being deeply discounted a full 50%!!

Unfortunately, this is now water under the bridge as far as these first two copies for GenTech goes. However, they have already committed to buying another 8 or 9 copies. THERE IS TO BE NO FURTHER DISCOUNT ON THESE COPIES. Have you received their new purchase order yet? Unfortunately, they are probably under the impression that they will get the conference discount on these additional copies too. I'll have to touch base with Glenda so she can straighten all this out with them.

We need to get our act together before closing more new sales. What is the specific intent of offering a discount to conference attendees? It gets a little nebulous when we say "conference attendees receive a discount." Does the discount extend to any organization/person the attendee is associated with? Does the purchase need to be made on the spot to qualify? Does the discount have an expiration date? Are the discounted purchases limited to one per person?

These are just some of the questions that come to mind. If some rules aren't established here this is going to bite us again. GenTech placed the order more than 3 months *after* the conference. Since they are buying a relatively expensive product, it isn't reasonable to expect them to purchase it on the spot. Having said that, there should be an EXPIRATION DATE for the conference discount. I would suggest 30 to 60 days after the conference. And in the future we should make it clear the discount applies only to the first copy, *not* to subsequent copies.

Let's establish some good guidelines so we are all on the same page. We want to avoid any future misunderstandings and maintain the good will of our customers.

Ken

At 05:15 PM July 8 Glenda wrote:

Ken,

I've been going back and forth with GenTech over this for a good while, but after making a few other concessions, I think the fires are out on this one for now.

I agree fully with your concerns. Next time we offer something like this, let's spend a few minutes thinking it through first. Shouldn't take all that long—you came up with a great list of questions to consider. I'm *sure* that would take a lot less time than all this has!

Glenda

We need not dwell on more precise definitions for now—there is plenty of opportunity for that in the rest of the book.[1] More important is why your business should focus on business rules. I will answer that question in this part of the book.

---

1. For an in-depth discussion of definitions for *business rule*, refer to What Is a Business Rule? in Chapter 13.

When Is a Door Not a Door?

The Business Rule Difference

One of the interesting things about consulting with different organizations on business rules and publishing a journal[2] on that subject is that a lot of really silly rules cross my desk. I think you might enjoy some of these, so I have included several small selections in Part III.

One reader recently forwarded a rule that raises some interesting questions. He observed that in his apartment building the doors to the stairwells all have signs on them that say, "Doors must be kept closed at all times." His question was, "Is a door you must never open really a door?" If the rule is followed religiously, he noted, the door might as well be considered part of the wall.

DOORS MUST
BE KEPT
CLOSED AT
ALL TIMES

---

2. *Business Rules Journal;* see the Web site at *http://www.BRCommunity.com.*

Before addressing that tongue-in-cheek question, let's do some analysis on this rule. I think we can safely assume that the rule as stated is actually a shorthand form. A more complete and accurate version might be, "You may use this door for entry and exit, but it must be closed behind you." If we wanted to be very complete, we might explain the basic motivation for the rule by adding, "This is a fire door."

Further analysis of this simple rule reveals some fundamental ideas of the business rule approach.

- The rule was posted, that is, written down. Why? The answer lies in the motivation for the rule. Its purpose is to protect the inhabitants of the building against the dangers of fire. *When a rule becomes important enough, it is always written down.*
- The rule was written in plain English. If the rule were difficult to understand or encoded in such a way that many of the inhabitants could not readily interpret it, the rule would not serve its purpose very well. *A rule important enough to write down is worth writing plainly.*
- A procedure for this situation is not really needed. We could write one, of course, but in this case it would probably be trivial. ("Approach door; grasp doorknob with hand; twist doorknob in clockwise direction; pull/ push carefully. . . .") Nonetheless, the rule is still crucial. *Rules can exist independent of procedures.*
- This rule—like all rules—serves to shape behavior. The posting of the rule reminds inhabitants, staff, and others to close the door, and presumably they are therefore less likely to forget or perhaps even block the door open. *The purpose of a rule is always to guide or influence behavior in desired ways.*
- The rule serves a purpose. It is neither frivolous nor arbitrary. Fire is a deadly risk, and all reasonable measures must be taken to protect against it. *Business rules never arise in a vacuum; there are always identifiable and important business factors motivating them.*
- The rule was posted right where the action is—that is, where actual use of the door occurs. This proximity to the action helps ensure that people follow the rule as events actually unfold. *The best way to ensure rules are followed is to get them right in front of people at the exact point where the guidance is relevant.*
- The rule is undoubtedly part of a larger body of regulatory fire code rules for buildings. Even though the rule might be posted thousands of times

for enforcement purposes, these postings arise from a single source. This ensures consistency. *If rules are important enough to be enforced, they are important enough to be single-sourced.*

- The body of fire codes was undoubtedly produced by experts experienced in the field and is backed by the political authority of the city or state. The regulations were *not* produced or mandated by an IT department! *Business logic should always be specified directly by those people who have relevant knowledge.*

- Because of the importance of the regulations to the well-being of the community, any and all changes to them must be reviewed, approved, incorporated, and disseminated carefully. Because new dangers and liabilities can be discovered at any time, this process should be as streamlined and efficient as possible. On the other hand, over time some rules may become obsolete and even dangerous. The bottom line: *Rules must be managed.*

The Basic Principles of the Business Rule Approach

- *Rules should be written and made explicit.*
- *Rules should be expressed in plain language.*
- *Rules should exist independent of procedures and workflows.*
- *Rules should build on facts, and facts should build on concepts as represented by terms.*
- *Rules should guide or influence behavior in desired ways.*
- *Rules should be motivated by identifiable and important business factors.*
- *Rules should be accessible to authorized parties.*
- *Rules should be single-sourced.*
- *Rules should be specified directly by those people who have relevant knowledge.*
- *Rules should be managed.*

These commonsense observations represent basic principles of the business rule approach. Your business undoubtedly has literally hundreds or thousands of such rules guiding its various business processes. Yet in practice, these basic principles are seldom followed. In many organizations, the problem is so severe that the overall guidance process has just about broken down.

Can you do something about it? *Yes!* This book will guide you toward solutions.

Now back to that question, "Is a door you must never open really a door?" The answer is obvious—yes, of course it is. A wall *without* a door will always just be a wall. If you need a door sometime in the future, you must remodel, and that means time and money (not to mention disruption for the inhabitants). If you have ever remodeled your home, you know exactly what I mean.

The wall *with* a door acts like just a wall until such time that the "must remain closed" rule is discontinued. Then, with relatively little delay, expense, or disruption, the wall can become a wall with a *functional* door.

Think of the business rule approach as a relatively inexpensive way to build potential doors for your business for all those many cases when they might one day be needed. That way you can avoid walling yourself off from best-fit solutions and quick-response opportunities. In a world of constant and accelerating change, *adaptability* is the name of the game. This is why your company should focus on business rules today!

CHAPTER TWO

Areas of Opportunity

Changing the Face of Business

Where Does the Business Rule Approach Apply?

The "Re's" of Business Rules

In my experience, business rule projects generally fall into one of the following major categories. Without exaggeration, I suspect one or more of these categories apply to virtually every organization of any size worldwide—including *your* organization!

Reengineering

The first category involves projects to reengineer business processes. The focus here is on a top-down, business-driven requirements process. Business rule development—especially for *core* business rules—is a critical part of such an approach for at least two reasons.

1. Business rules play a central role in strategizing, that is, in rethinking the business problem and in developing a full and optimal business solution up front. I will have more to say on that point later (see Chapter 4).
2. Business rules sharpen and complement other, more traditional deliverables (for example, workflow models). In short, business rules handle the *business logic* portion of redevelopment efforts.

Revitalization

At more or less the opposite extreme are projects with no intent to reengineer any business process. Instead, their focus is on the day-to-day problem of how to implement changing policies and directives coming down from above (and/or from outside regulatory or governmental bodies) into existing processes. This needs to be done in a timely and efficient manner.

Typically, these organizations currently lack any effective means to trace the higher-level policies and rules to their actual implementation in legacy environments and related procedures. Because the connections are lost, impact assessment and modification can be performed only slowly and painfully. These projects view the business rule approach as a way to *reestablish lost connections* by reinventing their rule management environments.

Redeployment

Just about every company these days is eyeing the Web as an environment for redeploying basic business services. To do that, a company must identify and encode the business logic that governs those services (that is, the business rules).

This type of project actually represents the larger problem of how to exploit new hardware/software environments more quickly and cheaply—in other words, how to rearchitect the technical environment. By no means is this problem limited to organizations that have been around for a good while. For example, I recently talked with the staff members of a dot.com company (still alive and kicking as of this writing). They were looking for a way to escape their "unlivable" *five-year-old* legacy hardware/software environment. Legacy time frames are continuously shrinking, so the business must find new ways to become ever more nimble about *migrating* business logic from one environment to another.

Recapture

There are actually several related "Re's" in this category—*reverse engineering, retention,* and *redocumentation*. This type of project is really motivated by fear (or risk avoidance, to put a more positive spin on it). The issue is how to avoid losing your business rules. Many business rules, for example, are buried deep in undocumented legacy systems. Here, the focus is on reverse engineering of the program code to get at the business rules—that is, on *rule mining*.

Other projects focus more on knowledge retention: identifying those workers who know the business practices, sitting them down in a room together, and extracting the rules on a facilitated basis. The objective is to record this knowledge before the workers are lost to retirement—or to the competition. I will have more to say on this point later (see Chapter 3).

Whichever way you choose to recapture the rules (whether by rule mining or by undertaking facilitated retention sessions), the objective is to *redocument your rules.*

Reempowerment

This is perhaps the most exciting area of business rule activity. Initially, this category focused on customer relationship management (CRM). (This focus is currently expanding—I'll say more about this later in this chapter.) Companies are using the business rule approach to handle highly individualized customer relationships on a huge scale.

For that, you must do three things.

1. You must record and manage the rules of engagement. (Many companies are so out of touch with their customers you could probably call this an attempt at *re*engagement.)
2. You must "operationalize" new or modified rules of engagement quickly—weeks or months of delay in programming is unacceptable.
3. You must manage the rules of engagement on the business side, not the IT side. In other words, you must *reempower* business users to manage the rules directly.

This area is clearly target-rich for business rules. As an idea of great potential for your business, it is worth examining more closely.

Let's Make a Deal

A Killer App for Business Rules

Let's take a closer look at the *reempowerment* category of business rule activity mentioned above. This type of project often focuses on opportunities in the general area of CRM—in particular, on making deals. Deals (or, more precisely, contracts and agreements) are how the company formalizes the "rules of engagement" with each customer.

Just about every company these days, of course, wants more and more customers—and highly individualized relationships with each and every one of them. Making the situation even more challenging is the fact that products and services in today's economy are also increasingly complex and/or differentiated. So the question becomes, how can you manage highly individualized or even one-of-a-kind agreements for increasingly complex and differentiated products with increasingly large numbers of customers? And, by the way, how can you do it economically, flexibly, and quickly?

One thing is for sure: you can't do it successfully the way it has been done in the past. The traditional approach might be summarized as follows. A manager, marketing representative, and/or lawyer comes to some agreement with a customer. Such agreement might be about the acquisition of a product or service as a whole (including options, timing, pricing, delivery, and so on) or about some specific aspect thereof (for example, discounts). Once formalized (for example, in a contract or letter of understanding), the agreement is then handed over to the programming staff (or, if simpler, to the operational staff) to implement and operationalize. Depending on the complexity and availability of resources, this might take weeks or months—a virtual lifetime at this crucial juncture in building the customer relationship.

There are at least three things fundamentally wrong with this approach.

1. *It is far too slow.* These days, operationalizing an agreement needs to take place in hours or days, not weeks or months.
2. *It cannot be effectively managed.* Even if the programming and/or implementation is done correctly (a very big if), the resulting code is far removed—almost completely disconnected—from the original agreement. Any resemblance in form is vague at best. Subsequent changes in the rules (inevitable these days) become slow, painful, and expensive affairs.
3. *The approach is deeply flawed from an organizational viewpoint.* Those workers in actual contact with the customers are displaced from those workers who have the skills to adjust the implemented rules of engagement. This leads to gaps, inefficiency, and frustration all around.

The business rule approach offers a potent two-part solution. First, deals are viewed as nothing more than collections of high-level business rules. (We call these *governing rules.*) The business rule approach has already evolved effective techniques to interpret and manage such rules.

Second, the programming of deals clearly must be *eliminated*. Business logic technology[1] addresses that problem by allowing the rules of engagement to be implemented much more directly.

This approach produces a huge additional advantage—much of the business rule activity can now go outboard. By this I mean it can be removed from the IT department and distributed to those directly in contact with the customers. This will empower those users to manage the rules of engagement directly. Now the deal making (and deal remaking) is done directly, through what I call *eDeals*. I believe enabling these power users for eDeals will prove a killer app for business rules—and, more importantly, for the business!

Reempowerment for the Company's Provisioning Processes

There's a Lot More to Reference Data Than Just Data!

A high-level manager at a large, well-established high-tech company recently summarized his company's operational problems in two succinct statements:

"We can't always deliver the products we announce correctly."

"We don't always know exactly who our customers are."

These problems posed serious risks to the company's ability to remain competitive.

A quick look at the company's fulfillment process revealed two obvious signs of trouble. First, the rate of complaints from the company's best customers was significant. Second, at several points in the process growing pools of workers had formed, focusing almost exclusively on problem resolution.

The manager's first impulse was to consider reengineering the fulfillment process itself. That course of action was a daunting one, however, because of the size, complexity, and distribution of the operation. It also promised only incremental improvements at relatively high cost.

Probing deeper, it became apparent that the real source of problems did not lie within the fulfillment process at all. The fulfillment process was highly

---

1. By *business logic technology*, I mean *rule engines, decision management platforms, business logic servers*, and so on. Since this discussion is nontechnical, I will not use any of these more technical terms in this part of the book.

dependent on other aspects of business operations, and these other aspects were simply not well organized.

In IT terms, applications supporting the fulfillment process were dependent on data feeds from other operational systems. IT therefore viewed the issue as a data quality problem and proposed a technical solution. From the business perspective, however, the real problem did not lie with the data but rather with the business processes that produced the data.

There were basically two such processes. First was the company's product release process. This process, which for more complex products typically stretched over many months, involved establishing valid product configurations based on a significant number of technical, packaging, and marketing guidelines (business rules). It also orchestrated the timing of releases across the large number of worldwide geographical areas of company operations. Each geographical area, of course, had its own local rules for releases, based on law, market factors, and customs. Also important was coordinating the ongoing review and approval process, which involves many levels of staff in different parts of the organization. The product release process had evolved in an ad hoc manner over many years' time and was highly fragmented. This produced flawed product and release data before even reaching the fulfillment process.

The second business process supporting the fulfillment process was the company's customer process—or, rather, the *lack* of one. The company had never evolved a global view of the customer base (at least at the operational level), and consequently the company had no focal point for managing the complexities of customer data (for example, subsidiary versus parent company, account versus customer, and so on). Rules about customer identification and data could not be effectively enforced at the source (that is, at the point of origin). Although the company's data warehouse did support a consolidated version of customer information, this data was aimed for *business intelligence* (that is, customer profiles, trending, competitive strategy, and so on) rather than for operational needs.

As a result of this analysis, the company began to focus more and more on the two upstream business processes: the product release process and the customer process. Its motto became the following.

 "Do it once, right at the source."

Doing it right at the source is another basic principle of the business rule approach. As the above case study illustrates, it means reexamining the business processes that provide essential business inputs (for example, product release information and customer information) for day-to-day operational processes. My name for these upstream support business processes is *provisioning processes.*

Provisioning processes present a high-yield opportunity to apply business logic technology. They are inevitably rule-intensive but are not themselves highly dependent on *incoming* data feeds. Also, they inevitably offer substantial opportunities for direct specification of rules by business-side workers.

From an IT perspective, provisioning processes produce what has traditionally been called *reference data*—data that historically often appears as codes and/or in look-up tables. Typical kinds of reference data, as suggested by the case study above, include *product configurations, product families, customers, geographical areas,* and so on. This is obviously just the tip of the iceberg. A more complete list is presented in Table 2–1. For each there is an associated provisioning process and a likely candidate for a business rule project.

The term *reference data,* unfortunately, does not do justice either to the problem or to the core issue of provisioning processes. From a business perspective, provisioning processes are critical to the effectiveness of operational activities. For example, in the case study above, at stake was no less

Table 2–1 Examples of Provisioning Processes

A provisioning process and the associated business rules might focus on . . .

- *Customers:* including segmentation
- *Companies:* suppliers, outlets, channels, and so on
- *Part types:* including substitution options
- *Product configurations:* often in the form of technical templates
- *Product types:* including option selections
- *Facilities:* including capacity and usage restrictions
- *Agreements:* any kind of service contract
- *Charts of accounts:* including currency conversions
- *Organizational charts:* including titles, ranks, and so on
- *Personnel base:* not limited to employees
- *Skill sets:* including certification requirements
- *Calendar:* including categorizations of time periods
- *Jurisdictions:* geographies, political units, and so on
- *Connections:* routes, links, networks, and so on
- *Diagnostic sets:* including sets of inspection criteria

---

than correct product configuration. This capacity, by the way, encompasses support for fast product *re*configuration—increasingly a must in today's competitive business environment.

From a business rule perspective, the core issue lies in standard business *vocabulary*—the terms the business uses to communicate (and potentially to automate) fundamental aspects of its knowledge.[2] It turns out there is a whole lot more to "reference data" than just data!

Business Rules as Customer Interface

New Ways to Link Up

The business rule approach is profoundly changing the way we think about supporting business-to-business and business-to-customer interfaces. The concept of *eDeals* (any kind of agreement automated as business rules) mentioned earlier is just one way in which this is happening. Here are several more.

- *Supporting the supply chain:* A parts supplier must package its goods for the convenience of the finished-goods manufacturers who use them. Convenience is naturally different for each manufacturer. How does each customer define convenience? Business rules!
- *Integrating support services:* An international package delivery service seeks to integrate its services seamlessly within the automated workstation environments of its customers worldwide. Imagine all the differences across (a) national and subnational boundaries, (b) hardware/software platforms, and (c) customized user interfaces. What approach is the delivery service using to establish a standard baseline? Business rules!
- *Setting customer expectations:* Local walk-in betting offices in a certain European country are required by law to make available to customers all the rules governing the placing of bets. These rules must cover every possible contingency. For example, what happens if your bet on a horse race includes some horse to show (come in third), but only two horses finish the race? (I am not really sure, but you probably end up losing your money somehow.) Basically, the betting rules let the customer know what treatment he or she can expect. By making transactions more transparent, you build trust. In general, how do you make business transactions transparent? Business rules!

---

2. Refer to Chapter 14 for more on this topic.

What about Web-Based Commerce?

Harnessing the Dynamics of an Open Rule Marketplace

Over the past several years, companies have asked us to apply business rule techniques to the relatively new area of *Web content management*. (I use *content* here in the sense of what information Web pages hold.) These are typically larger organizations, with many sources of product and pricing content and many Web-based channels (eChannels) through which that information needs to be published. And, as you might guess, these organizations also have large numbers of business rules.

What have we found in these cases? You might think that the problems we diagnosed were all essentially new ones and therefore that all our solutions would be new ones as well. Not unreasonable, but *wrong*!

The first thing we discovered was a classic case of out-of-control bridges and interfaces (data feeds). I say *classic* because this problem has been recognized as a fundamental problem in business systems for at least a quarter century [Ross 1978]. The Web environment does put a new face on the problem, but underneath, it is the same as ever.

This problem can be addressed by introducing a *universal content repository* to keep the total number of bridges and interfaces to a manageable level. For more about this rather simple classic solution, refer to the boxed item, The "Old" Issue of Scalability.

Does the business rule approach also support the new challenges of organizing a highly dynamic environment for Web content management? The answer is a resounding *yes*. Our experience suggests not only that the business rule approach supports them quite well but also that there might not

The "Old" Issue of Scalability

Understanding the Problem

The basic problem with bridges and interfaces (data feeds) is relatively straightforward. Suppose you have a large number of different data sources and a significant number of applications that use them. Typically, these data sources and applications will have accrued one by one in largely unplanned fashion over a number of years. I say years because that is how long it *used* to take—in Web time, it can now take only months or even weeks.

In such an unplanned environment, each application typically has its own interface to each data source it uses. In the worst case, this means that if there are m number of data sources and n number of applications, you must manage $m \times n$ number of interfaces. As the following sample numbers suggest, this total can spiral out of control very quickly as the environment grows over time!

m	n	m × n
1	1	1
2	3	6
5	15	75
10	25	250
and so on	and so on	and so on

Each interface must be managed. As these sample numbers suggest, the overhead associated with simply managing the interfaces can escalate rapidly. So too can the opportunities for misinterpreting and misusing the source data. Making changes in data definition also becomes increasingly more difficult since such change must be propagated faithfully across the ever-growing number of interfaces. In a word, this approach simply does not *scale*.

Correcting the Problem

The problem of scalability is one reason why the business rule approach puts such an emphasis on integrating and sharing data. In the ideal case, this solution reduces the number of data sources to $m = 1$. Now, the growth factor is simply additive. Each time you add a new application, the number of interfaces is simply $n + 1$, rather than $m \times n$.

Unfortunately, in the real world (yes, that does include the Web), things are usually not that simple, and m cannot be reduced to the minimum $m = 1$. A common solution is to provide an intermediate staging area—a database or repository into which the data from the m sources is imported and consolidated.

For m data sources, this approach means creating m import interfaces. An export interface is still also needed for each of the n applications. (Now these n export interfaces are from the staging area rather than from the original data sources.) Consequently, the total number of interfaces to be managed is $m + n$, instead of $m \times n$. Each new data source or application means simply $m + n + 1$ interfaces to manage. As the following sample numbers indicate, this becomes more and more significant as the number of data sources grows. In other words, this is an approach that *does* scale.

m	n	m $\times$ n	m + n
1	1	1	2
2	3	6	5
5	15	75	20
10	25	250	35
and so on	and so on	and so on	and so on

The Universal Content Repository

How does this discussion apply to the Web environment? Many companies are beginning to realize that they have a problem with *content* management. Often, there are a significant number of sources for this content (m) and an ever-expanding number of Web applications (n) that use it. In Web time, the $m \times n$ factor can spiral out of control almost before you know it.

The remedy, of course, is to create an intermediate staging area, which can be called a *universal content repository*. As before, this brings the $m \times n$ interface total back to the more manageable $m + n$ case. This is simply an old solution applied to a new problem, but as they say, sometimes the more things change, the more they stay the same!

even be any viable alternative. There are many ways in which this is true, but let me single out three especially important ones.

Developing the Vocabulary

The Web environment brings to the business many new concepts and, in many cases, strange new terms to go along with them (for example, *extranets*, *eMarketplaces*, *eMarketMakers*, *affinity sites*, *commerce engines*, and so on). The business rule approach places strong emphasis on defining terms and organizing concepts up front and on doing so in a *business-driven* manner. This emphasis on vocabulary and foundation business knowledge is just the thing to make sense of the muddle—and to help you do it before any coding starts.

Building for Change

In several of our recent projects, the focus was on building highly tailored eCatalogs that target individual eChannels. Often, these eCatalogs are specific to individual customers and/or promotion efforts. The number of possible variations in composition, pricing, frequency of distribution, and so on (not to mention all the exceptions and restrictions on them, legal and otherwise) is staggering. Furthermore, these variations must be adjustable in close to real time to keep pace with ever-changing business factors.

In the Web-based commerce arena, any architecture that cannot support such real-time adaptability is a nonstarter. What is the optimal approach for making an ever-changing array of selection options accessible and relatively easy to change? This is precisely the area where business rules and business logic technology excel.

Harnessing Marketplace Forces

Although a rule-based approach is essential for dynamic content management, it is not in and of itself sufficient. With so many rules and such rapid change in them, it is almost inconceivable that they can be defined effectively by a central group, no matter how highly qualified that group might be.

Having a central group manage all the rules mimics the top-down control practices of command economies (for example, communism). That approach is inherently flawed at real-world levels of complexity. In macroeconomics, the solution is open marketplaces in which thousands (or hundreds of thousands) of individual consumer choices constantly fine-tune the balance between supply and demand.

A corresponding approach must be adopted for the rules governing use of the universal content repository, covering all the choices to be made about content selection, organization, and delivery frequency for the eCatalogs. These rules must be pushed out to all the individual consumers of the content, that is, to all the individual business users responsible for the particular eChannels.

The term we use for business-side, rule-based specification of any kind of service agreement is *eDeal*. The particular manifestation of eDeals appropriate for Web content management is *eSubscription*. Each eSubscription establishes the parameters of a finely tuned pipeline (that is, eCatalog) of content for a particular highly focused Web commerce channel. The eSubscription is set up by the business staff closest to that particular business activity—the people in the best position to determine the optimal tactics and tradeoffs for each particular case.

What about the central group responsible for managing the universal content repository under this approach? To facilitate specifying eSubscriptions, this group would probably define generalized rule templates that reduce much of the business user activity to point-and-click selection of appropriate parameters.

The most important thing to remember about the central group, how-ever, is that it acts as neither creator (supplier) nor consumer of content. In-stead, it supports the inner workings of the content marketplace. Working in much the same manner as the support staff for stock or commodity ex-changes, the central group's basic role is as enabler of intrabusiness content exchange and as enforcer for the basic corporate rules of fair trade.

Reference

Ross, Ronald G. 1978. *Data Base Systems: Design, Implementation and Manage-ment.* New York: AMACOM.

CHAPTER 3

Serving Up Knowledge

The Need to Know

What Is Knowledge Management?

And What Does It Have to Do with Business Rules?

I am frequently asked whether the business rule approach bears any relationship to knowledge management. Although many in the field have failed to make the connection yet, the answer is *yes*. The following set of questions and answers reveals how the business rule approach and knowledge management are linked.

What is knowledge management about?

According to experts in the field, the central concerns are generally as follows:

- Organizing the process of capturing and leveraging enterprise knowledge in order to further business strategy
- Organizing knowledge to get the right answers the first time, *every* time
- Changing corporate culture to encourage the sharing of knowledge, by allocating power to those who share rather than to those who hoard
- Making sure that the company does not lose vital knowledge

- Enabling less experienced staff to answer questions as correctly as the most knowledgeable people in the enterprise
- Enabling people outside the company to answer questions on their own
- Answering every question well, even if the person who is asking cannot ask the question exactly right

Where have the early successes been?
The focus of attention has been on call centers and help desks, for the most part.

Where do new applications with the highest potential lie?
Self-service and Web applications offer a rich set of opportunities.

What new challenges do these applications present for designers?
The challenges for designers lie in building structured dialogs in environments where human intervention (which is expensive!) needs to be kept to a minimum and where *everything* is subject to rapid change. In short, such dialogs must be *smart*.

A *smart dialog* is characterized as follows.

1. The right question is asked at the right time.
2. Suggestions and heuristics appear automatically at the optimal points.
3. Nonviable options, alternatives, and/or conclusions are eliminated as soon as possible.
4. Opportunistic questions (for example, for cross-selling) are inserted dynamically.

How does knowledge management connect to business rules?
There are two major targets for applied knowledge management.

1. Workers *inside* the company. For these, you want to codify the knowledge of the company's best people and make it available to workers at lower levels of skill or experience. (*Lower* here generally also means lower *cost*.)
2. Customers and others *outside* the company. For these, you want to codify what middlemen know and to reduce or eliminate their involvement. This is sometimes called *disintermediation*.

In either case, you must codify the knowledge—and that means business rules.

Can business logic technology play a role in knowledge management?

There is huge opportunity for this kind of connection. The last three of the four characteristics of smart dialogs (above) could be easily rule-based. Is there any better technology to accommodate rapid change? *No!*

What is knowledge?

That is a question best left for others to answer. I do know this much, however: Business rules represent that part of enterprise knowledge you can *codify.*

How can the company prevent loss of knowledge?

As above, the answer is to codify the business rules so the knowledge is no longer *tacit.* By the way, a good layperson's definition of *tacit* knowledge is this: If you lose the person, you lose the knowledge. As discussed in the boxed item, Knowledge Walking Out the Door, this represents a far greater risk than many companies realize.

Knowledge Walking Out the Door

Many companies today seem unaware of one of the biggest risks they face—their own internal brain drain. A significant portion of the company's operational self-knowledge has disappeared already—*downsized, outsourced, reengineered,* or *early-retired* away. How many people still with the company have any real idea about how critical areas of the business actually work? Who can tell you the *real* criteria for making operational-level, day-to-day business decisions?

The answer, I often find, is only one or two key people for any given business area. Sometimes they are on the IT side, sometimes on the business side. The company's exposure in this regard can be quite significant.

If your company finds itself in that situation, what should you do? The solution is an initiative to harvest and manage the business rules of the at-risk area. This is sometimes called *knowledge retention.* Otherwise, all you might have left is the program source code—and you really do not want to have to go there to access your business rules!

Personalized, Never-Ending, On-the-Job Training

Knowledge Companions for 21st-Century Line Workers

Everyone is concerned these days about the accelerating rate of change and the urgent need to build business systems that prove more adaptable. A flip side to the issue of change, however, has received very little attention. That flip side has to do with *training.*

Remember the old story about telephone operators? Use of the telephone has grown at such a rate that if automatic switching had not been invented, it is said that by now everyone in the world would be a telephone operator. Growth in the rate of change in *business* today is just as fast. Workers are being thrown into new responsibilities and procedures at an ever-increasing rate. That means they must be trained by other workers. If this keeps up, sooner or later everyone in the world will have to become a trainer.

Clearly, that cannot happen. The only solution is to make training *automatic*—that is, built right into the business systems that support the workers' day-to-day responsibilities and procedures. Business rules can make that happen. Briefly, here is how that can be done.[1]

---

1. For more discussion, refer to Chapter 7.

The business rule approach features declarative expression of each rule. Consider the following rule: *A rush order must not include more than five items.* Suppose a worker violates this particular rule while performing some procedure. What error message should pop up on the screen?

Certainly not, as all too often happens today, some obscure system code or some message in computerese. Instead, the initial message should simply be the business rule statement itself. In the business rule approach, we like to say that the business rules *are* the error messages.

Another way to look at this is that the rule statement represents a *requirement* that is pure business logic. In the business rule approach, this kind of requirement is incorporated directly when building the system, then gets output directly to inform the worker when a violation in his or her work is detected. Think of that as a communication from a worker who knows the business logic to a worker who must follow that business logic—*without these workers ever communicating directly or possibly ever even coexisting in time or space.*

A *friendly* business rule system would go a step further. When an error is detected, the business rule system not only materializes the original business logic for the worker but can also offer a canned procedure so he or she can correct the violation immediately. (This assumes, of course, that the worker is both authorized and capable in that regard.)

For the business, this capacity means achieving *real-time compliance*, eliminating costly downstream detection and corrective action. It means that mistakes can be addressed immediately so they are not compounded as other actions are subsequently taken.

For the worker, it means being constantly (re-)exposed to the business logic on a highly selective, real-time basis. Remember, the business rule could have been changed just recently, maybe even in the last few seconds.

For these reasons, I view business rule systems as instructional knowledge companions that provide personalized, never-ending, on-the-job training for harried 21st-century line workers.

CHAPTER 4

What about IT Projects?

Where the Rubber Meets the Road

If We Had Already Started Coding . . .

Meeting Those Project Deadlines

Recently, we were talking to the chief developer at a large client organization about progress on a major reengineering effort there. The project in question targeted one of the organization's core business processes. Our concern was whether the project team members could meet a deadline some nine months out for delivering a large-scale prototype. We had just spent several intensive months developing a comprehensive business model, and they still had several months of system design left to complete.

This chief developer is very sharp—not one to commit to any answer lightly. For the longest while, he said nothing, lost in thought. Finally, eyeing the detailed business diagrams plastered on the walls all around, he said, "If we had already started coding, I would say we had no chance at all. But since we haven't started coding yet, I'd say the chances are pretty good."

I had to run that by several times in my mind before I caught his meaning. "If we had already started coding, *I would say we had no chance at all.*"

I knew he thought that the application coding itself was going to be pretty tough. It would involve using business logic technology, a worldwide distribution network, graphical user interfaces (GUIs), and some significant middleware.

He was saying that if they had to resolve all the business issues while coding, they would never pull it off in time—or probably ever. However, since the project team was tackling the tough business issues up front (including specifying the business rules), he thought they had a pretty good chance of completing the code by the target date.

In large measure, the business rule approach is simply about asking the right questions at the right times. It is about being business-driven in the project approach. How important is that? Ask lead developers who *really* know their stuff (and who are willing to give you a straight story). There is only one way to honestly meet a deadline—and that is to solve the business problem *first*.

Two Things Wrong with Traditional Business Systems Development

Yes, There Is a Better Way!

Is your company as successful as it would like to be in developing business systems? Probably not. Have you identified the reasons? Here are the two most common factors we see and what you can do about them.

Never-Ending IT Projects

Problem Statement: Why do so many projects miss their deadlines? Delivery dates are adjusted time and time again. Primary requirements are forever changing midstream, causing endless rework (sometimes called "maintenance"). Some projects seem to lurch from one gridlock to the next; others run headlong into belated showstoppers. "Always time to fix it, but never time to plan it" seems to be the norm. A distressing number of projects never deliver anything at all.

> *Is this really simply a fact of computer-age life, or does it perhaps suggest that primary requirements are not being gathered completely and accurately before development starts?*

Solution: The answer is relatively straightforward. First, you must develop a true business model. (I will say more about what *true* means in a moment.)

Then, you must faithfully follow a series of continuing checks and balances against that business model when developing your follow-on requirements.

IT-Driven Business

Problem Statement, Part 1: The capabilities of IT have advanced explosively in the past decade or two. Businesses continue to devote significant resources to take advantage of these new capabilities. And there is no end in sight.

> *How does the business decide which kinds of automation are really beneficial—and which are not? How can the business be sure it will use new technology for the maximum business benefit?*

Problem Statement, Part 2: In the early days of building business systems, the business side could essentially sit back and just let them happen. The advantages of automating were so compelling that you could do virtually no wrong. Now, for all practical purposes business and IT operate inseparably. When undertaking projects, the logical step then would be to put together seamless business/IT project teams and have them follow a business-oriented approach to developing requirements. Yet many companies are nowhere close to doing that today.

> *What will it take to ensure that projects focus on achieving maximum business benefit? Can a win-win solution be found such that project participation is also individually rewarding?*

Problem Statement, Part 3: Companies often do very little to induce, structure, or reward creative business thinking in their IT projects. Neither the business side nor the IT side is really challenged to close the gap. All too often, the business side still produces fuzzy, ill-focused "requirements," and the IT side continues doing "requirements" only a notch or two above programming.

> *How can this gap between business professionals and IT professionals in developing requirements be eliminated? How can the company bring meaningful structure to the process?*

Solution: Again, the answer is relatively straightforward. The business needs an organized approach that enables business professionals to drive the development of requirements. This approach must provide a roadmap that shows how to ask the right kinds of questions about the right things at the right times. It needs a business-driven approach.

What *Business-Driven* Really Means

Getting to the Right Mind-Set

Let's start with a given. Businesses do not exist to manage hardware/software environments; rather, hardware/software environments exist to support the business. This truth should be self-evident, but in the midst of such a fast-paced technological revolution, sometimes we lose sight of it. As a result, we often find the tail seeming to wag the dog.

Clear-headed people on both the business side and the IT side know it should not be that way. The IT projects the company decides to undertake should always be, in fact, *"of the business, for the business, and by the business."* Saying it is one thing; figuring out how to accomplish it, of course, is another.

Fortunately, the business rule approach offers the well-organized roadmap you need to put the business back in the driver's seat. Later in this chapter, I will outline the particular ways in which business rule methodology structures the requirements development process to accomplish this. First, however, we should carefully examine the relevant mind-set issues, listed below. These are equally important.

1. There should be only one kind of project. In days past, IT had its projects, and the business had its projects. These were seldom if ever woven together. Clearly this approach is outmoded in the 21st century. These days, virtually every business project involves some automation— and most IT projects have direct impacts on the business. We must therefore come to a *single* kind of project with a *unified* approach for the project team to follow.

2. The business side has the knowledge to solve business problems. Clearly IT can help develop solutions, but in large measure, IT's role should be focused on designing and implementing solutions.

3. The first two issues imply this third one. What the system shows the business side once implemented should look much like the requirements that the business side articulated during development. I do not mean that in a figurative sense—I mean it in a literal sense. Business knowledge *in*, and business knowledge *out*. As I suggested earlier, *the business rules should become the error messages.*

4. Achieving this requires that the business questions be asked first, before addressing the system and implementation issues. Although this seems like an obvious point, it often does not happen that way in practice.

5. Capturing business knowledge up front requires new participatory roles for the people on the business side. It requires deeper, more focused involvement on their part. It also requires commitment of the most valuable commodity of all—their time.

6. In return (this is important!), the people on the business side have the right to expect the most conservative use of their time possible and ready-made structures (thinking tools) to help them organize their business knowledge in optimal ways.

7. This requires a structured approach where the emphasis is on asking exactly the right questions at exactly the right times. In addition, the approach must lay out exactly the right form (type of deliverable) each kind of answer should take.

8. Finally, business questions are quite often highly complex in their own right. As with any complex problem, this means the questions and answers need to be carefully factored, that is, not jumbled together as rambling statements but specifically addressed to one particular aspect of the problem at a time.

More on What *Business-Driven* Really Means

The Business Model

When the rate of change increases to the point that the time required to assimilate change exceeds the time in which the change must be manifest, the enterprise is going to find itself in deep yogurt.

—John A. Zachman [1994]

Our solution[1] to the mind-set issues described above has been greatly influenced by the work of John Zachman and his Architecture Framework.[2] If you

---

1. *Our solution* refers to the techniques of Business Rule Solutions (BRS), LLC, in Proteus, the BRS business rule methodology.
2. For more information on John Zachman's thinking, refer to Zachman [2002] and collected articles by Zachman found in the *Business Rules Journal*, available at *http://www.BRCommunity.com*.

are familiar with that body of work, I can easily position our approach by saying it addresses rows 1 and 2 of the Framework in the exact six-abstraction
(column) manner he prescribes. (Our deliverables, however, are aimed primarily at the business-process level, rather than the enterprise level.)

If you are not familiar with Zachman's work, what I just said probably
sounds like Greek. Fortunately, knowledge about the Zachman Framework is
not a prerequisite for using the business rule approach. I can explain our solution to the mind-set issues this way. The focus is on developing a *business
model* for the scope of the project, with direct participation of the business
process owners, operational-level managers, and subject matter experts.[3]

Since these people constitute the audience for the business model, the
approach and techniques must be specifically tailored to their perspective.
This means banishing system and technical issues. Think of a business model
as a business blueprint that can be read both by business people and by software design architects.

A business model must also be carefully factored to ensure that the inherent complexity of creating business solutions can be managed. What are
these factors, and how does the business rule methodology address them?
Again, we follow Zachman's lead on this. He indicates that there are six basic
factors (abstraction) to consider. We address each head-on as follows.

- **Motivation—the "why" factor:** We address this factor first by creating a
  battle plan for the intended business solution. We call this deliverable a
  Policy Charter. It outlines the appropriate ends (for example, business
  goals) and means (for example, tactics) for solving the business problem.
  This includes core business rules—make-or-break policies needed to
  conduct business operations in their new form successfully. I will discuss
  this distinctive deliverable in more detail momentarily.
- **Function—the "how" factor:** We address this factor by developing
  business process models[4] that sequence the flow of tasks. The result is a
  beginning-to-end view of the transformations necessary to achieve operational business results.

---

3. See the section Why Business Rule Methodology Is Different in Chapter 13.
4. Since process and workflow models are common in techniques for business process
reengineering and business-oriented requirements development, I will not discuss them
at length in this book.

- **Structure—the "what" factor:** We address this "data" factor[5] by developing the standard business vocabulary of the targeted business area. These definitions are organized into a Concepts Catalog, which is essentially a glossary of terms. The Concepts Catalog is actually just one part of the larger problem—what shared operational business knowledge will be needed to run the to-be business. That knowledge is organized into what we call a *fact model*. This important type of deliverable is discussed in more detail in Chapters 5 and 14.
- **People—the "who" factor:** We address this factor by defining organizational roles and responsibilities, and the work relationships between them. Associated work products are also identified.
- **Time—the "when" factor:** We address this factor by examining the regimens needed to organize the aging of core concepts. These regimens consist of stages or states we call *business milestones*.
- **Location—the "where" factor:** We address this factor by building a Business Connectivity Map indicating business sites and their communication/transport links from the business perspective.

In addressing each of the individual factors of the business blueprint, we consciously and deliberately seek out the relevant elements of business logic—that is, the business rules—and record them. This is another area, rule management,[6] in which our approach is business-driven.

Although the business blueprint is business-oriented, it must nonetheless provide a comprehensive and complete set of requirements that system architects can subsequently use to design the actual system. The business model can be transformed directly into a first-cut system model. For system designers this means that most, if not all, of the relevant business questions have already been answered.

Developing a good system design is often quite difficult in and of itself. The business model is crucial input, giving the system designers an important head start on their work.

---

5. In a system model, *structure* could be taken to mean *data* structure, but in a business model, we think a better description is *basic knowledge* structure.

6. For more discussion of this important area, refer to the section What Rule Management Is About in Chapter 13.

The business model is also your best guarantee that the system designers (and then the implementers after that) will be far less likely to discover show-stoppers on the business side way downstream in the development process. The later that holes in the business solution are discovered, of course, the more expensive and frustrating on all sides it becomes to correct them. Avoiding such late-developing showstoppers on the business side is really the bottom line in what it means to be *business-driven*.

The Policy Charter

A Small-Sized Big Picture

Cost overruns are manageable if the project will achieve worthwhile benefits; however, failing to satisfy business goals is always unacceptable.

> —Gladys S. W. Lam [1997], Principal, Business Rule Solutions, LLC

Recently, a business project sponsor confided to us her frustration with the project team she had put together to kick off a project. Basically, her complaint boiled down to this: Despite many months of hard work, she felt like she was still missing the big picture. And if *she* was still missing it, she was pretty sure the team members were still missing it too.

The irony was that the team members *had* produced a "big" picture—a very big picture indeed! They had produced documentation covering features, workflows, data models, technical architectures, migration issues, support requirements, problem areas, "open" issues, and still more—hundreds and hundreds of pages of it. In all those pages, however, there was no answer to what the sponsor really wanted to know—the *why* of it all.

As we discussed this more, it became clear that the sponsor wanted a focused statement of what the new capabilities would mean to the business. Specifically, she wanted to know what business tactics (courses of action) and policies (core business rules) would be supported and why these would be best for meeting the business goals. In other words, the business sponsor wanted to see the underlying *motivation* laid out—not for the new system per se but for a new way of doing business.

She did not mean a business case. They had done a high-level cost/benefit analysis previously and had long since satisfied themselves on that score. The business sponsor wanted proof that the business implications had been examined and resolved before they went into actual design and development. That meant answering two fundamental business questions: one working *down* from the business goals, and the other working *up* toward those business goals.[7]

- *Working down from the business goals:* What are the most effective business tactics and policies[8] for achieving the business goals, and how would the associated risks and conflicts be resolved?
- *Working up toward the goals:* What is the business motivation for each tactic and policy, and given the business goals, why is each tactic or policy the most appropriate?

As you might already see, these are merely two sides of the same coin. They require what we call a *Policy Charter*, a key element of the business rule approach.[9] In our experience, a Policy Charter does not need to be all that large—just a small-sized big picture.

The True Business Analyst

The Go-To Guy for 21st-Century Business Systems

The key role in solution development for the 21st-century business is that of *business analyst.* Does your company have business analysts? Can you define the role they need to play? What they need to know? What they need to be able to do?[10]

A good starting definition for the role of business analyst is "business problem solver." (Read on to find out why that is not sufficient, however.) To perform the role of business problem solver, a business analyst must be a generalist. He or she must be able to grapple with a problem in any of a number

---

7. I do not mean project goals or project objectives, so to avoid confusion I will continue to say *business goal* rather than simply *goal.*

8. I mean *core business rules* here, but management tends to think in terms of setting policies (hence the name *Policy* Charter). Either term is acceptable in this context.

9. See also the section Why Business Rule Methodology Is Different in Chapter 13. For additional information, refer to Lam [1998]. For an enterprise-level approach, refer to the landmark work by the Business Rules Group [2000].

10. For an excellent look at the practical side of being an effective business analyst, refer to Seer [2002].

of dimensions, whether involving tactics and policies, infrastructure, organization, information systems—or, more likely, some mix of all the above.

To be a business problem solver, a business analyst also must be in touch with the reality of the "as is" business. Think of a business analyst as the person most likely to be able to tell you (or find out for you) how some aspect of the business *really* works—and what is wrong with it. To put that a little more strongly, if the business analyst *cannot* tell you (or find out for you), then he or she is simply not doing the job.

That is just for starters. Business analysts must also be able to visualize and develop "to be" solutions. To do that, they need the skills of a system analyst or of a business process engineer.

So which is it: system analyst or business process engineer? The correct answer is both—and neither. By *both,* I mean that a business analyst should feel comfortable with both the IT side and the business side of developing systems. Indeed, if a business analyst is *really* good, he or she might not even clearly understand the difference. After all, in the information age, what *is* the difference?

Here's what I mean by *neither.* On the one hand, a business analyst is definitely *not* a traditional IT system designer. More times than not, IT designers are really more interested in getting to the code than in rolling out a complete business solution or doing much planning.

Fortunately, many companies are beyond that point. Even so, they often still fall well short of having true business analysts (even if they use that term). For example, a business coordinator for system change requests is *not* a true business analyst. Yes, adding a field or two to a GUI in a legacy system is often no trivial matter. However, that rarely amounts to problem solving where competitive advantage or corporate survival is at stake. That is the kind of problem solving with which a *true* business analyst must contend.

On the other hand, I do not mean a high-level business process reengineering expert either. By *high-level,* I mean the type of business planner who is more comfortable with value chains and business strategies than with operational tactics and the nuts and bolts of business processes.

A true business analyst is someone who can help put together a full set of requirements, that is, a complete business model covering all aspects (factors) of the target area. The test for such a model is that you must be able to transform it (with a lot more work, of course) into a workable system design.

The assumption here, by the way, is that at least some of the design is likely to be automated.

This leads me back to the earlier point about why *business problem solver* fails to capture entirely what true business analysts are about. Certainly, they do fix business problems. Business analysts, however, must be equipped to develop solutions in terms of better infrastructure, not just in terms of direct fixes (even detailed ones) for the immediate problem at hand. *Better infrastructure* in turn implies longer, multifaceted projects. It also requires a structured approach to business analysis—that is, to the development of the comprehensive requirements necessary to create a workable "to be" world. That set of comprehensive requirements, of course, represents a business model.

The business rule approach provides the structured approach to business analysis needed in the 21st century. The business analyst then must be directly involved in capturing policies (core business rules), creating fact models, developing "to-be" workflows, and so on.

The other issue—how to support longer, multifaceted projects—requires a better understanding of basic project management tools (that is, time lines, budgets, resource allocation, and so on). This is the stuff good project managers bring to the table. Unfortunately, good project managers are also in short supply, but that is a different story for a different day.

References

Business Rules Group (Ronald G. Ross and Keri Anderson Healy, eds.). 2000. "Organizing Business Strategy: The Standard Model for Business Rule Motivation." Version 1, November 2000. Available at *http://www.BusinessRulesGroup.org*.

Lam, Gladys S. W. 1998. "Business Knowledge—Packaged in a Policy Charter." *DataToKnowledge Newsletter* (formerly *Data Base Newsletter*), May/June. Available at *http://www.BRCommunity.com*.

———. 1997. Originally from a lecture, quote reprinted with permission in *Data Base Newsletter* 25(2):5.

Seer, Kristen. 2002. "How to Develop Effective Business Analysts," Parts 1, 2, and 3. *Business Rules Journal,* May, July, and September (respectively). Available at *http://www.BRCommunity.com.*

Zachman, John A. 2002. *The Zachman Framework: A Primer for Enterprise Engineering and Manufacturing* (electronic book). Available at *http://www.zachmaninternational.com.*

———. 1994. Originally from a lecture, quote reprinted with permission in *Data Base Newsletter* 22(6):16.

Business Rule Concepts
The Mechanics of Business Systems[1]

Overview

Part II of this book explains the basic ideas of the business rule approach and explores the breakthrough innovations it offers. These culminate in Chapter 7, which presents revolutionary new ideas for organizing work in the 21st century.

To develop these ideas, I use an extensive analogy to the human body—in particular, the mechanical system of the human body. That analogy is presented in this Overview. As it will explain, the mechanical system has three fundamental components. Each of the three chapters in this part of the book examines one of these fundamental components as it relates to business systems.

The Marvelous Organism

The human body is marvelous in many respects, not the least of which is its mechanics. Roughly, support for the mechanics of the human body has three basic components, separate yet intimately interconnected, as follows.

> **Structure** is provided by the bones, which are organized and connected within the skeleton. The skeleton provides both a framework for carrying the weight of the other components as well as a semirigid scheme around which the other softer components can be organized.

---

1. Acknowledgment: I would like to thank Keri Anderson Healy, Editor of the *Business Rules Journal*, http://www.BRCommunity.com, for her editorial assistance and her many suggestions for clarifying and enhancing the original draft of this material.

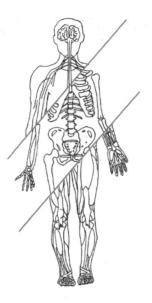

Mechanical Components
→ Structure: Skeleton
→ Power: Muscles
→ Control: Nerves

Power is provided through the muscles, which are connected to the bones. The muscles enable motion based on the framework provided by the skeleton. Since motion is what we see happening from outside the body, the muscles seem most directly responsible for the behavior we perceive.

Control is provided by the nervous system, which connects to the muscles. Nerves indirectly connect muscles to other muscles through long series of connections passing through the brain. Responses to all stimuli are coordinated through the firing of nerve impulses—no firing, no movement, and therefore no behavior.

These basic mechanical components are familiar to us all. In a moment, we will see how the mechanics of business systems can be viewed in the very same terms. As we examine the analogy, several observations about the mechanics of the human body are worth keeping in mind.

- All three components are *essential.* The human body literally cannot function without all three.
- The three components are all interconnected—that is, they are *integrated* with each other. For example, tendons connect muscle to bone. Successful behavior depends on this integration.

- Each of the three components is *specialized* for a particular role or responsibility. Each optimizes for its particular task. Mixing or combining the three components would provide a much less effective solution. Also, specialization provides for greater simplicity. Think about how much more complex bones would be if they incorporated muscles or how much more complex muscles would be if they incorporated nerves.
- The nervous system in some sense is the most important component because it provides control for the other two. The body is certainly capable of behavior without a well-organized nervous system—but not *effective, adaptive* behavior. Literally, you cannot operate at your best with only half a brain!

A New View of Business Systems

I believe that business systems should be organized in a manner similar to the mechanical system of the human body. Let's revisit the three components of that system, thinking now about the business (or some business capacity within it[2]) in place of the human body.

Structure

Structure is provided by organized—that is, *structured*—knowledge about the most basic things we can know about the business. These "basic things we can know" are often simply taken for granted—just like the human skeleton in everyday activity. They consist of core *concepts* of the business and the basic *logical connections* we make between them.

Think of these core concepts as bones and the logical connections as ligaments (that is, bone-to-bone connections).

- Just as each bone has a particular shape that is optimal for its purpose and location, so too must each core concept have a carefully crafted "shape." A concept's shape is given by its definition, which must be clear, concise, and well suited for its business purpose. Every bone or concept

---

2. By *business capacity* I mean some significant subset of the business, possibly encompassing one or more business processes and/or functional areas. To simplify matters, from this point forward in the discussion I will drop the additional *or some business capacity within it* whenever *business* appears and assume you understand I also mean any significant subset of the business.

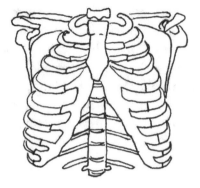

Mechanical Components
→ Structure: Skeleton
→ Power: Muscles
→ Control: Nerves

must also have a standard name. In the business rule approach, the standard names for concepts are called *terms*.

- Each ligament also has a particular shape that is optimal for its purpose and location. Similarly, each logical connection between concepts must have a standard "shape." In the business rule approach, these logical connections are called *facts*. Their standard shapes are given by *fact statements*, which reference the appropriate terms.

A drawing or diagram of the complete human skeleton helps us understand how all the bones fit together. To illustrate the overall structure of terms and facts, it is likewise helpful to create a drawing or diagram. Our name[3] for such a diagram is *fact model*.

A fact model provides a framework, in many ways like a skeleton, in two basic respects.

1. A fact model literally provides a standard scheme around which the other components can be organized—that is, the "basic things we can know" *in common* throughout the business.
2. A fact model carries the "weight" of the organization—that is, when eventually implemented as a database, it will carry the cumulative record of past interactions (the history).

---

3. *Our name* refers to the name that Business Rule Solutions (BRS), LLC, uses in Proteus, the BRS business rule methodology.

Mechanical Components
→ Structure: Skeleton
→ **Power: Muscles**
→ Control: Nerves

Power

Power is provided by processes, which operate on the terms and facts. Whereas the fact model provides structure, the processes enable activity.

When we think about a business system, the processes are often the first things that come to mind. They represent the most visible aspect of the business system because they literally *do* what the business needs to get done (for example, take the customer's order). However, viewing a business system as merely a collection of processes makes no more sense than viewing the human body as merely a collection of muscles. Any organism is much more than that—whether human or business.

Control

Control is provided by rules, which constrain processes (the "muscles") to act only in certain ways deemed best for the business as a whole. In the human body, there are literally hundreds of muscles, which must act in concert. If they do not, the resulting behavior at best will be less than optimal. At worst, serious damage can result (for example, hyperextension of a limb) that will significantly reduce the body's overall capacity to act.

Similarly, business systems literally consist of hundreds (or thousands) of "muscles" (processes), which must act in concert. If they do not, the business

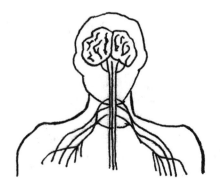

Mechanical Components
→ Structure: Skeleton
→ Power: Muscles
→ Control: Nerves

will also behave in a less than optimal fashion. In some cases, serious damage can result (for example, loss of customers, squandering of resources or opportunities, and so on) that will significantly reduce the business's overall capacity to act (that is, its competitiveness and/or effectiveness).

In the human body, we take many control actions of the nervous systems for granted. For example, who thinks about the impulses sent to the heart to make it beat—unless, of course, something goes wrong? Or who in the process of saying, "Ouch!" thinks much about the jerk reflex that causes the hand to move so quickly off the hot stove? As long as all runs smoothly, we can apply our mental faculties to a higher purpose—whether for working, solving problems, or simply planning a fun lunchtime getaway.

Similarly, while things run smoothly in the business, we can take the control actions of the rules for granted and concentrate on matters requiring a higher order of intelligence. Until a rule "breaks" somehow—and that is a very important possibility, of course—we can focus on the more creative aspects of business operation and strategy.

A business is very much like a human body—a living organism. Let's revisit the observations I made earlier about the mechanics of the human body, now applying them to business systems.

- All three components—structure (terms and facts), processes, and rules—are *essential*. A business literally falls apart—disintegrates—without all three.
- The three components are obviously interrelated. For example, processes act to record information about the things represented in the fact model.

These actions, in turn, are subject to the rules. Successful business behavior depends on effective *integration*. These fundamental interrelationships must obviously be taken into account.

- Each of the three components is *specialized* for a particular role or responsibility and optimized for its particular task. Mixing or combining them would provide a less effective solution. The business rule approach therefore recognizes the importance of factoring out the rules. We[4] call this *Rule Independence*. As a fringe benefit comes a huge simplification in the processes (the "muscles" of the business system). In the business rule approach it is legitimate for the first time to talk of truly *thin* processes—a long-standing goal among many information technology (IT) professionals.

- In many ways rules are the most important component since they provide control for the other two. The business and its systems are certainly capable of behavior without a well-organized set of rules—but not *effective, adaptive* behavior. Literally, rules are what make a business more than half-smart in how it operates.

The second point above emphasizes that the three basic components of business systems must interrelate in an integrated fashion. Just how they do that represents the new vision of business systems at the heart of the business rule approach. Some of the implications of this new vision are profound.

In the human body, each of the three individual components of the mechanical system also has its own inner workings. In fact, there are individual sciences focusing almost exclusively on each particular component.

Each of the three basic components in the business rule approach must also be understood individually. Each too has its own particular "physiology." These individual "physiologies" are examined one at a time in the three chapters that follow in this part of the book.

- Chapter 5 examines structure, as embodied in the core concepts of the business and their logical connections. In particular, this chapter explains fact models and what they represent.

---

4. At certain points in the discussions that follow in this part, I mention elements of methodology or deliverables that pertain specifically to Business Rule Solutions, LLC. When I use *we* or *our* in these contexts, please note that I am referring to the Principals of Business Rule Solutions.

- Chapter 6 examines control, as embodied in rules. This chapter provides exciting new insights about the inner workings of rules.
- Chapter 7 examines power, as embodied in processes. The business rule approach offers a new view of processes, one that is radical in its simplicity. Ironically, it is in that very simplicity that the big picture of business systems emerges in the business rule approach.

> . . . cyberspace is a new form of community. Remember its motto—No Rules? But soon there were etiquette rules called Netiquette posted in every chat room. *You can't have a sense of community without rules* [emphasis added].
>
> —Judith Martin (Miss Manners)[5]

---

5. From "10 Questions for Judith Martin," *Time Magazine,* December 2, 2002, Vol. 160, No. 23, p. 18.

Organizing Basic Business Knowledge

What You Need to Know about Terms and Facts

In the human body, structure is provided by the bones, which are organized and connected within the skeleton. The skeleton provides both a framework for carrying the weight of the other components as well as a semirigid scheme around which the other softer components can be organized.

A business system must have a corresponding structure. In the business rule approach, this structure is visualized by means of a fact model. Without any exaggeration, a good fact model is no less important to a business system than a strong and complete skeleton is to the human body.

A fact model appears to many IT professionals as more or less equivalent to a high-level data model[1] or class diagram.[2] It some ways it is, but in other, very important ways it is not. I want to highlight those differences for interested readers, so comparisons between fact models and data models appear at several points in this discussion as separate boxed items.

---

1. Sometimes also known as an *entity model* or *entity-relationship* diagram.

2. *Class diagram* is more or less the corresponding term in object orientation. I certainly understand that important distinctions can be made between a data model and a class diagram—and even that these distinctions themselves can be controversial. However, this discussion is informal. For the sake of simplicity, I will simply say *data model* from this point on and assume you understand I also mean class diagrams of a corresponding nature.

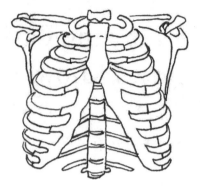

Mechanical Components
$\rightarrow$ Structure: Skeleton
$\rightarrow$ Power: Muscles
$\rightarrow$ Control: Nerves

To the Data Modeler: Data Models versus Fact Models

IT professionals might see a fact model as nothing more than simply a high-level data model. The distinction, however, is an important one. It revolves around the basic purpose—*who and what is the model for?*

Data Models

Many IT professionals use data models as the front-end basis for designing a database or as the data integration blueprint for building a data warehouse. No matter how the data model is developed, it ends up being used primarily as a system development tool. Once created, you are not likely to see business-side workers making continuous use of it thereafter.

Also, although many practitioners do recognize the importance of terminology in creating a good data model, data models in general tend not to be comprehensive about *business* vocabulary. Such parsimony probably arises for both organizational and technical reasons. This practice usually does not cause problems for data models since they are usually not used to support declarative specification of rules on a large scale. By *large scale*, I mean hundreds or thousands of rules.

Fact Models

In contrast with data models, to be successful, a fact model needs to become a central fixture of the operational business. The reason is simple: the fact model represents the basic vocabulary for expressing its rules. When these rules number in the hundreds or thousands, this vocabulary *must* be comprehensive.

This intense focus on business vocabulary in fact models often requires a special business-side support role for its ongoing coordination.[3] Such business-side specialists sometimes already exist in companies today, but rarely if ever do they work with data models.

Although a fact model should serve as an initial blueprint for data design, that use is not its primary purpose. Rather, the purpose of a fact model is literally to *structure basic knowledge of the business.* Creating a successful fact model[4] means capturing that business knowledge from the business-side workers and managers who possess it. This ability is central to the business rule approach. As discussed in Part I, the skill of distilling that business knowledge is essential for business analysts.

Unfortunately, many business-side workers and managers have been intimidated in the past by data models. I want to emphasize that there is no need whatsoever to view a fact model as representing anything technical.[5] It is true that a good fact model can be hard to create. If you have the relevant business knowledge, however, it should never be hard to understand. If it is, somebody is doing something wrong!

Terms and Facts

In the human body, the skeleton has two basic components: the bones and the ligaments that connect the bones. Even though the bones are larger and in a sense more basic, both components are essential.

A fact model represents the basic "skeleton" for the knowledge structure of a business system. As in the skeleton for the human body, a fact model likewise has two basic components: terms and facts. These are equivalent to

---

3. Half-jokingly, we call this role the *terminator.* Refer to Chapter 14 for additional discussion.
4. For an in-depth discussion of how to create a fact model, refer to Ross and Lam [2000].
5. I mean *technical* here in the sense of IT, not in terms of the products or services of the business. These products or services might, of course, be highly technical in their own right.

the bones and ligaments, respectively, in the human body. These terms and facts structure basic business knowledge—that is, they identify things that it is possible to know about.[6]

  Terms and facts structure basic business knowledge.

About Terms

A *term* is a basic word or word phrase in English or another natural language[7] that workers recognize and share in the business. A term carries a particular meaning for the business, which should be unambiguous given a particular context of usage.[8] Terms are always nouns or qualified nouns. Here are some examples.

customer	employee name	date
prospect	delivery date due	high-risk customer
shipment	manager	employee
order	gender	line item
invoice	status	quantity back-ordered

Our meaning of *term* comes straight from *Webster's*.[9] Note the key words "precise meaning" in this definition.

Term: *A word or expression that has a precise meaning in some uses or is peculiar to a science, art, profession, or subject.*

—*Merriam-Webster's Collegiate Dictionary, Tenth Edition*

---

6. Workers, of course, can know many things about the basic operations of the business. Terms and facts establish which of all those basic things the workers will *share*.

7. For convenience, I will drop the phrase *or another natural language* in the discussion from this point on, with the implicit understanding that the discussion applies to any language, not just to English.

8. We take a fact model to represent a single context of usage. This context of usage represents the scope that the fact model covers (sometimes called a *domain of discourse*). From this point forward in the discussion, I will drop *context of usage* when discussing the meaning of terms, with the implicit understanding that this qualification is nonetheless a highly significant one.

9. Refer to Chapter 16 for the meaning of *term* in formal theory.

It is important to note that the particular word or phrase selected as a term represents merely the tip of the iceberg with respect to meaning. More fundamental is the business *concept* for which the word or phrase stands. This concept *must* be defined. That is, the concept a term represents should never be taken for granted. As one practitioner put it, "The more self-evident the meaning of a term is, the more trouble you can expect." As an example, another practitioner from a medium-sized company rattled off six different (and conflicting!) definitions of *customer* from different parts of his organization.

In the business rule approach, a precise definition for each term must be given explicitly in business-oriented (that is, nontechnical[10]) fashion. All facts (and rules) that reference the term will depend on this meaning. Here is an example of a definition.

> ***Customer:*** An organization or individual person that has placed at least one paid order during the previous two years.

To be included in a fact model, a term should satisfy all three of the following fundamental tests.

> **Basic:** Terms in the fact model represent the most basic things of the business—that is, terms that cannot be derived or computed from any other terms. Any term that can be derived or computed should be expressed as the subject of a rule.

> **Atomic:** Terms in the fact model should represent things that are indivisible—that is, not composite—at least as seen from the business's point of view. Terms that have a collective sense (for example, *merchandise, personnel, inventory,* and so on) should be broken down into their atomic constituents before being represented in the fact model.

> **Knowable:** Terms in the fact model should always represent things we can know something about, rather than something that happens. In other words, a fact model is about *knowledge,* not about the actions, processes, or procedures that produce that knowledge. A fact model, for example, might show the terms *customer* and *order,* but it would not show the action *take customer order.*

---

10. Again, I mean *technical* here in the sense of IT, not in terms of the products or services of the business. The definition of some terms can be highly technical in a business sense.

In the business rule approach, the collection of all terms and definitions is called a *Concepts Catalog.*[11] In one sense, this label is merely a dressed-up name for a glossary. Because definitions are so crucial to organizing large sets of rules, however, this glossary needs to be automated. Such support permits changes in the terms to be coordinated directly with all the rules where they appear.

 Every term requires a definition, and every definition belongs in the Concepts Catalog.

Using the Concepts Catalog is the way to avoid a "Tower of Business Babel" when building complex business systems. Here then is a fundamental (and obvious) principle of the business rule approach: We will inevitably work more effectively if we all speak the same language!

 A fact model establishes common business vocabulary.

---

11. This is the term used in the current work (2002) of the Business Rules Group (*http://www.BusinessRulesGroup.com*). The Business Rules Group is using the term Concepts Model to refer to the combination of the Concepts Catalog and the associated fact model.

To the Data Modeler: Types versus Instances

The most basic terms in a fact model represent *types* of things rather than *instances* of those things. For example, a business might have 10,000 customers, but they are represented by the single term *customer*. Incidentally, since the term refers to the type rather than to instances, the term's singular form is preferred for the fact model (that is, *customer* rather than *customers*).

These prescriptions are generally the same as for data models. In data modeling, however, terms almost always represents types of things rather than instances of those things. This is not true for fact models.

Rules often reference things that data modelers would see at the instance level. As a simple example, the terms *male* and *female* might be handled in a data model using a *type code*—a special kind of attribute for distinguishing the type of instances (for example, M = male, F = female). Rules expressed at the business level, however, should reference *male* and *female*, not M and F. Therefore, *male* and *female* might be included in the fact model, whereas the tendency in data modeling probably would be not to include them.

Many such cases involve far more than just two instance-level terms. For example, an organization that inspects ships has thousands of rules that reference hundreds of individual parts of a ship. A health insurance company has thousands of rules that reference hundreds of individual health care treatments. Similarly, many organizations—perhaps even most—have thousands of rules that reference hundreds of individual instance-level terms related to their particular lines of business.

For that reason, standardization of terms at the instance level is often required in the business rule approach. Such standardization focuses on things whose instances can be predicted or prescribed in advance (for example, ship parts, health care treatments, and so on). Handling these more extensive cases requires extensions to fact models that we call *instance models*. As in the examples of ship parts and health care treatments, such instance models often (but not always) involve the product or service of the business. (Refer to Part IV for additional discussion.)

Standardizing instance-level terminology is even more of a business problem than is standardizing type-level terminology. This is something for which data modelers are often not prepared. Nonetheless, the business benefits are substantial—for starters, such standardization enables *knowledge transfer* and *knowledge automation*. These are hardly luxuries in a world where staffs are ever more volatile and where self-service is rapidly becoming the norm.

About Facts

Facts are given by simple, declarative sentences that relate appropriate terms, much as ligaments connect bones in the human skeleton. Here are some examples of fact statements.[12] Note that in each of these examples, a verb or verb phrase (italicized below) connects some of the terms listed earlier.

> Customer *places* order.
>
> Order *is included in* shipment.
>
> Employee *has a* gender.
>
> Manager *is a category of* employee.

Several observations are worth making.

1. Facts represent common or shared verbs and verb phrases of the business. In other words, a fact model extends the common business vocabulary in important ways.

    A fact model extends the common business vocabulary.

2. Every fact is always expressed using a complete sentence, generally following a strict subject-verb-object structure—for example, *Customer places order.*[13] This sentence provides a template, a structured way to talk about how the terms logically connect to each other.

    Facts structure the logical connections we want made between concepts.

3. The collection of all such sentences establishes the full and complete scope of the business system in a very important sense. Even if a worker

---

12. Since this discussion is informal, I will use the word *fact* instead of the more correct *fact statement* in the discussion that follows. The distinction is that the same fact can be given by statements in different forms and/or by statements in different languages (for example, French, Mandarin, and so on). In other words, there can be many different *fact statements* for exactly the same *fact.*

13. In formal terms, such sentences represent *predicates.* Every fact statement is a predicate. Refer to Chapter 17 for in-depth discussion. Incidentally, we do recognize unary facts.

or some automated process produces some other terms and facts, we will literally have no way to share such knowledge in a standard and consistent fashion unless the appropriate terms and facts have been included in the fact model.

A fact model establishes basic business knowledge to be shared.

4. The sentences merely establish facts; they place no constraints on instances of these facts. For example, *Customer places order* represents a fact.[14] It is inappropriate to state the following as a fact per se: *Customer must not place more than 15 orders.* This latter statement is more than a fact—it places a *constraint* on instances of the fact. Thus this latter statement is a rule—part of the control aspect of the business system, *not* part of the structural aspect. A rule represents the nerves, not the skeleton!

Facts recognize what it is possible to know, but given that, no other constraints.

5. Note how the facts are expressed using verbs (for example, *places*). It is important to remember that these verbs do not represent or label any action, process, or procedure per se (for example, *place order*). Any such operation represents a different aspect of the business system—the power or "muscle" aspect. Think of the fact model as providing the most appropriate way[15] to organize knowledge about the *results* of such operations. In other words, terms and facts organize what we can know as the result of actions, processes, and procedures taking place in the business.

Fact models organize basic knowledge about the results of operations, not about how these operations actually take place.

---

14. It actually represents a fact *type*. Since this discussion is informal, however, I will avoid using the somewhat arcane term *fact type*.

15. To be precise, *the most appropriate way* means anomaly free and semantically clear. These are criteria that can actually be tested. In relational theory, normalization prescribes tests (the normal forms) for this purpose. Refer to Chapter 11 in Date [2000].

Using Graphic Fact Models

You might have noticed that even though fact models are usually rendered graphically, no diagrammatic examples have yet been presented. This is not because they are not useful. Just the opposite is true; they are *very* useful. Rather, I wanted to emphasize that a fact model is about what we can *know*. *"What we can know" can always be expressed in natural language sentences.*

A fact model also represents a kind of requirement for business system design. (For more on terms and facts as a kind of requirement, refer to the boxed item.) The sponsor(s) of a business rule project must sign off on the fact model.

We want to stress, however, that sponsors should sign off on the *sentences*—not on graphic fact models. By the way, many system development techniques that use data models have this guideline more or less *backwards!*

 The principal deliverable of the fact-modeling part of a business rule project is a set of declarative sentences.

Terms and Facts as Requirements

Ask managers and workers in the business what they mean by *requirements* for developing business systems, and typically you get answers centered on functions to be performed or on the look and feel of how the system behaves through its interfaces (for example, GUIs). The answer "terms and facts" is almost never among the responses. Nonetheless, they are indeed a kind of requirement.

 Terms and facts are a type of requirement.

Terms and facts are not the *only* kind of requirement in the business rule approach, of course. Without them, however, you cannot provide real meaning or coherency (sense) to all the others, especially to the rules. For that reason, terms and facts actually represent the most *fundamental* kind of requirement.

Terms and facts literally do just that—they provide *meaning*. This meaning, of course, is abstract. It might not be as obvious as what a system does or how the system looks on the outside. Just because something is less obvious, however, does not mean it is any less important. Break a bone, and see what happens to the body's behavior!

 Terms and facts provide meaning and coherency to other kinds of requirements, especially rules.

Let's be very clear about this. A fact model can and should provide a first-cut blueprint for how data will be eventually organized in a database. This data design, however, is an end result—an objective toward which system developers must work. Up front, there is a lot of work to be done first. Consider another analogy.

When you pay an architect to create a blueprint, you expect a house that looks like the blueprint to eventually come out of the effort. Assuming that happens, at that point the blueprint reflects a reality—the house itself. But for the longest time (seemingly forever while you're waiting), the blueprint is nothing more than an organized attempt to determine your basic requirements. It does not really describe the house itself but what you (the owner[16]) *want* the house to be. And to be perfectly frank, deciding what you want the house to be is often the hardest part of all. That is why you hired architects to help you!

 A fact model is a blueprint for basic business knowledge.

---

16. I use *owner* deliberately here. *Owner* is the term John Zachman uses in the Zachman Architecture Framework for the audience of row 2. Row 2 in the Framework focuses on the enterprise model (or business model), in contrast to a system model (row 3) or a technology model (row 4). A fact model is a fundamental part of the business model in row 2.

Zachman, incidentally, suggests the term *semantic model* for the cell in row 2 that addresses the question *what* (that is, structure or data). We believe that a fact model plus the associated Concepts Catalog fits his prescriptions for a semantic model very closely. For more information on John Zachman's thinking, refer to Zachman [2002] and collected articles by Zachman found in the *Business Rules Journal*, available at *http://www.BRCommunity.com*.

Now it might seem that writing sentences should be a lot easier than creating structured fact model diagrams. Are we letting everyone off easy? *No!* Knowledgeable workers on the business side must originate and understand the sentences; business analysts and fact modelers must help clarify and express the sentences in plain business language. This is *hard*—not because English is hard, but because determining how to express what we know about the business in an understandable, agreed-to form can be hard!

Even harder than this is getting all the sentences to fit together as if in some large jigsaw puzzle. This is where the graphic fact model diagram plays an important role.

When creating a blueprint for remodeling your house, you can quickly see when the pieces are not fitting together. The eye often spots the problems quite easily. A fact model serves a similar purpose. In working with sentences, especially a large set representing the basic knowledge of a complex business, it is often hard to spot the redundancies and overlap. Representing the sentences graphically makes this easier.

Figure 5–1 presents a simple fact model in graphic form. The facts from this fact model are listed below. This list includes several facts that are *implicit* (that is, not labeled explicitly) in the graphic fact model. These implicit facts

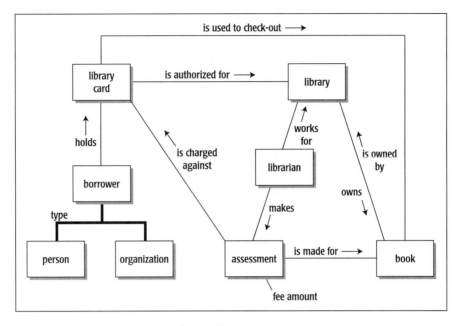

Figure 5–1   Sample fact model for a library

are discussed briefly in Fact Statements for Figure 5–1, along with some final notes on the differences between fact models and data models.

Fact Statements for Figure 5–1
Explicit
- *Library card is used to check out book.*
- *Library card is authorized for library.*
- *Library owns book. (Book is owned by library.)*
- *Librarian works for library.*
- *Librarian makes assessment.*
- *Assessment is made for book.*
- *Assessment is charged against library card.*
- *Borrower holds library card.*

Implicit
- *Person is a category of borrower.*
- *Organization is a category of borrower.*
- *Assessment has a fee amount.*

To the Data Modeler: More on Data Models versus Fact Models

"Is a Category of" Facts

Facts of the "is a category of" variety are often represented implicitly in a fact model. By *implicitly* I mean that the literal words "is a category of" are not actually shown on the model. Instead, the sample fact model in Figure 5–1 uses heavy dark lines to designate the two "is a category of" facts it includes.

Data model approaches vary in their treatment of "is a category of" facts. In some approaches, they are represented as subtypes of some business entity or data object. In others, subtypes are not recognized at all.

In any case, two important distinctions between fact models and data models should be made in this regard.

1. Because of the focus on comprehensive vocabulary in fact models, "is a category of" facts are generally used far more extensively than is subtyping in data models.
2. In fact modeling, no assumptions whatsoever are made about how an "is a category of" fact will be physically represented. In data models, in contrast, use of subtyping is often shaped (or indeed even constrained) by assumptions about the physical representation of "is a category of" facts.

"Has a" Facts

Facts of the "has a" variety are also often represented implicitly in the fact model. Again, by *implicitly* I mean that the literal words "has a" are not actually shown on the model. Instead, the sample fact model in Figure 5–1 uses a thin line for the one "has a" fact it includes (Assessment has a fee amount).

To avoid clutter, "has a" facts are sometimes omitted from the graphic fact model altogether unless they are involved in core business rules and/or computations central to the business problem. In one sense, "has a" facts represent detail that can be handled better elsewhere (for example, in a business rule repository). Indeed, they might never even be expressed as sentences. Still, it is important to recognize them as simply another kind of fact under the business rule approach.

Data models treat "has a" facts as representing attributes of some business entity or data object. Depending on the approach, such attributes might or might not be shown explicitly in the data model.

Cardinality and Optionality

Fact models do not represent certain kinds of specifications to which data modelers might be accustomed. For example, neither *cardinality* (also called *multiplicity*) nor *optionality* is ever represented for the explicit facts in a fact model.

These explicit facts roughly correspond to relationships in data models. Data-modeling techniques usually prescribe including some indication of cardinality for these relationships. For each relationship, this answers the question, "How many?" For example, can a given customer place many orders or only a single (one) order? Cardinality is important in database design; however, any type of cardinality except *many* is actually a form of rule. For example, consider the statement *An order must not be placed by more than one customer.* This statement actually represents a rule expressed for the fact *Order is placed by customer.*

The same is true about expressing the optionality of a relationship. Indicating a relationship to be mandatory (that is, not optional) is a form of rule.

The business rule approach emphasizes developing terms and facts *before* plunging deeply into the expression of any form of rules, including those pertaining to cardinality and optionality. Moreover, all rules should be stated explicitly (again, in sentences) so that their business motivations can be reviewed apart from system or data designs.

The Fact Model and Behavior

A good fact modeler seeks to ensure that each term or fact is represented in the fact model one and only one time and that it does not overlap any other term or fact. In other words, the fact model ensures that terms and facts are *unified* and *unique.* Later, this will provide a way to ensure that all rules are defined consistently and that different actions will operate in consistent fashion.

 By helping to ensure unification and uniqueness of terms and facts, the fact model ensures consistency in business behavior.

Like the skeleton in the human body, the terms and facts in a fact model should represent the *minimum* set needed to provide a suitable framework for the other components. There are no extra bones in the human body—every one has its specific purpose. Adding a bone here or there is not going to improve the body's mechanics. Anyway, bones are relatively expensive because, although essential, they represent overhead to the end result actually desired—namely, *behavior*.

Similarly, a few extra terms and facts here or there in the fact model will not help the business body operate. And they will prove expensive. A fact model helps ensure there are no extra terms and facts in the basic knowledge of the business.

 A fact model should represent a minimum set of terms and facts.

Some professionals believe that if they can get the behavior right, the structure will simply fall into place. That is not our experience at all. It's the body as a whole that matters. You can design a lot of very elegant appendages and a lot of fancy behaviors, but there had better be a well-considered skeleton to hold them all together!

References

Date, C. J. 2000. *An Introduction to Database Systems* (7th ed.). Boston, MA: Addison-Wesley.

Ross, Ronald G., and Gladys S. W. Lam. 2000. *The BRS Fact Modeling Practitioner's Guide: Developing the Business Basis for Data Models.* Houston, TX: Business Rule Solutions, LLC. Available at *http://www.BRSolutions.com.*

Zachman, John A. 2002. *The Zachman Framework: A Primer for Enterprise Engineering and Manufacturing* (electronic book). Available at *http://www.zachmaninternational.com.*

CHAPTER 6

Exercising Control

What You Need to Know about Rules

In the human body, control is provided by the nervous system, an organized collection of nerves that connect to the muscles. Responses to all stimuli are coordinated through the firing of nerve impulses—no firing, no movement, and therefore no behavior.

A business system must have similar control over behavior. In the business rule approach, this control is provided by rules.

Rules for Control

Rules are familiar to all of us in real life. We play games by rules, we live under a legal system based on a set of rules, we set rules for our children, and so on.

Yet the idea of rules in business systems is ironically foreign to most IT professionals. Say "rules" and many IT professionals think vaguely of expert systems or artificial intelligence—approaches deemed appropriate for only very specialized and/or very advanced kinds of problems. There is little recognition of how central rules actually are to the basic, day-to-day operations of the business.

Not coincidentally, many business-side workers and managers have become so well indoctrinated in *procedural* views for developing requirements that thinking in terms of rules might initially seem foreign and perhaps

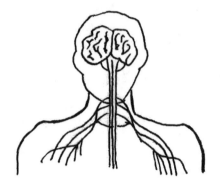

Mechanical Components

→ Structure: Skeleton
→ Power: Muscles
→ Control: Nerves

abstract. Virtually every methodology is guilty in this regard, whether for business process reengineering, system development, or software design. This is unfortunate for at least two important reasons.

1. Thinking about the control aspect of any organized activity in terms of rules is actually very natural. For example, imagine trying to explain almost any game you can think of—chess, checkers, baseball, football, tennis, and so on—without explaining the rules on which the moves in the game are based. Even if it were possible (that's doubtful!), explaining things that way would certainly not be very *effective*.

2. Business-side workers and managers have the knowledge it takes to create good rules. What *they* know makes all the difference in the world in playing the business game.

The business rule approach not only depends on good rules but also offers new insights into what they are about. Without any exaggeration, good rules are no less important to a business system than a robust, finely tuned nervous system is to the human body.

The first step in understanding the central role of rules in the business rule approach is simply to relate them to the issue of control. The boxed item, Sample Rules, presents a light sampling of typical rules,[1] each catego-

---

1. Since this discussion is informal, I will use the word *rule* instead of the more correct *rule statement* to refer to expressions of rules. The distinction is that the same rule can be given by statements in different forms and/or by statements in different languages (for example, French, Mandarin, and so on). In other words, there can be many different *rule statements* for exactly the same *rule*. (I made the equivalent distinction in Chapter 5 between *fact* and *fact statement*.) Obviously, it is desirable to use consistent conventions in creating rule statements. Such conventions are provided by RuleSpeak, as discussed in Part III.

rized according to the kind of control it addresses. Note how far-ranging these categories of control really are. *Every* aspect of operational control in a business system—or indeed in the business itself—can be addressed by rules.

 Rules provide control in the business rule approach.

Sample Rules

Restrictions
> *A customer must not place more than three rush orders charged to its credit account.*

Heuristics
> *A customer with preferred status should have its orders filled immediately.*

Computations
> *A customer's annual order volume must be computed as total sales closed during the company's fiscal year.*

Inference
> *A customer must be considered preferred if the customer places more than five orders over $1,000.*

Timing
> *A customer must be archived if the customer does not place any orders for 36 consecutive months.*

Triggers
> *"Send-advance-notice" must be executed for an order when the order is shipped.*

The second step in understanding rules—a crucial one—is to understand how they relate to terms and facts. In the business rule approach, rules build directly on terms and facts. Actually, a rule should simply add the sense of *must* or *must not* to terms and facts that have already been defined in the fact model and Concepts Catalog. In business problems involving hundreds or thousands of rules—not at all uncommon—there is no way to achieve consistency across such large numbers of rules without a common base of terms and facts. This important principle of the business rule approach is discussed in Part III, which explains how to express rules in appropriate fashion.

 Rules build directly on terms and facts.

The third step in understanding rules—also a crucial one—is to understand how rules relate to events. It is to that subject that we now turn.

Rules and Events

Business systems have addressed the validation and editing of data since the first computer programs for business were written many years ago. Unfortunately, the programming view of editing and validating data is a very procedural one, simply because traditional computer programs work that way. With respect to rules, however, the procedural view is a very limiting one. It definitely represents a case of "can't see the forest for the trees."

Rules in the business rule approach must be perceived and expressed *declaratively*, independent of processes and procedures. Appreciating the importance of this principle is key. It inevitably moves us away from seeing requirements for business systems as essentially a programming problem and toward viewing them as a true *business* problem. Happily, this view is also greatly simplifying. Suddenly, the forest emerges from the trees.

Understanding this fundamental principle of the business rule approach requires careful examination of the relationship between rules and events. Intuitively, we know that rules must be enforced when certain events occur. (If nothing happens, rules cannot be violated, and therefore the rules can remain dormant.) But what exactly is the connection between rules and events?

First, it is important simply to recognize that rules and events are not the same. This might seem obvious, but it is nonetheless a common source of confusion.

 Rules and events are not the same.

To understand this, we must probe into events more deeply. What is an event? There are at least two ways of looking at events, both correct.

1. **The business perspective**: For the business, an event is when something happens that requires the business to respond, even if only in a trivial way. (Usually, the response is *not* trivial.) For example, a customer might place an order. This is an event that requires a well-organized response. Often, as discussed in Chapter 7, we try to organize our response to such business events in advance—for example, with workflow models, procedures, scripts, and so on.

2. **The IT perspective:** For the business system, an event is when something happens that needs to be noted or recorded[2] because knowing about the event is potentially important to other activities, either those occurring during the same time frame or those that might happen later. In the business rule approach, of course, such recording is always based on predefined terms and facts—that is, primarily on the basis of the fact model. A business system can support the fact model in several ways (for example, as a database design, a class diagram, and so on). To simplify matters, let's just say there is some data somewhere in the business system that must be updated (created, modified, or deleted) to record the event. Otherwise, the business cannot know about the event.[3] For convenience, I will call these *update events*.

Now, how do events connect with rules? Suppose the following rule is specified for the business: *A customer must be assigned to an agent if the customer has placed an order.* Figure 6–1 shows the relevant terms and facts for this rule.

The rule itself has been expressed in a declarative manner. This means, in part, that it does not indicate any particular procedure or process to enforce it. It is simply a rule—nothing more and nothing less.

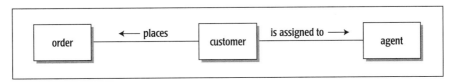

Figure 6–1   Terms and facts for the customer rule

---

2. More precisely, an *event* can be defined as any change in state. However, this discussion is informal and such an exacting definition unnecessary here.

3. Except perhaps informally, based on interpersonal or intersystem messages.

Declarative also means that the rule makes no reference to any business event or update event where it potentially could be violated and thus need to be tested. The rule does not say, for example, "*When* a customer places an order, then. . . ."

This observation is extremely important for the following reason. "*When* a customer places an order" *is not the only event when the rule could potentially be violated.* Actually, there is another event when this rule could be violated. In business terms this other event might be "*When* an agent leaves our company. . . ." The corresponding update event might be "*When* an agent is deleted. . . ."[4] This other event could pose a violation of the rule under the following circumstances: (a) The agent is assigned to a customer, and (b) that customer has placed at least one order.

In other words, the rule could potentially be violated during *two* quite distinct kinds of events. The first, "*When* a customer places an order . . .", is rather obvious. The second, "*When* an agent leaves the company . . .", might be much less so. Both events are nonetheless important because either could produce a violation of the rule.

This example is not atypical or unusual in any way.[5] In fact, it is quite commonplace. In general, *every* rule (in proper declarative form) produces[6] two or more kinds of update events when it could potentially be violated.

 Every rule produces two or more update events when it could potentially be violated.

About Violations of Rules

What happens when an event occurs that might violate a given rule? At least two things should happen, as follows.

1. No matter which event it is, at that point the rule should *fire*[7] so that the prescribed test or constraint can be applied.

---

4. The specific update event that poses a potential violation of the rule is actually the deletion of an instance for the "is assigned to" fact.

5. Rules do exist that are specific to individual update events, but these rules represent the exception, rather than the general case.

6. I mean *produces* in the sense of can be *analyzed to discover.*

7. I use the term *fire* in this discussion to mean loosely both *execute* (to evaluate the relevant condition[s]) and, if necessary, *take appropriate action.* Sometimes *fire* is used to refer only to the former.

2. Assuming the rule is about preventing errors,[8] a message should be returned to the end user (that is, the business worker) to explain why the violation occurred.

What should the error message returned to the business worker say? *The error message should contain exactly the same text as was originally given for the rule.* In the example above, this means the error message will literally read, "A customer must be assigned to an agent if the customer has placed an order."[9]

To put this more strongly, in the business rule approach the rule statement *is* the error message. As discussed in Part I, we believe that the architecture of business systems should always be viewed first and foremost as a *business* problem—not as a technical problem.[10] This treatment of error messages in the business rule approach supports that goal in a fundamental way. It also has important implications for the front-end requirements-gathering process, as discussed in the boxed item, Rules as Requirements.

 The rule statement is the error message.

Rules as Requirements

In the business rule approach, the principal error messages end users will see once the system is operational should be the very same rules that knowledgeable workers on the business side gave as requirements during the earlier design of the business system.[11] The error messages and the requirements are literally one and the same. Well-expressed rules during the requirements process mean well-expressed error messages; poorly expressed rules during the requirements process mean poorly expressed error messages.

Continued

---

8. That is, the rule does not perform an automatic computation, inference, and so on. Later in this chapter I will call rules that prevent errors *rejectors*.

9. Additional text can be provided, of course, to explain the relevance of the rule to the specific event, to suggest corrective measures, and so on.

10. In a truly *friendly* business rule system, when a rule is violated, a procedure or script can be made available to the end user to assist in taking immediate corrective action. This opportunity is discussed in Chapter 7.

11. The actual rule statements can be refined or supplemented, of course, during prototyping and/or system testing (or afterward).

Several observations about this principle are worth making. First, direct assistance in expressing the rules up front will prove extremely valuable to the workers involved. We see this as an important skill for the business analyst, a role described in Part I.

Second is the potential for closing the requirements gap between the business side and the IT side that still plagues so many companies. In traditional approaches, much is usually lost in the translation of up-front requirements to the actual running system. In the business rule approach, the business side gets back whatever it puts in. This is exactly as it should be for a business-driven approach.

 The business rule approach helps to close the requirements gap.

In summary, what does this analysis reveal about the relationship between rules and events? First, it illustrates the basic point that rules and events, while related, are not the same. Second, it illustrates that there are always potentially multiple events when any given rule could be violated. Figures 6–2 and 6–3 provide additional examples to reinforce this crucial point. In the business rule approach, rules are central—*not* events.

 In the business rule approach, rules—not events—are central.

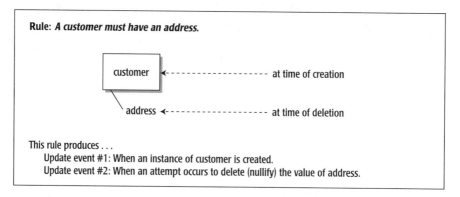

Figure 6–2 Multiple events for a simple rule

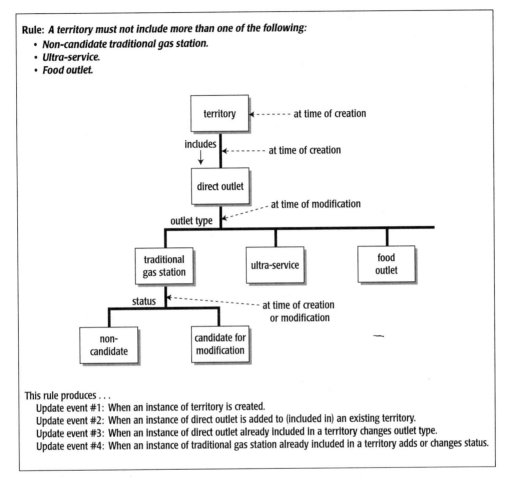

Rule: *A territory must not include more than one of the following:*
- *Non-candidate traditional gas station.*
- *Ultra-service.*
- *Food outlet.*

This rule produces . . .
    Update event #1: When an instance of territory is created.
    Update event #2: When an instance of direct outlet is added to (included in) an existing territory.
    Update event #3: When an instance of direct outlet already included in a territory changes outlet type.
    Update event #4: When an instance of traditional gas station already included in a territory adds or changes status.

Figure 6–3   Multiple events for a more complex rule

Implications of Rules Playing the Central Role

Let's examine some of the implications of this central role for rules. On the technical side, discovering and supporting update events becomes a crucial implementation concern. Fortunately, business logic technology[12] can often

---

12. By *business logic technology,* I mean *rule engines, decision management platforms, business logic servers,* and so on. Since this discussion is focused on concepts rather than technology, I will not use any of these more technical terms in this part of the book.

do this automatically—a huge boost to productivity in building reliable business software.

 Automatic support for identifying and supporting update events for rules is an important feature for business logic technology.

The emphasis on rules and their separation from events opens many new doors of opportunity for both IT and the business. Among these opportunities are the following.

Simple consistency: The two or more update events when a rule might be violated are likely to be embedded in at least two different processes or procedures. (In the earlier example, this might include *Take an order* and *Drop an agent*.) Often, these events will be embedded in many more different processes or procedures than that. Yet for all of these, there is only a *single* rule. That same rule should fire when any of the update events occur in any of the processes or procedures where the rule might be violated. By this means, the business rule approach ensures complete consistency in the "editing criteria" applied across all these procedures. It also ensures there are no holes arising from omissions for less than obvious kinds of events.

Adaptability: Separating the rule from the processes and procedures where it can be violated allows the rule itself to be specified *in one place*. One-place specification (single-sourcing) means the rule will be easier to find—and to change quickly—once the business system is implemented.[13]

Reengineering: Business processes and procedures are generally organized as responses to business events. Declarative rules, however, are specified in *eventless* fashion. They are the pure essence of the business—the Rule Book for the business game. (Refer to the boxed item, About the Rule Book, for additional discussion.) This clarity opens up altogether new horizons for reengineering business processes.

---

13. This includes prototypes in which end users test-drive new processes and procedures *before* implementation.

Rules are key to reengineering business processes.

About the Rule Book

The Rule Book[14] should not be paper-based but rather automated. That way it can play a very active role not only during the system development project but once the new business system becomes operational as well. Software tools are now available that enable direct *business-side* management of rules, opening unprecedented opportunities for the business. (Refer to Chapter 13 for more about rule management.)

Does the Rule Book complicate matters for the business? *No!* A business system is no more complicated by having independent rules than are the games of chess, baseball, and football by having their own independent rule books. I believe the value of Rule Independence speaks for itself.

Rather, the point we take is the following. Your approach for developing requirements should put the Rule Book on at least an equal footing with deliverables for developing processes and procedures (such as workflow models, use cases, scripts,[15] or other techniques). These latter deliverables are needed to produce the raw power to do work—muscles for the business to flex. A Rule Book represents a well-developed nervous system, a way to ensure your business works *smart*.

Ways in Which Rules Can Exercise Control: Functional Categories of Rules

Rules come in three basic varieties with respect to the type of control they exercise: *rejectors*, *producers*, and *projectors*. All rules fall into one of these three functional categories, which are discussed briefly below. Chapter 10 provides a more complete classification including relevant subcategories. Additional discussion appears in Part V, Appendix C.

---

14. A Rule Book is a key deliverable of Proteus, the Business Rule Solutions, LLC, business rule methodology.

15. We use the term *script* for any detailed procedure workers can follow. Scripts are discussed in Chapter 7. BRScripts are a rule-based form of specifying procedures in Proteus.

Rejectors

Many rules are naturally rejectors—that is, left to their own devices,[16] they simply reject any event that would cause a violation to occur.[17] The specific sequence of activity would occur more or less as follows.

1. An end user initiates a procedure to do some work, for example, *Take a customer order.*
2. The end user's activity produces an update event to record the results of the work, for example, *Create an instance of order.*
3. The update event causes a rule to fire, for example, *An order must have a ship-to address.*
4. The rule checks whether the end user has actually given a ship-to address with the order. Suppose the end user has *not* done so.
5. The rule causes the update event to be rejected—that is, the action fails, and the order is *not* created.[18]

This analysis reveals the following important point about rejectors. In their native form, rejectors are very narrow-minded. Either the end user plays by the rules, or the work will not be accepted. If there is any question about the quality of the work—that is, about the quality (consistency) of the data that would result from it—the work will simply be rejected (until correct). In other words, rejectors *insist* upon data quality and do so by active, real-time interventions in ongoing work.[19]

 Rejector-type rules address data quality.

---

16. Often, such rules are not left entirely to "their own devices." For example, when a rule fires and a violation is detected, a user-friendly business rule system might automatically offer a script that the user can follow to correct the violation. Such capability is discussed in Chapter 7.

17. Rejectors are constraints, but then, formally, so are projectors. It is therefore misleading to use the term *constraint* exclusively for rejectors, even though this practice is common among IT professionals, especially those involved with database technology.

18. For simplicity, I am ignoring the opportunity to invoke an appropriate script at this point to allow the user to correct the violation immediately.

19. In general, a rule cannot *directly* prevent a user from doing something wrong inside a process. A process is more or less like a black box whose semantics are unknown. However, the rule can prevent the *results* of the process from being recorded. In other words, the rule can reject the data that the process "wants" to leave behind once it finishes executing if the rule is not satisfied with the results.

This brings me to another point. The business rule approach emphasizes real-time enforcement of rules—in other words, *real-time compliance.* The objective is to coordinate ongoing activities, to ensure optimal (that is, correct) results on an as-you-go basis in doing work. Rejectors therefore play a high-profile role in the business rule approach.

 The business rule approach emphasizes real-time compliance.

Producers

A producer-type rule never rejects update events. Instead, it always accepts them and automatically calculates or derives something for the end user. In performing this computation the producer uses all relevant data, whether old or new (that is, resulting from the most recent update event). For example, in taking an order, a producer-type rule might recompute the current order total each time a new line item for the order is entered.

Producers automate computation. In other words, no programming is required to implement them. The results computed from a producer are guaranteed to be both current and correct.[20] Moreover, since producers are generally multievent like all rules, rule-based computation means there is no chance of missing less than obvious kinds of events where recomputation needs to occur.

Producers are really simply *functions* defined in a declarative manner. Producers seem much friendlier than rejectors because they do not inhibit update events but rather provide additional mileage from them. Their overall purpose is to boost end-user and programming productivity.

 Rule-based functions enhance productivity.

Projectors

A projector-type rule is the exact opposite of a rejector in a fundamental way. Specifically, a projector-type rule never rejects update events. Instead, like producers, it always accepts them and automatically takes some other action—that is, produces some other event—as a result.

---

20. That is, correct given how the rule was specified. If the rule was specified imprecisely, the results, of course, might not be as intended.

In general, a projector can be expressed as *if this, then that too.* In other words, a projector literally projects "this" to "that."[21] There are actually many kinds of automatic events that projectors can cause, but among the most important are the following.

- *Inference:* Infer new facts—that is, knowledge—from existing facts, providing automated assistance in making decisions.
- *Triggers:* Execute processes and procedures automatically.

Like producers, projectors seem much friendlier than rejectors because they do not inhibit update events but rather provide additional mileage from them.[22] Also like producers, projectors provide automatic value-adding behavior; that is, they eliminate given behavior as an end-user responsibility, providing automated assistance in performing operational work.

 Projector-type rules provide automatic value-adding behavior.

Projectors extend the overall range of rules significantly. The complete spectrum of rules is examined more closely in the boxed item.

The Spectrum of Rules

The business rule approach covers the entire spectrum of rules, from the simplest kind of validation rules to the most advanced forms of inference. The goal is a unified approach to the capture and management of all such rules.

---

21. The projection from "this" to "that" might or might not be immediate when the event occurs. This depends on the particular business logic technology and on how it is used. In the classic use of expert systems, for example, the firing of rules was often delayed—that is, not inline with actual ongoing events. More recent practice, however, has emphasized firing rules on a more immediate, inline basis. In general, this approach proves much more effective for operational business purposes.

22. This is not entirely accurate. For example, a projector can be used to switch on (that is, enable) a rejector-type rule in appropriate circumstances. The net result would be potential rejection of update events in those circumstances.

To illustrate the extremes in this spectrum of rules, consider the following situation that might occur in a baseball game. Suppose it is the bottom of the seventh inning, with two outs, two strikes on the batter, and two base runners. The score is tied. The batter is left-handed.

Rejector: A validation rule might ensure that the batter still gets only three strikes even if the pitcher is changed.

Producer: A computation rule might compute the batter's hit percentage in similar prior circumstances.

Projector: Inference rules might help choose the best relief pitcher under the given circumstances.

Logic Traces

In the latter two cases above, especially for projectors, the results might very well prove unexpected or nonintuitive. This can often happen when larger sets of inference rules are involved in automatic "reasoning" performed by business logic technology. The user (in this case, say, the pitching coach) would be entirely justified in wanting to ascertain *how* the results were produced.

Continued

To pursue this, the user must be able to audit the result,[23] preferably in real time if the situation permits. This means being able to work (or trace) backward from the result through the chain of rules that fired to produce it. The business logic technology must, of course, support this need—a capability called *logic traces*.

Logic traces allow decision-making logic to be directly audited.

Several scenarios are possible as the user traces back through the logic. A subject matter expert might find flaws that need correcting, or he or she might have new insights about where improvements can be made. Someone less expert about the particular decision will simply learn more about the basic knowledge of the business.

This is an important way in which a business rule system is instructional. Even more than that, logic traces take business rules to the next higher level—a step closer to what in Part I were called *knowledge companions*. All this is possible because business rule systems always ensure that business logic is visible to authorized users.

The business rule approach always supports visible logic.

Expanding the Coverage of Rules

Suggestions and Guidelines

As discussed earlier, the business rule approach emphasizes rules as a principal way to exercise control. Rules can also be used, however, to *influence* behavior rather than to control it directly. Such rules act more as guidelines or heuristics—that is, as *suggestors* [Ross 1997]—instead of hard-and-fast rules. An example illustrates such use.

Consider the sample rule discussed earlier: *A customer must be assigned to an agent if the customer has placed an order.* Let's make a simple change in the wording, switching *must* to *should*. The rule now becomes: *A customer should*

---

23. Assuming, of course, that the user is properly authorized.

be assigned to an agent if the customer has placed an order. The original rule has now been converted into a suggestor. The boxed item (The Form, Fit, and Function of Suggestors) examines important details about this transformation.

The Form, Fit, and Function of Suggestors

Form

The form of the suggestor remains exactly the same as before the transformation. The only modification is that the word *must* has been changed to the word *should*. This consistency in form represents an important aspect of the business rule approach. Put simply, if you have a way to express rules for behavior, then you already have a language for expressing guidelines for behavior. The consistency in form also again suggests the potential of the business rule approach for knowledge management.

 Suggestors are expressed in the same form as other rules.

Fit

The firing of the suggestor remains exactly as before. Specifically, a suggestor fires upon the occurrence of any of the two or more kinds of update events in which the suggestor could be "violated." Also, like any rule, the suggestor should not be embedded in the procedures that produce those events. This allows for easy change in the suggestor. Such adaptability again is the result of Rule Independence.

 Suggestors fire the same way as other rules.

Function

Apart from the word change, the enforcement level of the suggestor is the only thing that differs after the transformation. Rules, of course, take whatever action necessary for enforcement. For the given rule, normally this would mean rejecting any update event that would cause a violation. As a suggestor, no such enforcement action is taken. The update event is *not* prevented. Instead, the end user is just informed of the guideline.

Continued

A suggestor is merely a rule that fires but is not currently enforced.

As always, the rule statement should pop up on the end user's screen. For the suggestor, however, the text is not an error message but merely a guideline. It informs the worker that under the given circumstance, some particular action (update event) is, or is not, appropriate. In other words, suggestors impart business knowledge to influence how work is conducted, but they do not attempt to control the work outright.

  A suggestor imparts business knowledge to influence how work is conducted.

Handling Exceptions

When introduced to the business rule approach, the first reaction some people have is that their business has far more exceptions to rules than rules per se. They question how all these exceptions can be handled in any organized fashion. This is a valid concern.

The business rule approach offers no silver bullet to the *business* problem of having too many exceptions to rules. It does, however, offer a very simple *technical* answer. This technical answer, in turn, does have implications for business process reengineering and for streamlining business operations. I will comment briefly on that momentarily.

First, let's examine the issue of exceptions to rules from the technical point of view. Consider the following rule: *A library card must not be held by more than one borrower, unless one of the borrowers is Bill Gates.* This rule includes a clear-cut exception. The normal rule for library cards is *A library card must not be held by more than one borrower.* Loosely stated, the exception is *Don't enforce this normal rule if Bill Gates is one of the borrowers who holds the library card.*

Careful examination of this exception reveals something quite interesting. Reword the exception to delete *Don't enforce* and incorporate the more rule-like *must be disabled.* The exception now reads as follows: *The normal rule for library cards must be disabled if Bill Gates is one of the borrowers who holds the library card.* What emerges is another rule!

Specifically, what emerges is a projector. This new rule "watches" for events that could affect evaluation of the condition *if Bill Gates is one of the borrowers who holds the library card.* If the condition is found to be true, the new rule takes an action automatically in response. The particular action it takes is to disable (switch off) the original rule, so that it will no longer be enforced for that particular library card. The bottom line is that *the exception to the rule is simply another rule!*

As a technical matter, the business rule approach *always* views exceptions to rules as simply more rules. This puts exceptions to rules on the same playing field as all other rules. This recognition has important consequences on the business side too, as examined briefly in the boxed item, The Cost of Exceptions to Rules.

    Exceptions to rules are always expressed as rules.

The Cost of Exceptions to Rules

Recognizing that exceptions to rules merely represent more rules is crucial for a business reason—one that touches on requirements development, on business process reengineering, and, indeed, on the business itself. Briefly, the reason is simply this: *All rules cost something.*

    All rules cost something.

The cost of rules is not simply the direct cost of their implementation and maintenance in business systems. The real cost often lies hidden in the associated documentation, training, administration, and time—the time it takes to communicate the rules and the time it takes to change the rules. In the 21st-century business, of course, time is among the most precious of commodities. Your business does not need *more* rules—it probably needs fewer (*good*) rules!

    Having fewer (good) rules is generally better than having more rules.

Rules and Guidance in the Business Rule Approach

To conclude this discussion, let's revisit the question of how rules provide control in the business rule approach. In the human body, nerves connect to muscles, the source of power for behavior. The nerves guide and control the muscles and, by that means, the resulting behavior. However, the nerves are not actually embedded within the muscles themselves.

In a business rule system, rules are like the nerves. They connect to processes—the source of power for behavior. The rules control the processes and, by that means, the resulting behavior. However, as we have discussed, the rules should not actually be embedded within the processes.

Processes or procedures connect to rules via update events. When a process or procedure attempts to satisfy some business event, the corresponding update event will occur. This can fire one or more rules, which will determine whether the event is undertaken correctly or will produce a desired outcome. Depending on the result, appropriate action will be taken. The exact nature of the action depends on the type of rule.

Control is externalized from the processes or procedures and is established in a separate rule layer or component. This permits *direct* management of the rules, which in turn permits much closer tie-in to the business side. This idea of Rule Independence is a centerpiece of the business rule approach. The various principles underlying Rule Independence are enumerated at the end of Chapter 7, after the additional implications for processes and procedures are reviewed.

 Rule Independence is key to business-driven systems.

Looking briefly ahead to those implications, one result is simplicity. To borrow a popular IT buzzword, taking out the rules means the processes and procedures become *thin*. The direct benefits of thin processes and procedures are significant in their own right. On a far grander scale, however, we believe Rule Independence can revolutionize how work in the company is organized and conducted. That potential is examined in the next chapter.

Reference

Ross, Ronald G. 1997. *The Business Rule Book* (2nd ed.). Houston, TX: Business Rule Solutions, LLC. Available at *http://www.BRSolutions.com*.

CHAPTER 7

Doing Work

What You Need to Know about Processes

In the human body, power is provided through the muscles, which enable motion. Motion results in the behavior that we see from the outside. On the inside, however, the muscles are connected to the skeleton, which provides a framework. The muscles are also connected to the nerves, which provide control. Without these other two vital internal components, meaningful behavior would be impossible.

A business system must have similar "power." This power—the power that produces the "motion" of the system—is provided by processes.

In general, a process takes some input (often provided by an end user working through some computer screens) and transforms it into some desired output. The process operates according to an algorithm provided by its designer or programmer. Simple as that. The only problem is that in traditional approaches, the processes are *not* all that simple. In fact, they are quite complex and therefore quite difficult to change.

The business rule approach offers powerful innovations for processes. By taking the rules out of the processes, it can produce processes that are relatively simple—ones that *can* be changed as the need arises.

 The business rule approach produces processes that are easier to change.

Mechanical Components

→ Structure: Skeleton

→ Power: Muscles

→ Control: Nerves

This simplification has repercussions far beyond IT—indeed, it has far-reaching consequences for the business as a whole. In particular, it can change the very nature of *work* in the business. We like to say that rules can revolutionize work. This chapter suggests how that can happen.

 Rules can revolutionize work.

Challenges Facing Businesses Today

Before examining how the business rule approach enables this innovation, let's review some of the challenges facing 21st-century businesses, particularly as they relate to business processes.

Time shock: As the rate of change accelerates, workers are constantly thrust into new roles and responsibilities. They must be guided through unfamiliar procedures as thoroughly and as efficiently as possible—but with minimum human intervention. The business pays a price, either directly or indirectly, if getting the workers up to speed is too slow (or too painful).

Training: The flip side of time shock is the issue of training—*how* to get the workers up to speed. Training is an expensive and time-consuming affair. Yet as the rate of change accelerates, more and more (re)training is required. What is the solution? Training must be built into the business systems that support workers in carrying out daily processes and procedures. We believe *business rules*—not computer-assisted training or anything like that—can help make that happen. We like to say that business rule systems are instructional. Later in this chapter, I show how this goal can be achieved.

Adaptability: In the National Football League (NFL), if a play is not working for a team, it will be gone from its play book within a couple of games (possibly along with a coach or two!), and a new play will be substituted for it. In effect, the plays are essentially throwaways—cheap enough to discard readily, with minimum disruption or cost to the team. The reason NFL plays are throwaways is that the knowledge necessary to run them is embodied elsewhere—in the scoreboard,[1] in the skills of the players, in the heads of the coaches, and most importantly, in the NFL rule book.

Similarly, businesses need to view their own procedures as throwaways—that is, cheap enough to discard and replace readily when the procedures no longer work well (that is, no longer make "yardage" for the business). Today, this generally means throwing away whole applications (or legacy systems) and replacing them with new ones, either built in-house or purchased from an outside source. Such replacement, of course, is far too expensive to do frequently. So businesses are stuck with procedures that work poorly (and only seem to get worse with time), often watching helplessly as the competition introduces better ones.

 Throwaway procedures are a must for the business to remain competitive.

What can a business do about these challenges? In the discussion that follows, I explain how business rules can fundamentally change how work is organized and managed in the business. The implications are indeed far-reaching.

---

1. The names of the variable information posted on the scoreboard are terms that represent the most basic knowledge constructs of the game of football—for example, *quarter, time, score, down*, and so on.

Putting Business Rules to Work

It is generally true that the more you know, the better you can do. If this were not the case, businesses would not spend resources on training and education. We would not spend the first decade or two of our lives in school, or bother to read, or even have libraries. There would be no dictionaries, no encyclopedias, no phone directories, and no Web.

Business rules are about *knowing*—that is, about basic business knowledge. Specifically, as explained in Chapters 5 and 6, business rules represent the terms, facts, and rules of the business. *Knowing* seems passive. So what do business rules have to do with *doing* work? This is no idle question. After all, it's doing the work that gets the product out the door and into the customers' hands.

A time-tested maxim in training is always *to build on what you know*. There are several ways in which this idea applies to developing a new approach for work (that is, the *doing*) in the business rule approach. To understand these ways better, let's restate the maxim in two parts as follows. First, always build on what you know. Second, always build on what you already know how to do. Each of these two points is examined in detail in the remainder of this chapter.

 Always build on what you know—and already know how to do.

Building on What You Know

Let's briefly review some of the basic ideas of the business rule approach so we can apply them to rethinking how work in the business should be organized.

Basing Procedures on Terms and Facts

A basic principle of the business rule approach is that terms and facts (the most basic forms of knowing) should be shared and defined independently of the doing. As discussed in Chapter 5, this objective is supported by developing a fact model and Concepts Catalog.

Procedures should always comply with these predefined terms and facts; that is, procedures should always reuse these terms and facts instead of developing their own, private versions. So the first and most basic aspect of understanding how work is organized in the business rule approach is the principle that no procedure ever defines "data" on its own (if it intends to share it). Do not underestimate how dramatically this principle in itself simplifies procedures under the business rule approach.

 Sharing common terms and facts simplifies procedures.

Basing Procedures on Rule Independence

The business rule approach shifts into high gear, of course, by recognizing that rules are also part of knowing. Like all parts of knowing, rules should not be embedded in the doing. We call this *Rule Independence*.

Only a relatively small portion of traditional applications literally support the actual steps of a procedure (that is, the doing) from a business perspective. Most of the code is devoted to editing, validations, derivations, and calculations—in other words, to supporting business rules.[2] When you take the rules out of traditional application logic, the result is a *thin process*.

I mean *thin* in the following sense: The process or procedure prescribes *only* the necessary series of steps to accomplish the desired work result. Excluded are all the rules—and all the error handling when violations of rules occur. (I will get to that crucial aspect a bit later.)

 Rule Independence results in thin processes.

Now, an initial image of work (that is, doing) in the business rule approach emerges. Work should be viewed literally as a series of steps needed to accomplish a work result.

A play in football is a good analogy. If you have ever seen a diagram of a football play in a play book, it is literally represented as a series of orchestrated steps needed to accomplish the desired result (to advance the ball). It is nothing more and nothing less. No rules—nor penalties for violating these rules—are embedded within the play. A play simply focuses on *doing*.

---

2. The code also addresses the issue of control (made largely unnecessary by rules), certain housekeeping chores (which generally also could be expressed as rules), and the detection and management of events (which can be taken over by the business logic technology).

For business systems, I can be more precise about the "plays" the business runs. In the business rule approach, we call them *scripts.*[3] "A series of steps" is a good description of what a script looks like; "a prescribed series of requests" is an even better one. Refer to the boxed item, More on Scripts in the Business Rule Approach, for additional discussion. Scripts, of course, *never* include embedded rules (nor the violation-handling activity for such rules).

 A script is a procedure consisting of a series of requests with no embedded rules.

More on Scripts in the Business Rule Approach

We like to describe a script as a prescribed series of requests. The word *series* is self-evident, but the words *prescribed* and *requests* deserve closer examination.

Prescribed means that the given series of steps *can* be followed to achieve the desired results, but not that they *must* be followed. For example, there might be one or more other series of steps that can be followed to achieve the

---

3. These are called *BRScripts* in Proteus, the business rule methodology created by Business Rule Solutions, LLC.

same results. To say *must be followed* represents a rule about sequencing,[4] and even that type of rule should not be embedded in the process or procedure.

By *requests* I mean requests for action. When the request is made to some software component, this action is taken in the form of executing some program. Such software components might include any of the following:

- Database management systems (to create, retrieve, modify, or delete data)
- GUIs or other screen objects
- Service providers, such as print routines
- Interfaces to legacy systems
- Special-purpose rule technologies

Examples of situations in which scripts could be applied include the following. Note that, as is typical, these scripts target bread-and-butter business activities. In each case, the script would provide a pattern for doing the operational-level work.

- Take a customer order.
- Evaluate a medical claim.
- Book a reservation.
- Assign a professor to a class.

 Scripts provide patterns for doing work.

Often a script is undertaken in response to something a human or organization does (for example, a customer places an order). A script can also be undertaken in response to some timing criteria (for example, time to bill customers) or some predefined condition (for example, inventory quantity on hand is below a certain threshold). In the latter two cases, appropriate criteria for initiating the scripts automatically can be expressed as rules.

---

4. *Sequencing* is not quite the right word here. Since rules are declarative, *required antecedents* is probably more precise.

Including People in Scripts

Do scripts specify requests only among software components? *No!* In many respects, the most important source or recipient of requests in scripts is a real person. After all, real people still do a significant amount of the actual work. It would be rather shortsighted to leave them out.

 Scripts involve real people too.

These people might be either *inside* the company (that is, workers) or *outside* the company (for example, customers). Although all these people might be "users" of the business system, for scripts we prefer the term *actors*. The term *user* suggests outside beneficiaries of system services, whose own work and interactions are outside scope. *Actor*, in contrast, suggests someone whose own activity or role is integral to understanding and doing the work. An actor is someone whose own work is definitely within scope.

 An actor's work is within scope.

What can human actors do to get work done? They can perform actions, of course. They can also make requests for action—requests to software components and, either directly or indirectly, to other actors.

This begins to bring the new image of work in the business rule approach into sharper focus. Work is performed as human actors and software actors interact with each other, following scripts. In the thin-process, throwaway world of scripts, the emphasis is on choreographed collaboration between actors, both human and machine.

 Business rules enable adaptable, throwaway collaborations involving people and machines.

Implications for the Business Side

Does all work have to be scripted? *No!* The boxed item, About Unscripted Work, explores that issue further.

> ### About Unscripted Work
>
> Not all work must be scripted in advance. In fact, in a dynamic business environment, not all events and circumstances can even be predicted, much less prescripted.[5] This fact has several important implications.
>
> - Ad hoc database access will always be a significant factor for business systems. This is an additional reason why it is so important to define terms, facts, and rules independently of processes and procedures.
> - Criteria must be identified to determine when it might not be cost-effective to script work in advance, even when some event *can* be predicted. Scripting work for low-frequency events performed by only a few actors, for example, is often not cost-effective.
> - The Rule Book (in automated form, of course) can be used to guide work in a timely fashion that has not been scripted in advance. The lack of a script might occur either because the event could not be predicted or because scripting the work in advance would not be cost-effective. Having the Rule Book for such situations is a crucial advantage of the business rule approach.

Building scripts for predictable, repetitive work, however, is quite useful. Remember, because the scripts are thin, the collaborations they prescribe need not be static but, rather, can be dynamic and constantly evolving. This is exactly what 21st-century businesses need to meet the challenge of rapid change.

This approach is consistent with current thinking about how IT should be used to transform organizational structures. Deep hierarchies, with many layers of middle management, are out. Flattened hierarchies, with empowered end users and flexible patterns of collaboration, are in.

Another current business trend centers on automating the extended value chain, crossing organizational boundaries between suppliers, producers, and

---

5. It could be argued that this fact makes business systems notably different from other kinds of computing problems such as real-time systems, process control software, systems software, and so on.

customers. The real goal here is *compacting* the value chain, allowing direct, dynamic interaction between empowered actors anywhere along the way.

It is interesting to note that both of the above trends involve eliminating certain types of organizational roles. In the case of reengineering, the target has often been middle-level managers. In the case of compacted value chains, the target is *middlemen in general*, and with that focus, the goal is *disintermediation*.

All such roles served in times past not only to filter information—the responsibility commonly ascribed to them—but also to know and enforce business rules. In their absence, having a Rule Book becomes all the more critical. Otherwise, how can the business communicate its rules and ensure that the behavior of all actors remains consistent with the business goals? The importance of this principle is examined more closely in the boxed item, Eliminating the Human Actors in the Middle.

     The Rule Book retains knowledge for the business.

Eliminating the Human Actors in the Middle

As middle-level managers were eliminated in the reengineering and downsizing initiatives of the 1980s and 1990s, they essentially took knowledge about many business rules with them. Indeed, we commonly now hear the complaint that *the systems seem to be running the business.*

As a result, many companies are facing tough choices in trying to regain that lost knowledge. One approach is to attempt to mine the business rules from the legacy code (not an easy prospect!). The alternative is either reengineering the business systems from scratch or replacing them with expensive (and often painful) implementations of packaged software. An important lesson can be learned from this: Never lose your business rules!

     Never lose your business rules!

Any business initiative whose direct or indirect effect might be to eliminate human actors "in the middle" should call on business rule techniques. Following this principle is a wise—and probably *essential*—safeguard for your business in the 21st century.

Back to Training

Let's now reconsider the problem of training in the 21st-century business. At any given time, actors participating in scripted collaborations might be found at virtually any stage of time shock. Significant time shock can occur when switching to new scripts, changing roles within the same script, or even performing the very same role for the very same script as the rules change.

Sometimes, you might find the actors completely up to speed; other times, it might seem they have suddenly dropped in from another planet. Most of the time, they will probably be somewhere in between. This poses daunting problems not only for training the actors but also for building the business systems that support them.

IT professionals tend to design toward the more advanced workers, either by necessity or by choice. This tendency often leaves the novice hopelessly befuddled when trying to use the system. This is a long-standing problem in software development.

An alternative is to build an additional stripped-down version for the novice worker, heavily laden with "help." This alternative doubles development work and creates significant maintenance and upgrade problems. This solution is not really best for all the in-between users—which, for whatever reason, usually includes most of us. And, of course, the help never really seems to help at all!

The solution is more or less obvious. If software were clothing, it would be called *one-size-fits-all*. The key is an environment that *stretches* as the end user grows in capabilities.

With respect to organizing work, *one-size-fits-all* means that the same script must be usable for actors at any stage of time shock. This is no small challenge, but the business rule approach to organizing work provides an innovative solution. The key lies with remembering that *all* potential errors (that is, mistakes that end users can make in matters related to the business) are handled by rules, which are *separate* from the scripts. The rules, and the necessary activity to handle violations of them, are invoked (that is, become visible to the actor) only when mistakes are actually made. The net effect, as explained in the boxed item, One-Size-Fits-All Software Environments, is to make the environment seem very different to the novice user than to the advanced (that is, up-to-speed) user.

One-Size-Fits-All Software Environments

A novice benefits directly when work is already scripted simply because there is a ready-to-use template to follow when performing the work. Even better, this template was presumably created on the basis of best practices—the how-to knowledge of those workers who already know what works best.

The novice (or time-shocked) actor will inevitably make *lots* of mistakes when performing a script. To this actor the business rule software environment seems big. Actually, all the rule violation activity that makes the system seem so big represents inline, automatic *training*—a business investment in getting (or keeping) that actor up to speed. In other words, business rule systems are instructional by design.

 Business rule systems are instructional.

The advanced actor, in contrast, can be expected to make *few or no* errors when performing a script. For this actor, the same business rule software environment will seem small. In fact, if sufficiently knowledgeable and properly authorized, the advanced actor might elect not even to use a predefined script to do the work. Instead, the actor might elect to wing it—that is, make the appropriate requests on the fly. The rules, of course, will still catch violations if the actor makes any mistakes.

Even for the advanced actor, however, the work environment might not stay small all the time—especially if the rules themselves are in rapid flux. That possibility, of course, is a likely one for the 21st-century business. These days, *no* worker can safely assume immunity from time shock.

 No worker is ever immune to time shock.

The key to one-size-fits-all scripts, of course, is Rule Independence—that is, capturing and implementing the rules separately. Even that, however, is not enough. Something more is necessary to guide and instruct actors effectively in doing work (that is, in performing scripts). In particular, the error messages human actors get back from the system when a rule is violated should succinctly state the business rule that the error represents. Only by this means can the actor get up to speed on the business itself.[6]

As indicated in Chapter 6, in the business rule approach the rule statements *are* the error messages! As workers bump into the rules, they learn simply by reading from the Rule Book then and there.[7]

  Workers learn by reading the Rule Book inline as the need arises.

Building on What You Already Know How to Do

In real life, there are generally two ways in which we build on what we already know how to do. These two ways are discussed from the business rule perspective below. The first is relatively straightforward; the second brings business rule thinking about organizing work to its culmination. Both pertain to *reuse* of scripts when doing work.

Reuse of scripts implies reuse of software as a given. Our goal, however, is *business*-level reusability. Focusing narrowly on *software*-level reusability misses this bigger picture.

  The business rule approach focuses on business-level reusability, not just software reusability.

Normal Reuse of Scripts

The most obvious form of reusing what we already know how to do is simply invoking one procedure or script from within another. The invoked procedure or script indicates how one step is to be taken within that larger procedure or script, whose purpose is broader or more general. Here are some simple examples from real life.

This Reusable Procedure . . .	Can Be Reused In . . .
Tying your shoes	Getting dressed
Making spaghetti sauce	Cooking an Italian dinner
Driving a car	Visiting your in-laws

---

6. Rule traces are another important capability in this regard.
7. Assuming the workers are authorized, of course.

This Reusable Procedure . . .	Can Be Reused In . . .
Throwing a football	Running a play
Typing	Using a computer program

Such reuse of scripts is commonplace when building business systems. For example, the script *Fill out address* can be reused in many other, broader scripts, potentially including *Take customer order, Record prospect information, Create shipment, Hire employee*, and so on. This form of reuse is obvious and very important for many reasons, including the following:

- The software to support it need not be rewritten but can be reused as is, saving time in development and maintenance.
- Reuse of any kind produces consistency, which in turn generally raises productivity.
- A worker who already knows the invoked script need not learn anything new to do that part of the work. This head start is highly desirable for time-shocked workers.

Such normal reuse of scripts involves no special use of rules. The business rule approach simply adopts it as a given.

 Normal reuse of scripts whenever possible is a given.

Abnormal Reuse of Scripts

Abnormal reuse does not imply abnormal scripts (whatever that might mean). Rather, it implies that a script already used in normal circumstances also gets used under abnormal circumstances. Such abnormal reuse is the final, crucial piece in rethinking work for the 21st-century business. Real life again provides good examples.

Procedure	Normal Circumstances	Abnormal Circumstances
Climb a tree	Recreation	Escape a vicious dog
Kick a soccer ball	Play a soccer game	Kick a penalty shot
Heat an item in a microwave oven	Warm up leftovers	Melt crystallized honey
Make a telephone call	Talk to your spouse	Call 911 for emergency assistance
Write in longhand	Sign a check	Take notes when your laptop is down

To understand abnormal reuse, it is important to understand exactly when abnormal circumstances occur. In many approaches, defining where and when abnormal circumstances occur is something of a mystery. The business rule approach, in contrast, is quite precise in this regard: *Abnormal business circumstances occur when and only when a worker makes a request resulting in a violation of a rule.* By implication, if no rule is violated, the circumstances are *not* abnormal. By the way, satisfying all rules does not necessarily mean the circumstances are *desirable.* It might simply mean some rules are missing.

Rules then *by definition* indicate the threshold between normal and abnormal business circumstances. Rules and only rules (actually, just rejectors) perform this role.

 Rules always define the threshold between normal and abnormal business circumstances.

Supporting abnormal reuse of scripts is therefore straightforward. It comes about as follows:

1. The worker executes a script.
2. The worker makes a request under that script.
3. The request produces an event.
4. The event fires the appropriate rules, if any.
5. Suppose one of these rules (a rejector) detects a violation in the work. *What happens here is the crucial piece. One more capability is required so that the reuse can occur, as follows.*
6. When the rule detects a violation, the business logic technology has been directed (by the designers of the script) to invoke *another* script automatically.
7. This other script offers the capability needed for the original worker (or possibly some other worker) to correct the error that caused the violation.
8. If that work is undertaken (not a given) . . .
9. And if the work is accomplished successfully such that the violated rule is now satisfied . . .
10. Then the original work can continue under the *original* script from where it earlier left off.

The simple example below illustrates the above activity step-by-step.

Normal script: *Take customer order*

Rule: *An order must be placed by a customer.*

If the rule is violated, the script to be invoked is: *Record customer information*

Actual work activity:

1. The order entry clerk executes the *Take customer order* script.
2. The order entry clerk makes out an order but fails to indicate any customer for it.
3. The update event is attempted.
4. This fires the rule: *An order must be placed by a customer.*
5. The rule detects a violation in the order.
6. The business logic technology has been instructed to pass control to the *Record customer information* script in this circumstance.
7. The order entry clerk is offered the opportunity to perform this other script.
8. The order entry clerk elects to do so.
9. This work successfully corrects the original violation of the rule.
10. The order entry clerk resumes work under the original script (*Take customer order*) from the point it was interrupted. (For example, the next action might be to schedule the order's fulfillment.)

An important comment about this example is that the script designated to handle the abnormal circumstance (*Record customer information*) is presumably the script otherwise used in *normal* circumstances for that kind of work. It would almost certainly therefore be familiar to the order entry clerk.

This represents a general principle for designing abnormal reuse of scripts: *If at all possible, any script invoked by a rule in abnormal circumstances should be a script already used for the same kind of work under normal circumstances.* In plain English, that simply means keep it as simple for the worker as possible!

Note that the script selected for the abnormal circumstances can be modified (or even replaced) *independently* of the script for normal circumstances. The latter script also can change (or be replaced) independently of the former. And all these changes can occur independently of the rule—that is, they can be accomplished with no impact on the rule itself. In these ways, abnormal reuse achieves the full potential of business rules for organizing work in 21st-century businesses.

 Business rule systems support change at a very granular level, and are therefore highly adaptive.

None of this adaptability would have been possible, of course, if the rule had been embedded within the script itself. Here, Rule Independence yields yet another major benefit—a new kind of firewall to limit the impact of procedural changes.

 Rules offer a new kind of firewall to limit the impact of procedural changes in the business.

In short, rules *will* revolutionize work! It is therefore altogether fitting that I close Part II with the Business Rule Manifesto.

Business Rules Manifesto
The Principles of Rule Independence[8]

By Business Rules Group
http://www.BusinessRulesGroup.org

1. Rules are a first-class citizen of the requirements world.
2. Rules are essential for, and a discrete part of, business models, system models, and implementation models.
3. Rules are not process and not procedure. They should not be embedded in either of these.
4. Rules build on facts, and facts build on concepts as expressed by terms.
5. Terms express business concepts; facts make assertions about these concepts; rules constrain and support these facts.
6. Rules must be explicit. No rule is ever assumed about any concept or fact unless a rule has been specified explicitly.
7. Rules are basic to what the business knows about itself—that is, to basic business knowledge. Rules need to be nurtured, protected, and managed.

8. Version 1.1, November 23, 2002. Edited by Ronald G. Ross.

8. *Rules are about business practice and guidance; therefore, rules are motivated by business goals and objectives and are shaped by various influences.*

9. *Rules should be expressed declaratively for the business audience, in natural-language sentences. If something cannot be expressed, then it is not a rule.*

10. *Rules are best implemented declaratively. Rules are based on truth values.*

11. *Rules are explicit constraints on behavior and/or provide support to behavior.*

12. *Rules generally apply across processes and procedures. There should be one cohesive body of rules which should be enforced consistently across different areas of business activity.*

13. *The relationship between events and rules is generally many-to-many.*

14. *A rule statement is distinct from the enforcement level defined for it. These are separate concerns.*

15. *Rules should be defined independently of responsibility for the who, where, when, or how of enforcement.*

16. *Rules often require special or selective handling of detected violations. Such rule violation activity is activity like any other activity.*

17. Rules define the boundary between acceptable and unacceptable business activity.

18. To ensure maximum consistency and reusability, the handling of unacceptable business activity should be separable from the handling of acceptable business activity.

19. Exceptions to rules are expressed by other rules.

20. Rules always cost the business something. This cost must be balanced against business risks.

21. Rules should arise from knowledgeable business people.

22. Business people should have tools available to help them develop and manage rules.

23. In the long run, rules are more important to the business than hardware/software platforms.

24. Rules should be managed in such a way that they can be readily redeployed to new hardware/software platforms.

25. A business rule system is never really finished because it is intentionally built for continuous change.

26. Rules, and the ability to change them effectively, are key to improving business adaptability.

PART III

Best Practices
for Expressing Rules
BRS RuleSpeak

Overview

BRS RuleSpeak is a set of practical guidelines that can assist business workers and IT professionals with all of the following tasks:

- Express rules in clear, unambiguous, well-structured business English
- Clarify business logic
- Find a middle ground between (a) high-level policies and directives and (b) rule specifications at an implementation level
- Improve communication about business rules between the business side and IT
- Bridge between business analysis and system design

In one way or another, each of these goals addresses difficulties in developing *requirements*. This problem is best described in the words of an experienced practitioner:

> *Another chronic problem is the difficulty of finding a common language to assure that business clients, analysts, and developers can truly communicate. Asking clients to sign off on a project is meaningless if the proposed process logic or database structure is presented in a form that they are not trained to understand. For developers, the communication medium must allow sufficient rigor to support system design and the creation of code.*

RuleSpeak provides an innovative solution. It shows how to express rules[1] in the clearest, most unambiguous form. Many users of RuleSpeak will be in IT; however, the structured English of RuleSpeak can be understood and "spoken" by large segments of the business community too.

I have divided the discussion of RuleSpeak into the following chapters.[2] Note that information about how to capture the rules themselves is not discussed in detail here.[3]

- Chapter 8 discusses the basic dos and don'ts of expressing rules. This lighter treatment is suitable for a general audience.
- Chapter 9 reviews the basic ideas of RuleSpeak and explains what it is and what purpose it serves. Included in this chapter are usage notes to ensure the best possible expression of rules.
- Chapter 10 presents the BRS Rule Classification Scheme. This chapter, a relatively brief one, provides the scheme for organizing the actual rule sentence templates presented in Chapter 11 and for organizing decision tables as discussed in Chapter 12. It also serves as a general reference point concerning the functional categories of rules.
- Chapter 11 provides the actual RuleSpeak rule sentence templates, with many examples to illustrate. These templates, which are based on the BRS Rule Classification Scheme, cover a broad range of cases.
- Chapter 12 discusses the use of decision tables to express business logic, explaining the RuleSpeak approach through relevant examples and prescriptions.

---

1. For convenience, I will often use *rule* in the discussion that follows in this part instead of the more correct *rule statement*, except where such use might cause confusion. As discussed in Chapter 6, the distinction is that the same rule can be given by statements in different forms and/or by statements in different languages (for example, French, Mandarin, and so on.). In other words, there can be many different *rule statements* for exactly the same *rule*.
2. At certain points in the discussions that follow in this part, I mention elements of methodology or deliverables that pertain specifically to Business Rule Solutions, LLC. When I use *we* or *our* in these contexts, please note that I am referring to the Principals of Business Rule Solutions.
3. Proteus, the Business Rule Solution's business rule methodology, provides comprehensive techniques and guidance to assist with this area.

CHAPTER 8

Expressing Rules

The Dos and Don'ts

Expressing and communicating rules effectively is not simply a matter of following certain conventions by rote but rather requires a certain underlying mind-set. In other words, people undertaking the task of writing rules for the business should be properly oriented. This chapter provides a series of basic guidelines for that purpose. Presented in the form of dos and don'ts, they also establish assumptions on which the other chapters in this part of the book are based. All of these guidelines, by the way, are aimed at the *business* expression of rules—not IT expression per se. This orientation is consistent with the fundamental principles of the business rule approach.

Not How, Not Where, Not Who, Not When

Proposed rule: *A group must not include both union members and nonunion members.*

Acceptable? Yes.

Discussion: Removing the specifics of *how, where, who,* and *when* produces rules in declarative form. A rule statement should include no indication about any of the following:

- *How* the rule will be enforced
- *Where* the rule will be enforced (for example, within what implementation components)

- *Who* (that is, which actor) is responsible for enforcing the rule
- *When* (that is, which events) should cause the rule to be tested

Declarative expression of rules allows the most flexible rethinking of requirements and reengineering of business processes.

Not Procedural

Proposed rule: *Check the product number in database SRU [the Sandals R Us database].*

If the product number is equal to 422 [the part number of flip-flops]
and the product description is equal to "plastic flip-flops,"
    then set the new product number in database ASC
    [The Athens Sandal Company database] equal to 1547
    and set the product description equal to "Fun-in-the-Sun Flip-Flops"
else if the product number in database ASC is equal to 423 through 495 [the part numbers of all orthopedic sandals]
    then set the new product number equal to 1647
    and set the product category equal to "Good for You, Too Sandals"
else if . . .

—Example of "business rules" from a recent software vendor white paper

Acceptable? No.

Discussion: This "rule" is obviously not in declarative form. Use of the control word *else* (among other things) indicates that the "rule" outlines processing logic rather than business logic. This type of rambling statement for expressing rules should be carefully avoided. It does not isolate individual pieces of business logic, nor does it communicate well for the business side.

Not Inscrutable

Proposed rule: *No savings and loan holding company, directly or indirectly or through one or more transactions, shall acquire control of an uninsured institution or retain, for more than one year after other than an insured institution or holding company thereof, the date any insured institution subsidiary becomes uninsured, control of such institution.*

—From the Code of Federal Regulations

(chosen as the winner of the annual "Legaldegook" contest by the Plain Language Committee of the State Bar of Texas)

Acceptable? No.

Discussion: The most basic test for a good rule statement is that it can be readily understood by any business worker who reads it—and that it always produces the same interpretation.

Not Impossible

Proposed rule: *Regardless of anything to the contrary in this booklet, if your medical insurance terminates for any reason including death, you . . . may elect within 30 days . . . to continue such medical insurance.*

—From the booklet "Group Insurance for I-14 Employees"

(consolidated group trust of a major insurance company)

Acceptable? No.

Discussion: Rules can be impossible for many reasons, including status (as above), time constraints, direct conflicts, and so on. Obviously, rules that are impossible should be avoided.

Always Built on Terms and Facts

Proposed rule: *A customer may* place *an order only if the customer* holds *an account.*

  Fact: A customer places an order.

  Fact: A customer holds an account.

  Terms: Customer, order, account

Acceptable? Yes.

Discussion: The business rule approach prescribes that rules always build on facts and that facts always build on terms. A rule really lies in the "must-ness" (or the "should-ness") of its expression. For the most part, everything else in the rule should represent terms and facts.

A structure to organize these underlying terms and facts is therefore an essential tool in expressing rules. As discussed in Chapter 5, this requires a fact model. The fact model serves as your reference source for standard term and fact names. This is illustrated in Figure 8–1, which shows a rule based on the same fact model that appeared in Figure 5–1.

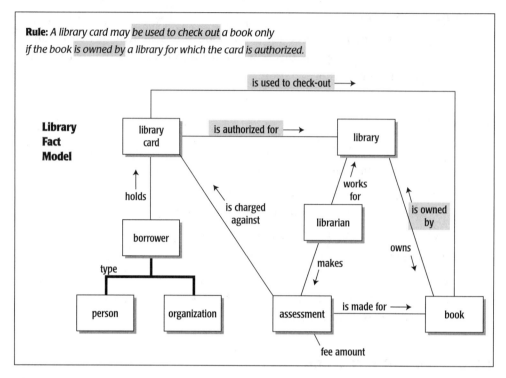

Rule: *A library card may be used to check out a book only if the book is owned by a library for which the card is authorized.*

Figure 8–1   A rule whose wording is based directly on a fact model

Standard term and fact wordings should be used faithfully in expressing rules. This practice ensures basic consistency and helps to avoid ambiguities—issues that rapidly become primary in importance as the set of rules grows larger and larger in number.

No AWOL Facts

Proposed rule: *An order must not be shipped if the outstanding balance exceeds credit authorization.*

Acceptable? Probably not.

Discussion: There seems to be AWOL[1] (hidden or missing) facts in this rule.

---

1. From the military term *AWOL*, which stands for "absent without leave."

- Outstanding balance of what? Order? Customer? Account? Shipment?
- Credit authorization of what? Order? Customer? Account? Shipment?

Ambiguities can result whenever references to relevant facts are omitted from a rule. First clarify the facts, then revise the rule. The appropriate facts for the rule above might be as follows.

Fact: *Customer* has credit authorization.

Fact: *Customer* holds account.

Fact: *Account* has outstanding balance.

An appropriate revised rule based on these facts appears below.

Revised rule: *An order must not be shipped if the outstanding balance of the customer's account exceeds the customer's credit authorization.*

No Fluff

Proposed rule: *Programmers must always work on a system.*

Acceptable? Could be better.

Revised rule: *Programmers must work on a system.*

Proposed rule: *Shipments must have a status at all times.*

Acceptable? Could be better.

Revised rule: *Shipments must have a status.*

Discussion: Words and phrases added for emphasis just add clutter. They should be avoided to keep the rule statements as succinct as possible. For example, assume a rule implies *always* or *at all times* unless explicit qualification is given.

No Plural Subjects

Proposed rule: *Programmers must work on a system.*

Acceptable? Could be better.

Revised rule: *A programmer must work on a system.*

Proposed rule: *Shipments must have a status.*

Acceptable? Could be better.

Revised rule: *A shipment must have a status.*

Discussion: Use a singular subject for all rules. This is the first of many points below about the importance of carefully identifying and expressing the *subject* for every rule. Selecting an appropriate subject is a critical step in expressing rules well.

Careful about Iffy Starts

Proposed rule: *If an employee is retired, then he must not be assigned an employment counselor.*

Acceptable? Could be better.

Revised rule: *A retired employee must not be assigned an employment counselor.*

Discussion: Always start a rule with an appropriate subject. If qualification is necessary (for example, an *if* clause), place it at the end of the rule.[2]

This guideline also applies to timing clauses. An additional example illustrates this.

Proposed rule: *By the close of registration, a student must be enrolled in at least two courses.*

Acceptable? Could be better.

Revised rule: *A student must be enrolled in at least two courses by the close of registration.*

Discussion: *Close of registration* refers to an event. An event is a *when*, which is not appropriate as the subject of a rule. This event (or more precisely, the appropriate point in time) can be included in the rule as a timing clause, as illustrated above, to indicate when enforcement of the rule should begin.

No AWOL Subjects

Proposed rule: *No less than two people in booths between 9 A.M. and 1 P.M.*

—Restaurant in Alameda, CA

Acceptable? No.

Discussion: What is the subject of the original rule? It is AWOL—missing. The implied "There may be . . ." is not a subject! Identifying the appropriate

---

2. This guideline is discussed more in Chapter 9.

subject is an important step in moving from informal expression of a rule, where the context is obvious, to more formal expression.

Revised rule: *A booth must not be occupied by a party of one between 9 A.M. and 1 P.M.*

This step often leads to additional insights about the true meaning or implications of a rule. For example, since *zero* number of people is probably an acceptable (and necessary) clarification for the original rule, the revised rule introduces the term *party*.

Careful about Actors as Subjects

Proposed rule: *A customer may make a withdrawal only if his or her account is active.*

Acceptable? Probably not.

Discussion: Only customers? What about preauthorized third parties? What about the bank itself? What about other actors?

Carefully examine any rule that indicates an actor as a subject. Does the rule really pertain only to that actor? Often, the answer is no. If not, substitute a nonactor subject; for example, in the revised rule below, *withdrawal* is substituted for *customer*. Be careful not to confuse rules, which express constraints or guidance for behavior, with workflows or procedures, which indicate what actors actually do.

Revised rule: *A withdrawal from an account may be made only if the account is active.*

No Commands

Proposed rule: *Don't ship orders if the outstanding balance of the order exceeds the customer's credit authorization.*

Acceptable? No.

Discussion: What is the subject of this rule? The implied subject is *you*. *You* represents an actor—a very vague one at that!

The command form of rules is common in communication between actors. In general, commands suffice as long as the actors share the same context. For rules, however, communication contexts can never be taken for granted.

Rules must establish their own contexts—that is, their expression should communicate universally to all actors within the scope of the business problem.

Again, the crucial step is to ask what term is the appropriate subject for the rule. This question might result in the following revision of the rule above.

Revised rule: *An order must not be shipped if the outstanding balance of the order exceeds the customer's credit authorization.*

No CRUD

Proposed rule: *Update product cost when the cost of any component changes.*

Acceptable? No.

Discussion: The implied subject of this command is again *you*. In this case, however, the command verb *update* represents a system event. Is the implied *you* the system? If not, then who?

System events should never be used as the subjects for rules. (*CRUD* stands for *create, retrieve, update, delete*—all system events.) As before, the crucial step is to ask what term is the appropriate subject for the rule. For computation rules such as the one above, a term representing the result of the computation should be indicated as the subject, as in the following revision.

Revised rule: *A product's cost must be computed as the sum of the cost of all its components.*

Another problem with referencing an event as the subject of a rule is that most rules need to be tested during *more* than one event.[3] If a particular event is referenced as the subject of a rule, the other events might be missed in interpreting or enforcing that rule. In the original rule statement above, for example, the additional events *when a component is added to a product* and *when a component is removed from a product* are probably also relevant since they too can affect a product's cost. The revised rule covers these other events as well.

Careful about Events as Subjects

Proposed rule: *When an order is created, it must have a promised shipment date.*

Acceptable? Could be better.

---

3. This topic is discussed in Chapter 6.

Discussion: *When* always indicates an event. As discussed above, rules are usually not specific to a single event. Should not an order continue to have a promised shipment date? Would it be appropriate just after an order is created to delete the promised shipment date? This rule is almost certainly not specific to the event indicated by *when*. Therefore, the reference to the event should be removed from the rule. This removal actually results in a simpler statement, as follows.

Revised rule: *An order must have a promised shipment date.*

Stating a rule in an *event-less* fashion is an important step in ensuring consistent and complete enforcement across all relevant events. The rule above is a very simple one. For most rules, the other relevant events will be less obvious—and more numerous!

Careful to Qualify

Proposed rule: *A project team member should not be rotated off the project until finished.*

Acceptable? Could be better.

Discussion: To what does the qualification *until finished* apply? The project team member is finished? The project is finished? Be careful about the placement of a qualification relative to the term it logically qualifies. Make that term explicit as needed to avoid ambiguity.

Revised rule: *A project team member should not be rotated off the project until the project is finished.*

Be especially careful about time-based qualifications. To avoid ambiguity, include an explicit reference to the event being qualified as needed. The example below further illustrates this point. An event referenced in this fashion should not, of course, be indicated as the subject of the rule.

Proposed rule: *A purchase order must be approved by at least two managers during a snowstorm.*

Acceptable? Could be better.

Revised rule: *A purchase order taken during a snowstorm must be approved by at least two managers.*

Careful to Extract Embedded Computations

Proposed rule: *The sum of all payment amounts applied to an order must be greater than or equal to the amount due for the order.*

Acceptable? Could be better.

Discussion: This rule includes both a computation and a constraint on the result of that computation. Extracting the computation is highly desirable for the following reasons.

- It enhances *clarity.*
- It allows the two resulting rules to be validated and changed *independently* of each other.
- It permits *reuse* of the computation logic by other rules. These other rules can simply reference the result of the computation by name, ensuring logical consistency across all the rules.
- It *isolates* the logic of the computation to a single rule, no matter how many times this logic is reused by other rules. This segregation facilitates change.

The computation embedded in the rule above should therefore be expressed as a separate rule. The subject of this rule should be the result of the computation. The original constraint on that result (*must be greater than or equal to*) should be expressed as a second rule. These revisions are illustrated below.

Extracted computation rule: *The amount paid for an order must be computed as the sum of all payment amounts applied to the order.*

Revised rule: *The amount paid for an order must be greater than or equal to the amount due for the order.*

Careful to Isolate Your Logic

Proposed rule: *A customer whose outstanding balance exceeds $1,000 on each of his or her last three successive invoices must not place an order for an item whose cost exceeds $500.*

Acceptable? Could be better.

Discussion: The specific conditions found in a rule can often be named. Sometimes a standard or common-use name already exists in the business. Such conditions should be broken out as separate rules and then the names of the conditions substituted for the conditions in the original rule. This has several important advantages paralleling those resulting from extracted computations.

- It leaves the original rule simpler, thus enhancing *clarity.*
- It allows the two or more resulting rules to be validated and changed *independently* of each other.
- It permits *reuse* of the condition's logic by other rules. These other rules can simply reference the name of the condition, as appropriate. The result is a higher degree of logical consistency across the rules.
- It *isolates* the logic of the condition to a single rule, no matter how many times this logic is reused by other rules. This segregation facilitates change.

The significant conditions in the rule above should be expressed as separate rules. The subjects of these rules should be the names of the conditions. The constraint from the original rule (*must not place*) should be expressed as yet another rule. These revisions are illustrated on the next page.

Extracted rule: *High-risk customer means the outstanding balance exceeds $1,000 on each of the customer's last three successive invoices.*

Extracted rule: *Big-ticket item means the item's cost exceeds $500.*

Revised rule: *A high-risk customer must not place an order for a big-ticket item.*

And No Etc.

Proposed rule: *A territory must not include any noncandidate traditional gas station if it includes any ultra-service or food outlet; must not include any ultra-service if it includes any noncandidate traditional gas station or food outlet; etc.*

Acceptable? No.

Discussion: Including *etc.* or similar indefinite words (for example, *vice versa*) in rules invites misinterpretation. Often, as illustrated below, a much simpler way can be found to express the rule.

Revised rule: *A territory must not include more than one of the following:*

- *Noncandidate traditional gas station*
- *Ultra-service*
- *Food outlet*

The Lighter Side of Rules[4]

Try This On . . .

Notice: This garment meets the general wearing apparel requirements of the Flammable Fabrics Act; however, it is flammable and should not be worn near sources of fire.

　　　　　　　—Tag on an item of apparel from a Massachusetts clothing outlet

User-Friendly Rule . . .

Visitor should be not ironed—cooked—washed.

　　　　　　　—Guest rule posted in a Vietnamese hotel

---

4. Editor's note: This material was forwarded to the author via e-mail. Original source unknown.

About Those Really Exclusive Clubs . . .
Members and non-members only.

—Sign posted at a discotheque entrance

Give Me a Break . . .
Gasoline must not be sold to anyone in a glass container.

—Sign at a Santa Fe gas station

Unhelpful Hint . . .
Exit access is that part of a means of egress that leads to an entrance to an exit.

—Government fire-prevention pamphlet for homes for the elderly

Strange Labor Rule . . .
No children allowed.

—Sign posted at the entrance to a Florida hospital's maternity ward

Beat the Heat . . .
River inhabited by crocodiles. Swimming prohibited. Survivors will be prosecuted.

—Sign posted on the Ramganga River,
Corbett National Park, Uttar Pradesh, India

Better Left Unsaid . . .
Bags should be used in case of sickness or to gather remains.

—Instruction on a Spanish airline's air sickness bag

Continued

Say Again . . .
Members of the immediate family of an authorized exchange patron who are
not otherwise authorized admission to AAFES-Eur facilities in the company of
the authorized patron except for those members of the immediate family who
reside in the country where the AAFES-Eur facilities are located.
—U.S. Air Force regulation

On Being in Two Places at Once . . .
No refreshments shall be supplied to any member after the above-named
hours, and none shall be supplied for consumption off the club premises except to a member on the premises at the time.
—Bylaw in a private social club rule book

Ask about Pants . . .
No shirt, no shoes, no service.
—Sign posted on the wall of a beach restaurant

A Definition to Remember . . .
For purposes of paragraph (3), an organization described in paragraph (2)
shall be deemed to include an organization described in section 501 (c) (4), (5)
or (6) which would be described in paragraph (2) if it were an organization described in section 501 (c) (3).
—The Internal Revenue Service

CHAPTER 9

Developing Rule Statements

The Basics of BRS RuleSpeak

About the Rule Sentence Templates

A rule sentence template is a basic sentence structure or pattern in English[1] that can be used to express a rule in a consistent, well-organized manner. Each RuleSpeak template is aimed toward a particular kind of rule based on its functional category. These categories are discussed in Chapter 10. The actual rule sentence templates are presented in Chapter 11.

The purpose of the templates is to ensure that written rules are more readily understood. The templates also help ensure that different practitioners working on a large set of rules express the same ideas in the same way. Such consistency would not result if rules were expressed in a free-form manner.

The templates are not technical in nature. In other words, they do not represent a formal language for implementing rules at the system level (for example, in business logic technology[2]). Rather, they are aimed toward improving communication at the *business* level.

---

1. Templates could be offered for other languages (for example, French, Mandarin, and so on); however, this discussion addresses only English.
2. By *business logic technology,* I mean *rule engines, decision management platforms, business logic servers,* and so on.

They also address a key challenge in rule management—tracing changes to rules to and from the business side.

Using the templates to express rules requires a measure of discipline. This discipline can be achieved through a modest amount of practice and through an understanding of certain fundamentals about rules discussed in this chapter. Such discipline will not constrain creative development of rules but rather will enhance it greatly.

Success Factors in Using the Templates

What is important—and what is *not* important—when you apply the Rule-Speak templates? Obviously what is *not* important is how you will actually implement the rules using a particular programming language or business logic technology. Appreciating this distinction can be difficult for those responsible for actually implementing the rules. They often tend to want to go too deep too soon. This tendency often works against analysis and management of the rules from the business perspective.

It is also important to understand the level of rules to which the templates should be applied. The templates are not aimed at the automated level of rules. They are also not aimed at the highest level of governing rules (that is, the language of laws, regulations, contracts, policies, and so on). Rather, the templates are aimed at *operating rules*. Refer to the boxed item, The Levels of Rules, for the important distinctions between these three levels of rules.

The Levels of Rules

In the broadest sense, rules fall into one of three levels with respect to the purpose and style of their expression, as described below. RuleSpeak is aimed at expressing the intermediate level, operating rules. This is the critical transformation stage between governing rules as handed down from the business side and rules suitable for implementation in technology platforms (that is, automated rules).

Governing rule: Examples of governing rules include legal statements (for example, laws, acts, statutes, and so on), formal regulations, binding agreements (for example, contractual obligations), higher-level business policies or directives, and so on. Governing rules are often aimed at guiding or constraining the business, regulating its interactions with external parties, and/or limiting its exposure to risks or threats. Governing rules often must be interpreted into one or more operating rules to be applied in an actual business process or used for system design.

Operating rule: An operating rule is a declarative statement in well-structured business English, suitable for direct application to a business process and for consideration in a system design. An operating rule should be unambiguous and stated in a manner directly relevant to the internal workings of the business. Operating rules can be derived or interpreted from governing rules or sometimes reverse-engineered from automated rules.

Automated rule: An automated rule is a specific rule of the business, stated in a form recognizable by business logic technology, a programming language, an application generator, or similar technology. An automated rule is the implementation counterpart to an operating rule.

Operating rules guide and control the business on a day-to-day basis. Often, operating rules must be interpreted from governing rules in order to clarify them, remove ambiguities, and achieve the right perspective for the business area to which they apply. The templates facilitate such interpretation by providing predictable formats of expression. This is also true, by the way, if operating rules are being harvested bottom-up from existing implementations or documentation or captured on a facilitated basis from business-side workers.

Fundamental Concepts

Understanding several fundamental ideas about rules will greatly help you express rules effectively. These fundamental ideas are briefly discussed below.

Every Rule Has a Functional Category

The functional category of a rule reflects how the rule reacts to events. These categories, which are presented in Chapter 10, are intrinsic, definitive, and nonoverlapping. For that reason, they provide a sound foundation for a comprehensive set of sentence patterns. The RuleSpeak templates presented in Chapter 11 directly reflect these categories.

Every Rule Should Have a Subject

In good English construction, every sentence has a subject. Although this subject might be implied or the sentence inverted, more often than not an explicit subject appears as the first word or phrase in the main body of the sentence. Such sentences are usually direct and, if well written, easy to follow.

RuleSpeak strongly encourages you to place an explicit subject at the very beginning of each rule statement. Such a lead-in subject is desirable for rules in every functional category. This approach promotes overall clarity and consistency.

Some rule languages—often at the level of business logic technology or programming languages—feature *If ... then ...* syntax. In such languages, the true subject does not appear until the *then* clause.

We find that the *If ... then ...* syntax proves unfriendly for many kinds of rules.[3] The best construction for computation rules, for example, is always to put the result of the computation (the subject) as the very first thing in the sentence. By this means, what the rule computes is clear from the start. The *If ... then ...* syntax is also often unnatural for basic kinds of validation rules.[4] For example, it is much more natural simply to say *Customer must have an address* than *If customer exists, then customer must have an address*.

Every Rule Should Use a Rule Word

Every rule can be stated by using one of the following keywords. These keywords are called the *rule words*. It is very important that every rule statement includes one.

- *Must* (or *should*), including *must not* (or *should not*)
- *Only*, often as in *only if*

Every Rejector Has a Flip Side

Every validation rule[5] has a flip side—that is, circumstances to which the rule does *not* apply. Any statement that identifies such circumstances is called a

---

3. Refer to Part V, Appendix D for more discussion.
4. I really mean *rejectors* here.
5. Again, I mean *rejector* here.

permission statement. Such a statement indicates that workers are not constrained by any rule in that situation and, therefore, are free to exercise judgement or discretion in taking relevant actions.

Permission statements should be recorded if they represent an important clarification of policy or if they represent resolution of some particularly difficult business issue. Whenever recorded, they should, of course, be stated in a fashion consistent with rules. Here is an example.

> **Rule:** *Orders on credit over $1,000 must not be accepted without a credit check.*

> **Permission statement:** *Orders on credit $1,000 or under may be accepted without a credit check.*

> **Comment:** Note how the permission statement addresses the reverse of the condition (over $1,000) included in the rule. Note also that the permission statement does not include a rule word.

Also worth noting is that a permission statement can sometimes essentially represent an exception to some other rule and therefore can actually appear to be a rule itself. For example, suppose the original rule above had omitted the qualification *over $1,000.* Then the permission statement would represent an exception and therefore should be viewed as a rule.

This is another reason it can be useful to record permission statements, especially during the early phases of rule capture when the rules are not likely to be stated so precisely. (*Precisely* here means considering all possible conditions—for example, *over $1,000.*)

Every Permission Statement Should Use a Permission Word

Just as there are special rule words for rules, there are also special permission words for permission statements, as follows.

- *May*
- *Need not*

Any permission statement can be expressed using one of these forms. Several examples follow.

> **Permission statement:** *An account may be held by a person of any age.*

> **Permission statement:** *An employee need not be a manager.*

> **Permission statement:** *A customer need not place any orders.*

Any Rule Can Be Qualified

Any rule can include a qualification (that is, a condition) indicating the circumstances under which the rule should be enforced. Such qualification should start with either the word *if* or *when*, as appropriate.[6] Here is an example.

> **Rule:** *A shipment must be insured if the shipment value is greater than $500.*

The word *if* should be used if the qualification is continuous over time. The word *when* should be used only if the rule is to be enforced at a particular point in time, as shown below.

> **Rule:** *A student's semester-fees-owed must be set to $3,065 when the student registers for a semester.*
>
> **Comment:** This rule will be enforced only at the point in time when the student registers for a semester. At any other time, the rule will not be enforced—that is, the value of the student's semester-fees-owed need not be $3,065.

An *if* clause should not be used in a rule if some term exists that refers to the condition and this term can be used as the subject of the rule. An example illustrates.

> **Rule:** *An employee must not have an employment counselor if the employee is retired.*
>
> **Revised rule:** *A retired employee must not have an employment counselor.*
>
> **Comment:** The *if* clause has been eliminated in the revised rule, which uses the qualified term *retired employee* as its subject. The resulting expression is more compact and readable.

Any Rule Can Include a Time Bracket

You can indicate a time bracket as qualification for a rule by using one of the following time words.

---

6. We prefer that the *if* or *when* be set off by a comma, to clearly indicate the start of the qualification. Here is an example: *A shipment must be insured, if the shipment value is greater than $500.* However, this is a relatively minor point, and since shorter rules generally read better without it, we do not usually insist on it.

- *Before* (date/time)
- *On or before* (date/time)
- *During* (named date/time . . . for example, summertime)
- *By* (date/time)
- *After* (date/time)

Some examples appear below.

Rule: *A student must not live off-campus before his or her junior year.*

Rule: *A student must not join clubs on or before the close of registration.*

Rule: *A student must live on-campus during summertime.*

Rule: *A student must be enrolled in at least two courses by the close of registration.*

Rule: *A student must be enrolled in at least two courses after the close of registration.*

Any Rule Can Reference a Value

For clarity, specific values included in a rule can be enclosed in single quote marks. Here is an example.

Rule: *Normal-tax-return-due-date must be set to 'April 15.'*

Comment: This rule references the value *April 15.*

Basic Usage Notes

Based on experience, we have found that certain conventions work better than others for expressing rules. The related issues are discussed below. These usage notes help explain the particular wording for rules you will see in the RuleSpeak templates in Chapter 11.

Using *Shall*

Some organizations prefer using the word *shall* in place of the word *must*. This is basically a cosmetic choice. However, we prefer the word *must* since we find it generally more appropriate for the operating-rule level.

Using *Should*

Any rule can be stated by using *should* instead of *must*. This choice reflects an assumption or decision about the enforcement level of the rule. Generally, *should* suggests the sense of "enforce or do *if possible*," whereas *must* has the sense that there is no choice about whether enforcement will occur. We generally use whichever word conveys the best sense for the rule as currently understood. Although *should* is not illustrated explicitly in the templates, its usage is always optional.

Using *May*

Unfortunately, the word *may* can be used in English in several different ways. The resulting ambiguity is particularly troublesome for expressing rules. Consider the following examples.

1. *A volunteer organization may not make a profit.*
   In everyday conversation, *may* often conveys the sense of *might*. Is the sentence above simply an observation ("A volunteer organization *might* not make a profit"), or is it a legitimate rule ("A volunteer organization *must* not make a profit")? Especially taken out of context, the sentence is ambiguous.
2. *A plane may take off only if given clearance by air traffic control.*
   The second sense of *may* is that of permission being granted or denied. Such use of *may* for expressing rules is a valid and often necessary one.
3. *A car may be started only if the car is not in gear.*
   Here *may* is probably being used incorrectly. Rather than expressing a rule that grants or denies permission (for example, to the driver), the sentence actually simply describes a fundamental characteristic or capability of a car. Since *capacity* is at issue, the word *can* should be used instead. The sentence above should therefore be rewritten as *A car can be started only if the car is not in gear.* This sentence does not express a rule.

To summarize, to express rules we never use *may* in the first or the third sense above. That is, we never use *may* to mean either *might* (that is, that something might occur or be true) or *can* (that is, that some capacity does or does not exist). The only valid use we recognize for *may* is in the second sense above—that is, where permission is being granted or denied. We deem this sense the correct one for rules.

Using *No*

The word *no* in conjunction with *must* can produce awkward rule statements. This occurs when the rule expresses an upper limit. An example illustrates.

> **Rule:** *An adjudicator must be assigned to assess no more than 15 claims.*
>
> **Comment:** The structure of this rule statement is unnecessarily awkward. The rule starts off with *must,* as if the adjudicator will be obligated either to have something or to do something. The *no* reverses that sense by indicating a limit (*no more than 15 claims*) that the adjudicator must not exceed. The rule can be made clearer by using *must not* rather than *must . . . no,* as the following revision illustrates.
>
> **Revised rule:** *An adjudicator must not be assigned to assess more than 15 claims.*
>
> **Comment:** The structure of this rule statement is better. The rule starts off with *must not,* which is reinforced, rather than contradicted, by the upper limit (*more than 15 claims*).

In general, the word *no* should always be avoided if possible in expressing rules. This guideline is also true where *no* is used in the sense of *zero.* Here is an example.

> **Rule:** *A team assigned to a high-security project must include no trainees.*
>
> **Revised rule:** *A team assigned to a high-security project must not include any trainees.*
>
> **Comment:** Note the use of *not . . . any* to replace *no* in the original version.

Using *Not . . . Not*

Double negatives, especially using two *nots,* often makes a rule's logic unnecessarily difficult. The *nots* can generally be eliminated by restating the rule in a more positive form, producing a version that is easier to interpret. An example illustrates.

> **Rule:** *A withdrawal from an account must not be made if the account is not active.*

Revised rule: *A withdrawal from an account may be made only if the account is active.*

Comment: Note the use of *may . . . only if* to replace the *not . . . if . . . not* phrase in the original version.

Do Double Dos Make a Not?[7]

A linguistics professor was lecturing to his class one day. "In English," he said, "a double negative forms a positive. In some languages though, such as Russian, a double negative is still a negative. However," he pointed out, "there is no language wherein a double positive can form a negative."

A voice from the back of the room piped up, "Yeah. Right."

Using *Or* and *And*

In complicated rules, mixed series of *ors* and *ands* can easily produce confusion and misinterpretation. (Strict series of only *ands* or only *ors* raise an additional question, which is discussed later in this chapter.) Embedded parentheses can be used to clarify the intended logic; however, the resulting expressions often remain difficult for business-side workers to follow.

To alleviate this difficulty, we recommend eliminating the *ors* and *ands* in favor of bulleted lists of conditions. To introduce any such list of bulleted conditions, use one of the following two phrases.

1. For *or*, use *At least one of the following is true.*
2. For *and*, use *All of the following are true.*

These phrases and lists of bulleted conditions can be nested (with appropriate indentation) as required.

Rule: *A credit check must be performed for a customer if all of the following are true:*

---

7. Editor's note: This material was forwarded to the author via e-mail. Original source unknown.

- *A credit check has not been performed for that customer in the last 6 months.*
- *The customer places an order for which any of the following is true:*
    - *The order total is more than $500.*
    - *The outstanding balance of the customer's account plus the order amount is more than $600.*
    - *The account designated for the order is not older than 30 days.*
- *A waiver has not been authorized.*

Comment: This rule has been specified without *ors* and *ands* by using lists of appropriately indented, bulleted conditions. To introduce lists of bulleted conditions, the phrases *at least one of the following is true* and *all of the following are true* have been used as appropriate.

Several related observations should be made. We recommend avoiding the words *both* and *either* for lists of only two bulleted conditions because if additional bullets are added in the future to such a list, the sense of *both* or *either* will no longer apply. Two examples illustrate this.

Rule: *An order may be accepted only if both of the following are true:*
- *A delivery address is given.*
- *The customer's credit is good.*

Comment: It is very likely that additional conditions will be added to the bulleted list of conditions specifying whether an order should be accepted. Therefore, we recommend replacing *both* with *all*, as shown below.

Revised rule: *An order may be accepted only if all of the following are true:*
- *It includes at least one item.*
- *It indicates the customer who is placing it.*

Rule: *An order may be shipped only if either of the following is true:*
- *Payment for the order has been received.*
- *The customer's credit is good.*

Comment: It is possible that some additional condition(s) (for example, *A valid credit card number is given*) will be added to the bulleted list of conditions specifying whether an order may be shipped. Therefore, we recommend replacing *either* with *at least one*, as shown on the next page.

Revised rule: *An order may be shipped only if at least one of the following is true:*

- *Payment for the order has been received.*
- *The customer's credit is good.*

More on the Lighter Side of Rules[8]

In a laundromat: Automatic washing machines. Please remove all your clothes when the light goes out.

In an office: After the tea break, staff should empty the teapot and stand upside down on the draining board.

On a church door: This is the gate of heaven. Enter ye all by this door. (This door is kept locked because of the draft. Please use side entrance.)

In a safari park: Elephants Please Stay in Your Car

On a repair shop door: We can repair anything. (Please knock hard on the door—the bell doesn't work.)

In a London loo: Toilet out of order. Please use the floor below.

On a hair dryer: Do not use while sleeping.

On a frozen TV dinner: Serving Suggestion . . . Defrost

On the bottom of a dessert box: Do not turn upside down.

In the instructions for an iron: Do not iron clothes on body.

On a children's cough medicine: Do not drive car or operate heavy machinery.

On a Korean kitchen knife: Warning. . . . Keep out of children.

On a Japanese food processor: Not to be used for the other use.

On an airline snack pack of nuts: Open packet, eat nuts.

On a Swedish chainsaw: Do not attempt to stop chain with your hands.

---

8. Editor's note: This material was forwarded to the author via e-mail. Original sources unknown.

Special Usage Notes

Using Rule Types in RuleSpeak

Rule types are names for specific kinds of rules based on the nature of the test they perform. Common examples include the following.[9]

- Mandatory
- Mutually exclusive, mutually inclusive, mutually prohibited, and so on
- Unique
- Ascending, descending
- Frozen

Use of such rule types in rule statements is optional. Whenever such a rule type is used in a rule, it has a very specific effect on the structure of the rule statement—namely, the subject and object(s) of the sentence get switched around, as illustrated below.

> **Rule that does not include a rule type:** *An employee must have an employee-name.*

> **Rule that includes a rule type:** *Employee-name is mandatory for an employee.*

---

9. Refer to Chapter 18 for additional discussion.

Comment: Note how the subject and object get switched around from the original version of the rule when the rule type *mandatory* is added into the sentence.

Because a rule statement can have multiple objects, the surrogate words *the following* can be used as the subject of the sentence in which a rule type appears. This indicates that a list of relevant items and conditions will subsequently appear in the rule. Several examples illustrate.

Rule: *The following are mandatory for an employee:*
- *Employee-name*
- *Employee-SSN*
- *Employee-address*
- *Employee-hire-date*
- *Employee-salary*

Rule: *The following are mutually exclusive for an order:*
- *Requested-pick-up-date-time*
- *Promised-delivery-date-time*

Rule: *The following must be frozen for a closed order:*
- *Which customer placed the order*
- *All line items of the order*
- *Order-total-amount*

Using *A, Some,* and *Each*

Use of the word *a* (or *an*) in a rule statement is imprecise with respect to quantification[10]—that is, whether *at least one* or *all* is intended. This problem can be corrected by disallowing the word *a* (or *an*) altogether, and substituting the word *some* if *at least one* is meant, and the word *each* if *all* is meant. The discussion and examples below explain.

We leave to the practitioner to decide whether this usage guideline should be followed in expressing rules. The improved clarity that results from using *some* and *each* in rules is significant. On the other hand, *a* and *an*

---

10. I use the word *quantification* deliberately here. Predicate calculus (refer to Part V) offers two quantifiers, EXISTS (the *existential quantifier*) and FORALL (the *universal quantifier*), which correspond very closely to the cases of *at least one* or *some,* and *all* or *each,* respectively, as discussed here.

are very natural in English. Disallowing them can be counterproductive, especially during start-up activity. For that reason, we elected not to eliminate them in all the examples included in this text.

Rule: *A service representative must be assigned to a high-volume customer.*

Comment: The second *a* in this rule almost certainly is not intended to indicate at least one high-volume customer but rather all high-volume customers. Therefore, substituting *each* for this *a* would be appropriate. On the other hand, the first *a* probably does not mean *all* (that is, that all service representatives must be assigned to each high-volume customer). Therefore, substituting *some* for this *a* would be appropriate. The revised rule appears next.

Revised rule: *Some service representative must be assigned to each high-volume customer.*

To test this revision, let's restate the rule with the subject and object of the sentence reversed, again using *some* and *each* as appropriate. The reversed rule is as follows.

Reversed rule: *Each high-volume customer must be represented by some service representative.*

Comment: This reversed version of the rule expresses the same intention as the rule above.

Which of the two latter versions of the rule is preferred? In general, we prefer a subject that can be qualified by *each* rather than *some*. This way the rule statement starts off with clearer intention—that is, the rule indicates up front that it applies to each and every instance of the subject of the sentence.

It should be noted, however, that there are circumstances in which this guideline cannot be followed, as the following, less restricted version of the rule illustrates.

Rule: *Some high-volume customer must be represented by some service representative.*

Comment: This rule (a bit strange) is satisfied if at least one high-volume customer (not all) is represented by at least one service representative (again, not all).

It should also be noted that *each* can appear more than once in the rule, as illustrated by the following revised version.

Revised rule: *Each high-volume customer must be represented by each service representative.*

Comment: This rule (again, a bit strange) is satisfied only if all high-volume customers (not just one) are represented by all service representatives (again, not just one).

Using Strictly ANDed and ORed Conditions

A rule can include a direct list of bulleted conditions that are strictly ANDed. By *direct* I mean that the list is not subjected to an *if* clause. By *strictly ANDed* I mean that the list contains no *ors* at the same level of logic as the *ands*. Such a rule can be broken into an appropriate number of separate rules, each addressing only one of the original conditions.[11] The resulting rules are more atomic but usually *not* better for business-side communication and validation. The following example illustrates this kind of rule.

Rule: *A claim must indicate all of the following:*
- *The active policy that covers it*
- *The claimant*
- *The health care provided*
- *The health care provider providing the health care*
- *The injury/illness*
- *The initial date of the injury/illness*

Comment: This rule has a directly ANDed list of six bulleted[12] conditions. The rule can be broken into six individual rules, as follows.[13] Nonetheless, we prefer the original consolidated version above for communication and validation.

---

11. This reduction to atomic form is permitted under an assumption in rule theory that is sometimes called the *universal and*. This assumption simply means that since all rules must be satisfied, an implicit *and* must therefore be considered to exist for all rules within scope (or more formally, within the *universe of discourse*).

12. Rather than bullets, it might be desirable to provide item identifiers (for example, a, b, c, and so on) in case exception-type rules need to be expressed that are selective with respect to individual items.

13. In formal rule theory, the implicit *ands* would appear for the *right-hand expression* of the rule. (Refer to Chapter 16.) Such rules can always be reduced to individual rules, as illustrated by this example.

Rule 1: *A claim must indicate the active policy that covers it.*

Rule 2: *A claim must indicate the claimant.*

Rule 3: *A claim must indicate the health care provided.*

Rule 4: *A claim must indicate the health care provider providing the health care.*

Rule 5: *A claim must indicate the injury/illness.*

Rule 6: *A claim must indicate the initial date of the injury/illness.*

A rule can also include a list of bulleted conditions subjected to an *if* that are strictly ORed. By *strictly ORed* I mean that the list contains no *ands* at the same level of logic as the *ors*. Such a rule can also be broken into an appropriate number of separate rules, each addressing only one of the original conditions. The resulting rules are more atomic but, again, usually *not* better for business-side communication and validation. Here is an example.

Rule: *An order must be credit-checked if any of the following is true:*
- *The order total is more than $500.*
- *The outstanding balance of the customer's account plus the order amount is more than $600.*
- *The customer's account is not older than 30 days.*
- *The customer's account is inactive.*
- *The customer is out-of-state.*

Comment: This rule has an implicitly ORed list of five bulleted conditions subjected to an *if*. The rule can be broken into the following five individual rules, as follows.[14] Nonetheless, we prefer the original consolidated version above for communication and validation.

Rule 1: *An order must be credit-checked if the order total is more than $500.*

Rule 2: *An order must be credit-checked if the outstanding balance of the customer's account plus the order amount is more than $600.*

Rule 3: *An order must be credit-checked if the customer's account is not older than 30 days.*

---

14. In formal rule theory, the implicit *ors* would appear for the *left-hand expression* of the rule. (Refer to Chapter 16.) Such rules can always be reduced to individual rules as illustrated by this example.

Rule 4: *An order must be credit-checked if the customer's account is inactive.*

Rule 5: *An order must be credit-checked if the customer is out-of-state.*

Here You Have It . . .

The subject of a sentence and the principal verb should not, as a rule, be separated by a phrase or clause that can be transferred to the beginning.

—A line in the famous writing manual *The Elements of Style*[15]

---

15. Strunk, William, Jr., and E. B. White. 1979. *The Elements of Style,* 3rd ed. New York: MacMillan, p. 29.

CHAPTER 10

Functional Categories of Rules

The BRS Rule Classification Scheme

The BRS Rule Classification Scheme reflects how rules react to events. A given rule can react in one of only three possible ways to an event—hence there are three fundamental categories of rules in the scheme.

These three categories, which are defined in Table 10–1, are *rejectors*, *producers*, and *projectors*. Because these three categories are intrinsic, definitive, and mutually exclusive, they provide a sound foundation for the comprehensive set of rule sentence templates in RuleSpeak. They also have well-defined subcategories, as the table also indicates. These subcategories provide an even richer basis for organizing the templates—as well as for gaining a better understanding of your company's rules.

Table 10–1 The BRS Rule Classification Scheme

Functional Category/ Subcategory	Common Name	Definition
1.0. Rejector	Constraint[a]	Any rule that tends to disallow (that is, reject) an event if a violation of the rule would result. Rejectors shield the business from incorrect data (or incorrect state)—that is, from information that violates business rules. For example, a rejector might be specified to prevent a customer from placing an order or on credit if the customer has a poor payment history.
2.0. Producer	—	Any rule that neither rejects nor projects events but simply computes or derives a value based on some mathematical function(s).
2.1. Computation rule	—	Any producer-type rule that computes a value following standard *arithmetic* operations (for example, sum, multiply, average, and so on) specified explicitly. A computation rule provides a precise formula for how a computed term is to be calculated. For example, a computation rule might be given to compute a customers' annual order volume.
2.2. Derivation rule	—	Any producer-type rule that derives a truth value (that is, true or false) based on *logical* operations (for example, AND, OR, NOT, EQUAL TO, and so on) specified explicitly. A derivation rule provides a precise definition for a derived term—that is, a truth-valued term whose value (true or false) is always established by the specified logical operations. For example, a derivation rule might be given to indicate whether a project is at risk depending on whether the project is over budget or understaffed.
3.0. Projector	Stimulus/ response rule	Any rule that tends to take some action (other than rejection) when a relevant event occurs. A projector never rejects events (as rejectors do); rather, it *projects* them—that is, causes some new event(s) to occur as a result. Projectors generally prescribe automatic system behavior, providing a productivity boost for workers. For example, a projector might be specified to reorder stock automatically if the quantity on hand drops below a certain point.
3.1. Enabler	Toggle	A projector that toggles something on or off.
3.1.1. Inference rule	—	An enabler that infers something to be true under appropriate circumstances. For example, an inference rule might be given to indicate that a person must be considered a woman if criteria for that person's age and gender are satisfied.

a. In formal rule theory, certain kinds of projectors (especially inference rules) are also considered to be constraints, so this common name can be misleading.

Term	Category	Description
3.1.2. Rule toggle	Exception-type rule	An enabler that turns another rule on or off under appropriate circumstances—that is, makes it capable or incapable of firing. For example, a rule toggle might be given to indicate that some normal operating rule is to be suspended under emergency circumstances.
3.1.3. Process toggle	—	An enabler that turns an operation, process, or procedure on or off under appropriate circumstances—that is, makes it capable or incapable of executing. For example, a process toggle might be given to indicate that a sensitive process cannot be executed while a security breach is suspected.
3.1.4. Data toggle	—	An enabler that creates or deletes instances of actual data under appropriate circumstances. For example, a data toggle might be given to indicate that a juvenile's criminal record must be erased when he or she reaches 18 years of age.
3.2. Copier	—	A projector that replicates (copies) actual values.
3.2.1. Imprint rule	—	A copier that sets the value of something that persists (for example, something in a database). For example, an imprint rule might be used to initialize the tuition owed by a student in a given semester to the base tuition for that semester when the student enrolls.
3.2.2. Presentation rule	—	A copier that establishes a value or parameter related to how data is to be presented (for example, on a screen, in a report, and so on). For example, a presentation rule might be given to indicate that an order is to be displayed on the screen in red if the order is overdue.
3.3. Executive	Trigger	A projector that causes an operation, process, or procedure to execute or a rule to fire.
3.3.1. Process trigger	—	A projector that causes an operation, process, or procedure to execute. For example, when an order is shipped, a process trigger might be given to execute a process that automatically sends the intended recipient a notification.
3.3.2. Rule trigger	—	A projector that causes a rule to fire. For example, when data about a shipment is displayed to the screen, a rule trigger might be given that fires another rule to predict the shipment's arrival date.

CHAPTER 11

Sentence Patterns for Rule Statements

The RuleSpeak Templates[1]

The BRS RuleSpeak sentence templates are presented below, with examples and comments. These templates are organized according to the functional categories defined in Chapter 10. Shorthand forms are suggested where appropriate. The entire set is summarized in Table 11–1 at the end of this chapter.

1.0. RuleSpeak Templates for Rejectors

A rejector is a rule that tends to disallow (that is, reject) an event if a violation of the rule would result.

1.1. "Must" Template

The most basic template is for rules that involve a *must* condition.

Examples:

Rule: *A shipment must have a status.*

Rule: *An order must indicate the customer that places it.*

Rule: *A purchase order taken during a snowstorm must be approved by at least two managers.*

---

1. Version 6.

1.2. "Must Not" Template

Rules expressed by using the must rule word can also involve conditions that are not permitted.

Examples:

Rule: *A freshman must not participate in any honors club.*

Rule: *A retired employee must not have an employment counselor.*

Rule: *The number of seats for a course section must not exceed 30.*

Rule: *An order must not be shipped if the outstanding balance of the customer's account exceeds the customer's credit authorization.*

Rule: *An order must not contain more than 99 line items.*

Rule: *A territory must not include more than one of the following:*

- *Noncandidate traditional gas station*
- *Ultra-service*
- *Food outlet*

1.3. "May . . . Only If" Template

Use of the word *may* rather than *must* is appropriate when the rule word *only* is used to express a rule. The *only* condition indicates the specific circumstances under which permission is granted.

Examples:

Rule: *A customer may purchase a pesticide from a supplier only if the supplier actually sells that pesticide.*

Rule: *A customer may place an order only if the customer holds an account.*

Rule: *A withdrawal from an account may be made only if the account is active.*

1.4. "May . . . Only [Preposition]" Template

Rules using the rule word *only* can be expressed without the additional word *if* when a preposition[2] immediately follows the word *only*.

---

2. Generally, these prepositions are actually included in the fact statements that underlie the rules. For example, the fact underlying the rule *A salaried employee may work only in a budgeted department* should include the preposition *in* (that is, *Employee works in department*).

Examples:

Rule: *A salaried employee may work only in a budgeted department.*

Rule: *A rush order may be approved only by a supervisor.*

Rule: *An account may be opened only on a workday.*

Rule: *A suspension may be imposed only for a serious offense.*

Rule: *A self-study award may be given only to a senior.*

Rule: *A tool properly stored may be used only with permission of the owner.*

Templates for Permission Statements

A permission statement is a statement indicating the absence of any rule under a particular set of specified conditions. Such a statement indicates workers are not constrained by any rule in that situation and therefore may exercise judgment or discretion in taking relevant actions.

A. "May" Template

A permission statement can be formed by using the permission word *may*.

Example:

Rule: *An order on credit totaling over $1,000 must not be accepted from a customer if the customer's credit has not been checked.*

Permission statement: *An order on credit totaling $1,000 or under may be accepted from a customer even if the customer's credit has not been checked.*

B. "Need Not" Template

A permission statement can be formed by using the permission word phrase *need not*.

Example:

Rule: *A customer must place at least one order.*

Permission statement: *A customer need not place any orders.*

2.0. RuleSpeak Templates for Producers

A producer is a rule that neither rejects nor projects events but simply computes or derives a value based on some mathematical function(s).

2.1. Templates for Computation Rules

A computation rule always involves one or more arithmetic operations.

Keyword phrase: *must be computed as*

Examples:

Rule: *A product's cost must be computed as the sum of the cost of all its components.*

Rule: *The amount paid for an order must be computed as the sum of all payment amounts applied to the order.*

2.1.1. Shorthand for Computation Rules

If desired, a computation rule can be expressed in shorthand form as follows.

Keyword: =

Examples:

Rule: *A product's cost must be computed as the sum of the cost of all its components.*

Shorthand version: *Product's cost = the sum of the cost of all its components.*

Rule: *The amount paid for an order must be computed as the sum of all payment amounts applied to the order.*

Shorthand version: *The amount paid for an order = the sum of all payment amounts applied to the order.*

2.2. Templates for Derivation Rules

A derivation rule always involves one or more logical (truth-valued) operations (for example, AND, OR, NOT, EQUAL TO, and so on). A derivation rule provides a precise definition for a derived term; therefore, the keyword *means* is always used for its specification.

Keyword phrase: *must be taken to mean*

Examples:

Rule: *At-risk project must be taken to mean the project is over budget or understaffed.*

Rule: *High-risk customer must be taken to mean the outstanding balance exceeds $1,000 on each of the customer's last three successive invoices.*

Rule: *Big-ticket item must be taken to mean the item's cost exceeds $500.*

Rule: *Midnight must be taken to mean the time is equal to12:00 PM.*

2.2.1. Shorthand for Derivation Rules

If desired, a derivation rule can be expressed in shorthand form as follows.

Keyword: *means*

Examples:

Rule: *At-risk project must be taken to mean the project is over budget or understaffed.*

Shorthand version: *At-risk project means the project is over budget or understaffed.*

✦   ✦   ✦

Rule: *High-risk customer must be taken to mean the outstanding balance exceeds $1,000 on each of the customer's last three successive invoices.*

Shorthand version: *High-risk customer means the outstanding balance exceeds $1,000 on each of the customer's last three successive invoices.*

✦   ✦   ✦

Rule: *Big-ticket item must be taken to mean the item's cost exceeds $500.*

Shorthand version: *Big-ticket item means the item's cost exceeds $500.*

✦   ✦   ✦

Rule: *Midnight must be taken to mean the time is equal to12:00 PM.*

Shorthand version: *Midnight means the time is equal to12:00 PM.*

3.0. RuleSpeak Templates for Projectors

A projector is a rule that tends to take some action (other than rejection) when a relevant event occurs. A projector (sometimes called a *stimulus/response rule*) never rejects events (as rejectors do); rather, it *projects* them—that is, causes some new event(s) to occur as a result.

3.1. Templates for Enablers

An enabler (also known as a toggle) is a rule that turns something on or off.

3.1.1. Template for Inference Rules

An inference rule always infers something to be true about the subject of the rule if the *if* condition is satisfied.

Keyword phrase: *must be considered*

Examples:

Rule: *A person must be considered a woman if the person is female and the person's age is 21 or over.*

Comments:

The subject of this rule is *person.*

The rule will infer something to be true about this subject (namely that a person is a woman) if the specified condition holds. In other words, the rule will toggle *woman* to true.

The specified condition is given by the *if* clause.

Rule: *The go/no-go decision must be considered no-go if the tank status is questionable.*

3.1.1.1. Shorthand for Inference Rules

If desired, an inference rule can be expressed in shorthand form as follows.

Keyword: *is*

Example 1:

Rule: *A person must be considered a woman if the person is female and the person's age is 21 or over.*

Shorthand version: *A person is a woman if the person is female and the person's age is 21 or over.*

Example 2:

Rule: *The go/no-go decision must be considered no-go if the tank status is questionable.*

Shorthand version: *The go/no-go decision is no-go if the tank status is questionable.*

3.1.2. Template for Rule Toggles

This template is the preferred form for expressing exceptions to rules at the atomic level of business logic. The subject of a rule toggle (exception-type rule) is always some other rule.

Keyword phrase: *must (not) be enforced*

Example:

Rule: *The one-borrower-per-library-card rule must not be enforced if one of the borrowers who hold the library card is Bill Gates.*

Comment: The subject of the rule, *one-borrower-per-library-card,* is the name of the rule that must not be enforced if the condition (*one of the borrowers who hold the library card is Bill Gates*) holds true. This rule can be of any kind—that is, a rejector, a producer, or a projector.

3.1.3. Template for Process Toggles

This form of toggle-type rule indicates that a process or procedure must not be executed (either by users, by rules, or by any other means) for as long as the condition(s) included in the rule, if any, hold true. The subject of such a rule is always a process or procedure.

Keyword phrase: *must be enabled/disabled*

Example:

Rule: *Send-appointment-notice must be disabled if the client's address is unknown.*

Comments:

The subject of the rule, *send-appointment-notice,* is the process to be disabled.

This process can be an operation, a method, an action, a procedure, and so on—anything that can be executed.

3.1.4. Template for Data Toggles

The subject of this kind of toggle-type rule is always some form of data.

Data toggles should be used only with great caution. The *created* form (see below) implies that data must be created from nothing. The result would therefore be arbitrary. (A copier-type rule should be used when the desired data *can* be identified—a much more likely circumstance. Refer to the discussion of copiers below.)

Keyword phrase: *must be created/deleted*

Examples:

Rule: *Lottery-winner-number must be created when lottery-date equals today's date.*

Comment: This rule essentially acts (hopefully!) as a random number generator.

✦ ✦ ✦

Rule: *Each outstanding case issue must be deleted when the case is closed.*

Comment: This rule will cause *the outstanding issues* data to be lost (deleted) at the point in time that a case is closed.

3.2. Templates for Copiers

A copier is a projector that replicates (copies) values.

3.2.1. Template for Imprint Rules

An imprint rule is a copier that sets the value of something that persists (for example, something in a database).

Keyword phrase: *must be set to*

Examples:

Rule: *Normal-tax-return-due-date must be set to April 15.*

Rule: *Applicable-sales-tax must be set to 8.25%.*

Comment: The value 8.25% is probably referenced by many rules. Instead of embedding the value in each of these many rules—not a good idea since the value might be changed—this imprint rule introduces a variable named *applicable-sales-tax* in which the current value can be held. All other rules referencing the value should use this variable name instead. By this means, the atomic piece of business logic is isolated to a single rule.

✦ ✦ ✦

Rule: *Applicable-sales-tax must be set to 8.25% if order-fulfillment-date = 2001.*

Comment: If the value of *applicable-sales-tax* is potentially reset each year, consider using a decision table instead of individually defined rules to set the year-by-year values. (Decision tables are discussed in Chapter 12.)

✦ ✦ ✦

Rule: *A student's-semester-fees-owed must be set to $3,065 when the student registers for a semester.*

Comment: Use of the time word *when* indicates that *student's-semester-fees-owed* is merely being initialized to a certain value at the given point in time. Presumably, this value will be incremented subsequently—for example, if the student registers for a particular course that has lab fees.

3.2.2. Template for Presentation Rules

A presentation rule is a copier that establishes a value or parameter related to how data is to be presented (for example, on a screen, in a report, and so on).

Keyword phrase: *must be displayed*

Following *must be displayed,* say where and how.

Examples:

Rule: *An order must be displayed to the screen in red if the order is overdue.*

Rule: *Potential Suppliers must be displayed in the Potential Suppliers Report in alphabetical order.*

Rule: *A client's–favorite-stock must be displayed to the screen when the client's–favorite–stock price varies by more than 8% over the past four hours.*

Comment: This last rule is an example of an *alerter.*

3.3. Templates for Executives

An executive (commonly known as a trigger) is a rule that under appropriate circumstances causes actual executions. A *process trigger* executes an operation, process, or procedure; a *rule trigger* "executes" a rule (that is, causes it to fire).

Executives differ from process toggles and rule toggles in the following way. Toggles merely enable (or disable) the process or rule, that is, make them capable (or incapable) of executing or firing. In contrast to executives, toggles do not *directly* cause actual executions (or firings).

3.3.1. Template for Process Triggers

The subject of a process trigger is always a process. This process can be an operation, a method, an action, a procedure, and so on—anything that can be executed. The word *when* is usually appropriate for process triggers since the process's execution is usually intended for a point in time, as given by the rule's condition.

Keyword phrase: *must be executed*

Example:

Rule: *Send-advance-notice must be executed for an order when the order is shipped.*

Comment: The subject of the rule, *send-advance-notice*, is the process to be executed.

3.3.2. Template for Rule Triggers

The subject of a rule trigger is always another rule. The word *when* is usually appropriate for rule triggers since the rule's firing is usually intended for a point in time, as given by the rule's condition.

Rule triggers should be used cautiously since *point in time* generally implies some event, and rules should normally be expressed without reference to any events. Rule triggers are sometimes used to indicate a preferred *firing order* for other rules—that is, that one rule should be fired before another when both can be fired in response to the same event.[3]

Keyword phrase: *must be fired*

Example:

Rule: *The projected-shipment-date-rule must be fired when a shipment is displayed to the screen.*

Comment: The rule *projected-shipment-date-rule* must be fired (evaluated) at the specific points in time (events) that a shipment is displayed to a user.

---

3. We do not necessarily endorse this practice. Scripting the desired order of firing is probably a more appropriate choice.

Snow-Blinded by Rules[4]

A man and his wife are sitting down to their usual cups of morning coffee, listening to the weather report coming over the radio: "There will be three to five inches of snow today, and a snow emergency has been declared. You must park your cars on the odd-numbered side of the streets." The man gets up from his coffee and replies, "Jeez, O.K."

Two days later, again they are sipping their morning coffee when they hear the weather forecast: "There will be two to four inches of snow today, and a snow emergency has been declared. You must park your cars on the even-numbered side of the streets." The man gets up from his coffee and replies, "Jeez, O.K."

Three days later, again they are sitting down with their cups of coffee and listening to the weather forecast: "There will be six to eight inches of snow today, and a snow emergency has been declared. You must park your cars on the—" and then the power went out and they didn't hear the rest of the instructions.

He says to his wife, "What am I going to do now?"

She replies, "Aw, just leave the car in the garage."

---

4. Editor's note: This material was forwarded to the author via e-mail. Original source unknown.

The Basic RuleSpeak Templates at a Glance

Table 11–1 provides a quick reference for the complete set of basic sentence templates in RuleSpeak. These templates are meant to provide basic structures for rule statements given in English so they can be captured and communicated consistently. The set of templates given in the table are not intended to constitute a formal or complete language.

As always in RuleSpeak, the templates are organized by a rule's functional category. Each category has one or more special *rule keywords*, each of which is the word or short phrase that appears distinctively in a particular sentence template for that category. (These special rule keywords appear in all capital letters in the table simply for emphasis.) The simple syntactical conventions used in the table are explained in the following list.

- The symbols < > indicate the syntactical item inside is mandatory.
- The symbols [ ] indicate the syntactical item inside is optional.
- The symbol / indicates that only one syntactical item of the two or more listed need be selected.
- *Condition* always involves a logical expression (something that must always be true or false). A *condition* is always based on one or more terms and facts (or data items) and may include logical operators such as AND, OR, and NOT.
- *Fact* inside brackets refers to the rest of the fact statement after the subject. For example, the <fact> for the fact statement *Customer places order* is "*places order.*" Also, in all cases where *<fact>* appears, an embedded condition is permitted. For example, "*places more than ten orders*" embeds the condition "*more than ten.*"
- Use of the keyword *should* in a rule statement indicates that the rule is a suggestor (that is, a guideline, heuristic, or suggestion).

Table 11–1 The Basic RuleSpeak Templates at a Glance

Category	Informal Description/ Purpose	Rule's Subject Must Be . . .	Template	Example
Rejector *Rule keywords:* MUST ONLY	A constraint for maintaining correctness (consistency) by preventing violations	Term or fact *(data item also permitted)*	<Subject> MUST/should [not] <fact> [if/while <condition>]. <Subject> may/should <fact> ONLY if/while <condition>. <Subject> may/should <fact> ONLY <preposition> <condition>.	*An order MUST indicate the date it was received.* *A student MUST not take more than four courses while on probation.* *A customer may place an order ONLY if the customer holds an account.* *A salaried employee may work ONLY in a budgeted department.*
Permission statement *Rule keywords:* MAY NEED NOT	A policy or clarification permitting a business practice	Term, fact, rule, or process *(data item also permitted)*	<Subject> MAY <fact/rule keyword> [if/while <condition>]. <Subject> NEED NOT <fact/rule keyword> [if/while <condition>].	*An order on credit totaling $1,000 or under MAY be accepted from a customer even if the customer's credit has not been checked.* *A customer NEED NOT place any orders.*
Computation rule *Rule keywords:* BE COMPUTED	A statement or arithmetic formula indicating how to calculate a numeric value	Computed term *(data item also permitted)*	<Subject> must/should [not] BE COMPUTED as <mathematical formula> [if/while <condition>]. *Shorthand:* <Subject> = <mathematical formula> [if/while <condition>].	*The amount paid for an order must BE COMPUTED as the sum of all payment amounts applied to the order.* *The amount paid for an order = the sum of all payment amounts applied to the order.*

Term type	Definition	Template	Example
Derivation rule *Rule keywords:* BE TAKEN TO MEAN MEANS	A statement or logical expression indicating how to determine a yes/no (true/false) result *(data item also permitted)*	<Subject> must/should [not] BE TAKEN TO MEAN <logical expression> [if/while <condition>]. *Shorthand:* <Subject> MEANS [not] <logical expression> [if/while <condition>].	*Big-ticket item must BE TAKEN TO MEAN the item's cost exceeds $500.* *Big-ticket item MEANS the item's cost exceeds $500.*
Inference rule *Rule keywords:* BE CONSIDERED	A rule that infers a conclusion from a particular set of circumstances *(data item also permitted)*	<Subject> must/should [not] BE CONSIDERED [a] <term> if/while <condition>. *Shorthand:* <Subject> is [not] [a] <term> if/while <condition>.	*A person must BE CONSIDERED a woman if the person is female and the person's age is 21 or over.* *A person is a woman if the person is female and the person's age is 21 or over.*
Rule toggle *Rule keywords:* UNLESS EXCEPT BE ENFORCED	A rule that turns another rule on or off in a particular set of circumstances, especially for making exceptions	Informal: <Rule statement>, UNLESS/EXCEPT <condition>. Formal: <Rule name> must/should [not] BE ENFORCED if/while <condition>.	*A library card may be held by at most one borrower UNLESS one of the borrowers who hold the library card is Bill Gates.* *The one-borrower-per-library-card rule must not BE ENFORCED if one of the borrowers who hold the library card is Bill Gates.*
Process toggle *Rule keywords:* BE ENABLED BE DISABLED	A rule that turns a process on or off in a particular set of circumstances	<Subject> must/should [not] BE ENABLED/DISABLED if/while <condition>.	*Send-appointment-notice must BE DISABLED if the client's address is unknown.*

continued

Table 11-1 *continued*

Category	Informal Description/Purpose	Rule's Subject Must Be . . .	Template	Example
Data toggle *Rule Keywords:* BE CREATED BE DELETED	A rule that deletes data (or creates it randomly) in a particular set of circumstances	Data item	<Data item> must/should [not] BE CREATED/DELETED if/while <condition>.	*Each outstanding case issue must BE DELETED when the case is closed.*
Imprint rule *Rule keywords:* BE SET	A rule that sets a stored data item to a particular value	Term or fact *(data item also permitted)*	<Term> must/should [not] BE SET to <term/value> [when/if <condition>].	*A student's-semester-fees-owed must BE SET to $3,065 when the student registers for a semester.*
Presentation rule *Rule keywords:* BE DISPLAYED	A rule that requires data to be presented in a certain manner (for example, on a screen or in a report)	Term or fact *(data item also permitted)*	<Subject> must/should [not] BE DISPLAYED [to/on/in <media>] <display manner> [if/while <condition>].	*An order must BE DISPLAYED to the screen in red if the order is overdue.*
Process trigger *Rule keywords:* BE EXECUTED	A rule that automatically executes a process or procedure in a given set of circumstances	Process or procedure	<Subject> must/should BE EXECUTED when <condition>.	*Send-advance-notice must BE EXECUTED for an order when the order is shipped.*
Rule trigger *Rule keywords:* BE FIRED	A rule that automatically fires another rule in a given set of circumstances	Rule	<Rule name> must/should BE FIRED when <condition>.	*The projected-shipment-date-rule must BE FIRED when a shipment is displayed to the screen.*

CHAPTER 12

Expressing Business Logic by Using Decision Tables

The RuleSpeak Approach[1]

In RuleSpeak, rule statements always have a subject. They also always include one or more other terms. In the context of decision tables, these other terms are known as *evaluation terms* or more generally as *decision criteria*. These decision criteria provide the basis for the *labels* of rows and columns of the decision tables.

Any specific value or value range (called a *bracket*) for an evaluation term will have a definitive effect on the rule's subject. This definitive effect is an *outcome*. The collection of all decision criteria and outcomes included in a decision table represents the decision table's *consolidated* business logic.

When Decision Tables Should Be Used

Often the need for a decision table to express consolidated business logic is recognized rather easily. In general, decision tables are useful where all of the following conditions are true.

- A significant number of rules are parallel—that is, they share the same subject,[2] have exactly the same evaluation term(s), and are equivalent (but not

---

1. Version 2.
2. This constraint does not apply to projectors.

identical) in effect. In other words, the rules[3] share a common pattern and purpose.

- Each evaluation term has a finite number of relevant values or brackets.[4]
- Given the different values of the evaluation term(s), the outcomes cannot be predicted by a single formula. (If a single formula could predict the outcomes, using a single rule or set of rules to give the unified formula is a better approach.)

Decision Tables Involving One Evaluation Term

Here is an example of a simple situation that meets all the criteria listed above.

> **Rule 1:** *Applicable-sales-tax must be set to 6.0% if year = 1995.*
>
> **Rule 2:** *Applicable-sales-tax must be set to 6.5% if year = 1996.*
>
> **Rule 3:** *Applicable-sales-tax must be set to 6.5% if year = 1997.*
>
> **Rule 4:** *Applicable-sales-tax must be set to 6.5% if year = 1998.*
>
> **Rule 5:** *Applicable-sales-tax must be set to 6.25% if year = 1999.[5]*
>
> **Rule 6:** *Applicable-sales-tax must be set to 7.0% if year = 2000.*
>
> **Rule 7:** *Applicable-sales-tax must be set to 8.0% if year = 2001.*
>
> **Rule 8:** *Applicable-sales-tax must be set to 8.15% if year = 2002.*

Note the following about the rules given above:

- These eight rules are exactly parallel in the sense described above.
- There is one evaluation term in each rule, *year.*
- Overall, this evaluation term has a finite number of relevant values (currently eight).
- The outcome is the value for the rules' subject, *applicable-sales-tax.*
- The outcome for each of the rules given its *year* value cannot be predicted by a formula.

---

3. Such a collection of rules is sometimes called a *decision set.*

4. To address an infinite set of values, the keyword *other* is often used to represent all values not specifically enumerated.

5. Note that the sales tax rate decreased in 1999 from the previous year. This decrease represents an apparently infrequent (and perhaps improbable!) tax cut.

The following decision table shows the consolidated business logic for the eight rules given above.

Rule: *Applicable-sales-tax must be set to the percent value in Table A for a given year.*

TABLE A

Year	Applicable Sales Tax
1995	6.0
1996	6.5
1997	6.5
1998	6.5
1999	6.25
2000	7.0
2001	8.0
2002	8.15

The original eight rules have been specified as a single table-based rule. The only evaluation term is *year*, which appears as the label at the top of the left-hand column. The relevant values of *year* appear in the left-hand column as labels for the rows. The appropriate outcomes (values of the subject, *applicable-sales-tax)* appear in the cells of the right-hand column.

Decision tables are also useful for finding missing rules—that is, for determining whether the consolidated business logic is *complete.* For example, if any cell in a decision table has no value whatsoever, then that outcome is possibly missing and should be addressed.[6] (If a majority of cells have no values, then the decision table format might not be optimal for representing the underlying business logic.) The crucial issue of completeness is discussed in greater detail later in this chapter.

Decision Tables Involving Two Evaluation Terms

The example above had a single evaluation term. The values of this evaluation term were listed as labels for the rows of the decision table. Where there

---

6. Automated rule analysis tools offer much more sophisticated capabilities. Corticon Technologies, Inc., has been a pioneer in this area.

are exactly two evaluation terms in a set of parallel rules, the values of the second evaluation term are shown as labels for the columns of the decision table. Again, the appropriate outcome for each two-way combination of values is indicated for the appropriate cell. An example using an extended version of the earlier rule illustrates such a decision table.

Rule: *Applicable-sales-tax must be set to the percent value in Table B for a given year and county.*

TABLE B

| | County | | | |
Year	Harkin	Lopes	Qwan	Quail
1995	6.95	8.2	7.35	4.0
1996	6.73	8.3	9.0	4.5
1997	6.15	8.4	9.0	5.0
1998	6.15	8.3	9.0	5.5
1999	6.15	8.4	6.75	6.0
2000	6.15	8.2	6.75	6.75
2001	5.75	8.2	6.75	7.0
2002	5.95	8.4	7.5	7.25

In this example, there are two evaluation terms: *year* (whose values appear as labels for the rows) and *county* (whose values appear as labels for the columns). The desired outcomes for the rule (the values of the subject, *applicable-sales-tax*) have been indicated as appropriate in the individual cells.

Decision Tables Involving Three or More Simple Evaluation Terms

Representing *more* than two evaluation terms using a two-dimensional media (for example, paper) is problematic.[7] If there are three or more evaluation terms, all but two (or fewer) of which are simple, the business logic can still be represented in the form used thus far. Two approaches are discussed below. Incidentally, there is more to understanding whether an evaluation

---

7. At this point, there is probably no viable substitute for an automated tool. Such tools include RuleTrack from Business Rule Solutions, LLC (*http://www.BRSolutions.com*) and Corticon Studio from Corticon Technologies, Inc. (http://www.Corticon.com).

term is "simple" than might be expected, as explained in the boxed item, A Word about "Simple" Evaluation Terms.

A Word about "Simple" Evaluation Terms

A simple evaluation term is one that has only a few values. For example, the term *gender* is simple—the possible values are just *male* and *female*. Another example is the term *is-order-overdue?* (or simply, *order-overdue*). This term has only two possible values: *yes* and *no* (or *true* and *false*).

The most important thing in this context is to recognize what "simple" does *not* imply. For example, simple values can be derived according to some logical expression (for example, "not weekend day or legal holiday") or computed according to an arithmetic expression (for example, "50% of flat rate + 1% of gross amount"). Indeed, such expressions can appear as a whole as the label for any given row or column of a decision table. (When used in this fashion, the expressions are called *decision criteria* rather than evaluation terms.)

A logical or mathematical expression can often be quite complex. An alternative to using the entire expression as a label within a decision table is to create a separate rule whose subject is an appropriate derived or computed term. This derived or computed term can then substitute for the expression in the decision table.

For example, the logical expression given above could be made into the following rule: *Workday means not weekend day or legal holiday.* Then *workday* can be used instead of *not weekend day or legal holiday* anytime this label is required for a row or column in a decision table. An added benefit is that the new term is reusable for other rules, including for labeling columns and rows in other decision tables. Since the associated logic is defined only once, it will always be applied consistently no matter how many times *workday* is used. This, of course, reflects a basic principle of the business rule approach.

Split-Row Decision Table

The first alternative for representing the business logic in such cases is to split rows and/or columns within a single array, as illustrated by the following example.

Rule: *Applicable-sales-tax must be set to the percent value in Table C for a given year, county, and commodity type.*

TABLE C

Year	County			
	Harkin	Lopes	Qwan	Quail
1995: Food	6.95	8.2	7.35	4.0
Other	9.0	9.1	7.35	9.0
1996: Food	6.73	8.3	9.0	4.5
Other	9.0	9.0	9.9	9.5
1997: Food	6.15	8.4	9.0	5.0
Other	8.55	9.5	9.9	8.0
1998: Food	6.15	8.3	9.0	5.5
Other	8.45	9.5	9.9	6.2
1999: Food	6.15	8.4	6.75	6.0
Other	8.45	9.6	8.2	7.75
2000: Food	6.15	8.2	6.75	6.75
Other	8.45	8.9	8.2	7.75
2001: Food	5.75	8.2	6.75	7.0
Other	7.75	8.2	8.3	7.0
2002: Food	5.95	8.4	7.5	7.25
Other	7.95	8.5	9.0	7.25

In this example, there are three evaluation terms: *year* (whose values appear as the outer labels for the split rows), *commodity type* (whose values appear in repeating sets as the inner labels for the split rows), and *county* (whose values appear as labels for the columns). The desired outcomes for the rule (the values of the subject, *applicable-sales-tax*) have been indicated as appropriate in the cells of the decision table. Note that there are only two values for the split-row evaluation term commodity type (*food, other*). Had there been very many more values than that, the table would quickly become quite lengthy and increasingly difficult to use.

Multiple-Array Decision Table

If the number of values or brackets is too large for a practical split-row decision table, multiple arrays[8] can be employed. In this case, there is one array

---

8. In this discussion, *array* is used in the mathematical sense—a number of elements arranged in rows and columns.

per relevant value or bracket of one (or more) of the evaluation terms. The values of each of the other two evaluation terms will appear as labels for the rows and columns in identical fashion for every array. All the cells of all the arrays represent the possible outcomes in the consolidated business logic.

Rule: *Applicable-sales-tax must be set to the percent value in Table D for a given year, county, and commodity type.*

TABLE D, ARRAY 1. FOOD

Year	County			
	Harkin	Lopes	Qwan	Quail
1995	6.95	8.2	7.35	4.0
1996	6.73	8.3	9.0	4.5
1997	6.15	8.4	9.0	5.0
1998	6.15	8.3	9.0	5.5
1999	6.15	8.4	6.75	6.0
2000	6.15	8.2	6.75	6.75
2001	5.75	8.2	6.75	7.0
2002	5.95	8.4	7.5	7.25

TABLE D, ARRAY 2. COMMODITIES OTHER THAN FOOD

Year	County			
	Harkin	Lopes	Qwan	Quail
1995	9.0	9.1	7.35	9.0
1996	9.0	9.0	9.9	9.5
1997	8.55	9.5	9.9	8.0
1998	8.45	9.5	9.9	6.2
1999	8.45	9.6	8.2	7.75
2000	8.45	8.9	8.2	7.75
2001	7.75	8.2	8.3	7.0
2002	7.95	8.5	9.0	7.25

In this revision of the previous example, there are again three evaluation terms: *year* (whose values appear as labels for the rows in each array), *commodity type* (whose values identify the separate arrays), and *county* (whose values appear as labels for the columns in each array). As before, the desired outcomes for the rule (the values of the subject, *applicable-sales-tax*) have been indicated as appropriate in the cells of the arrays.

Decision Tables Involving More Complex Sets of Decision Criteria

The most general case for decision tables involves one or more of the following:

- More than three or four simple evaluation terms
- Three or more evaluation terms that are not simple
- Some combination of these

Such decision tables can be represented using a special *header-and-body* format. The header of a decision table formatted in this fashion addresses the subject of the rule; the body presents the relevant conditions. Unfortunately, as discussed below, such decision tables are prone to anomalies, so they must be developed with care and then scrutinized closely. Here is an example.

Rule: *The delivery method for an order must be determined according to Table E.*

TABLE E

Decision Criteria	Delivery Method for an Order		
	Picked Up by Customer	Shipped by Normal Service	Shipped by Premium Service
Rush order	No	Yes	Yes
Order includes fragile item	No	Yes	—
Order includes specialty item	No	No	—
Order includes high-priced item	No	No	—
Order includes item involving hazardous materials	No	Yes	Yes
Category of customer	Silver	Gold	Platinum
Destination of order	—	Local	Remote

This decision table establishes the basis for determining the delivery method for an order, the subject of the rule statement. Three outcomes (possible values of the subject) have been included in the *header* of the decision table, at the top of each column. In the *body* of the decision table (the rest of the decision table below the header), seven decision criteria appear at left as labels for the rows.[9] Six of these decision criteria involve only two values (*yes, no* or *local, remote*), whereas one (category of customer) involves three (*silver, gold, platinum*). In any cell of the body of the decision table, a dash (—) indicates that that decision criteria does not matter in determining the outcome; that is, *any* value for that decision criteria will produce the same result. The choice (outcome) of delivery method for an order appropriate for the combination of decision criteria values given in any column of the body is indicated directly above it in the header.[10]

Representing the subject of the rule statement as the header in the decision table is consistent with the basic RuleSpeak guideline that the subject of a rule should always come first. For decision tables that involve more complex sets of decision criteria such as the above, we find that this approach is particularly helpful for achieving more complete and anomaly-free results.[11] The various aspects of this critical issue are explored later, after several additional notes about decision tables in header-and-body format.

- Different sets of decision criteria (that is, different columns in the body) can produce the very same outcome. (None are shown in the example above.) Appropriate formatting and/or color-coding of the header, and/or sequencing of the columns, can make this equivalence apparent. Such multicolumn equivalence in outcome is to be expected for larger tables.
- Each such set of decision criteria (that is, each such column) in the body produces one and only one outcome in the header.
- A logical AND (rather than OR) is always assumed for the set of all decision criteria in one column of the body.

---

9. This table therefore involves seven dimensions.
10. In this header-and-body format for decision tables, the combination of values in any one column of the body is considered a *label* for the outcome just above it in the header.
11. Some approaches to formatting decision tables recommend presenting decision criteria *before* outcomes. In other words, the contents of the header for a rule in RuleSpeak format would be shown at the bottom of the decision table. This reversed form essentially puts the decision table into *If-Then* format. Often this is made explicit by literally placing the word *If* above the decision table, then splitting the decision table into two parts so the word *Then* can be placed above the second part (the outcomes). We avoid this format for decision tables for the same reasons we avoid the *If-Then* format for expressing all rules at the business perspective.

- More than one header is permitted for a decision table in header-and-body format, representing other sets of outcomes based on the same sets of decision criteria in the body. (A logical AND is again assumed.)
- A decision table in header-and-body format with only a single header is in atomic form because both the second and third bullets above are satisfied. (These two bullets represent the fundamental criteria for whether a rule is in atomic form.) A decision table with more than one header is not in atomic form because the atomic form of rules does not permit ANDed outcomes (as per the second bullet).

Multiple headers should be used cautiously for the following reason. If a value of a cell in the body is changed, the revised set of decision criteria in that column may no longer produce exactly the same set of outcomes in the headers stacked directly above the revised column. Unless properly addressed (for example, by splitting the column), flaws in the business logic will result.

Completeness

The first issue in ensuring the quality of decision tables is completeness. In this context, completeness means that all appropriate situations have been addressed—that is, that all possible combinations of values for the decision criteria involving selective outcomes have been examined.

How complete is the sample decision table above? The header shows three outcomes, and the body includes three columns of values for the decision criteria, so obviously at a minimum the decision table addresses three possible combinations of decision criteria values. Actually, the body establishes the basis for a good number more than that for the following reason.

Several cells indicate acceptance of any value—for example, either *yes* or *no*—which renders the decision criteria for that cell essentially irrelevant to determining the outcome for the given situation. For example, column 1 includes one such cell, so that column actually provides the basis for establishing the outcome for *two* combinations—one if the value for the cell were *local* and one if it were *remote*. (As explained in the boxed item, The Completeness of Sets of Values Used as Decision Criteria, this assumption is by no means a trivial one.) Column 3 includes three such cells, so that column actually establishes the basis for 2^3 or 8 outcomes. Altogether, the body of the decision table actually establishes the basis for establishing 11 outcomes $(2 + 1 + 8 = 11)$.

The Completeness of Sets of Values Used as Decision Criteria

Our analysis of the decision criteria for this sample decision table assumes that there are only two possible values for destination of order: *local* and *remote*. This assumption would need to be validated, of course, with knowledgeable business workers. Verifying that all possible values for each decision criteria in a decision table have been discovered is another critical—and very basic—issue in ensuring the completeness of consolidated business logic.

The completeness of even the simplest value sets should not be taken for granted. For example, if the value set for a particular decision criteria is simply *yes* and *no*, but then situations are discovered where neither apply, the value set is not complete (and perhaps not very well developed either!). For example, it might be assumed that the only pleas a defendant at trial could enter were *guilty* and *not guilty*. Then a defendant pleads *no contest*. At least in the defendant's view, the distinction being made is a very real and significant one. In his or her logic, neither *guilty* nor *not guilty* applies—and it certainly *does* matter.

The bottom line is that "neither applies" in a decision table should never be confused with the use of dashes for "does not matter." This is quite clear if we return to the basic RuleSpeak statements for the columns. For example, column 3 in the decision table above should be worded as follows, simply omitting any reference to the dashed items altogether.[12]

An order must be shipped by premium service if all of the following are true:
- *The order is rush.*
- *The order includes an item involving hazardous materials.*
- *The category of customer that placed the order is platinum.*
- *The destination of the order is remote.*

continued

---

12. This should serve as a reminder that decision table formats are simply convenient representation tools for decision logic involving a significant number of largely parallel rules. There is really nothing inevitable, however, about every cell a decision table contains. A cell appears in a decision table because it *might* be relevant, not because it truly is.

If the dashes were taken to mean "neither applies," the proper rule statement would be quite different. Lacking any additional information, the proper statement might be worded as follows:

An order must be shipped by premium service if all of the following are true:
- *The order is rush.*
- *Neither yes nor no can be said about whether the order includes a fragile item.*
- *Neither yes nor no can be said about whether the order includes a specialty item.*
- *Neither yes nor no can be said about whether the order includes a high-priced item.*
- *The order includes an item involving hazardous materials.*
- *The category of customer that placed the order is platinum.*
- *The destination of the order is remote.*

It is not quite clear exactly what the latter version might mean, but one thing is clear. It certainly does not mean what the former version means!

What is the total number of *possible* combinations of decision criteria values? The total possible number of value combinations for the seven decision criteria can be calculated as follows: $2^6 \times 3 = 192$. This calculation reflects the fact that six of the decision criteria have two values each (*yes* and *no* for five of them, and *local* and *remote* for the other), whereas the seventh, category of customer, has three values (*silver*, *gold*, and *platinum*).

Having determined earlier how many combinations the decision table actually does address (11), we can now determine how many it does not: $192 - 11 = 181$. *So some 181 possible combinations have not been addressed at all!* We would therefore conclude that the development of this decision table (or, more accurately, of the associated business logic) is not even close to complete.

Validity

The sample decision table above is free of obvious anomalies such as subsumations or conflicts. These kinds of anomalies, common for decision tables involving more complex business logic, are illustrated in the decision table below.

Rule: *The delivery method for an order must be determined according Table F.*

TABLE F

Decision Criteria	Delivery Method for an Order				
	Picked Up by Customer	Shipped by Normal Service	Shipped by Premium Service	Shipped by Premium Service	Picked Up by Customer
Rush order	No	Yes	Yes	Yes	Yes
Order includes fragile item	No	Yes	—	—	—
Order includes specialty item	No	No	—	—	—
Order includes high-priced item	No	No	—	—	—
Order includes item involving hazardous materials	No	Yes	Yes	Yes	Yes
Category of customer	Silver	Gold	Platinum	—	—
Destination of order	—	Local	Remote	Remote	Remote

This new version is an exact replica of the previous decision table except for the two new columns added (for discussion purposes only!) on the right side. As before, a dash in any cell of the body indicates that that decision criteria is irrelevant to determining the appropriate outcome for the given combination of decision criteria values—that is, any value for that decision criteria will produce the same outcome.

Subsumation. Notice that column 4 in the new table is an exact replica of column 3 (including outcomes) except for only one difference—a dash is shown for category of customer. This dash indicates that the value platinum as shown in column 3 (or, for that matter, either of the other two values for category of customer, silver and gold) does not matter in determining the appropriate outcome, shipped by premium service, as indicated in the header. In other words, column 3—or, more precisely, the set of decision criteria values that are given there along with their associated outcome—is subsumed by column 4. Because column 3 adds no additional information for the consolidated business logic, it can be eliminated from the decision table altogether. In fact, it should be eliminated because leaving it in would open the door to specification conflicts.[13]

Conflict. Notice that column 5 in the new table is an exact replica of column 4 except for only one difference. The outcome indicated in the header for the former is picked up by customer, but the outcome indicated for the latter is shipped by premium service. Since the same customer order clearly cannot be picked up if it is shipped (or vice versa),[14] these two columns (that is, the outcomes for the given set of decision criteria values) are clearly in conflict. Such conflicts, of course, must be identified and resolved by knowledgeable business workers.

Appropriate Outcomes for Decision Tables by Functional Category of Rule

A key question for decision tables, of course, is *what goes into the cells?* The answer depends directly on the functional category (or subcategory) of the rule. The appropriate kind of outcome for each functional category is listed in Table 12–1.

---

13. The total number of combinations of decision criteria values covered by column 4 is calculated as follows: $2^3 \times 3^1 = 24$. So now (not considering column 5), the body of this decision table provides the basis for determining outcomes for 27 possible combinations of decision term values ($2 + 1 + 24 = 27$). That still leaves 165 ($192 - 27 = 165$) combinations not addressed. The consolidated business logic is still woefully incomplete!
14. That is, the outcomes are mutually exclusive.

Table 12–1 Appropriate Outcomes for Decision Tables by Functional Category of Rule

Functional Category of Rule	Informal Description/ Purpose	Appropriate Outcomes
Rejector	A constraint for maintaining correctness (consistency) by preventing violations.	An entry of *yes* or *no* (or nothing) indicating whether the rule should be enforced in the given circumstances.
Computation rule	A statement or arithmetic formula indicating how to calculate a numeric value.	The appropriate mathematical formula in the given circumstances. Alternatively, the name of another computation rule may be given.
Derivation rule	A statement or logical expression indicating how to determine a yes/no (true/false) result.	An entry of *yes* or *no* (or nothing), or an entry of *true* or *false* (or nothing), indicating the appropriate value of the derivation in the given circumstances. Alternatively, the name of another derivation rule may be given.
Inference rule	A rule that infers a conclusion from a particular set of circumstances.	An entry of *yes* or *no* (or nothing), or an entry of *true* or *false* (or nothing), indicating whether the given inference should be made in the given circumstances. The appropriate inference to be made can be shown instead.
Rule toggle	A rule that turns another rule on or off in a particular set of circumstances, especially for making exceptions.	An entry of *yes* or *no* (or nothing) indicating whether the given rule should be enabled (on) in the given circumstances. The appropriate rule that should be enabled (on) may be shown instead.
Process toggle	A rule that turns a process on or off in a particular set of circumstances.	An entry of *yes* or *no* (or nothing) indicating whether the given process or procedure should be enabled in the given circumstances. The appropriate process or procedure to be enabled may be shown instead.
Data toggle	A rule that deletes data (or creates it randomly) in a particular set of circumstances.	An entry of *yes* or *no* (or nothing) indicating whether the value(s) of the given data type should be created or deleted in the given circumstances. The appropriate value to be created may be shown instead.[a]

continued

a. The rule actually becomes an imprint rule in this case.

Table 12–1   *Continued*

Functional Category of Rule	Informal Description/ Purpose	Appropriate Outcomes
Imprint rule	A rule that sets a stored data item to a particular value.	The appropriate (set to) value to be applied in the given circumstances.
Presentation rule	A rule that requires data to be presented in a certain manner (for example, on a screen or in a report).	The appropriate graphical criteria (for example, color, sequencing criteria, and so on) in the given circumstances.
Process trigger	A rule that automatically executes a process or procedure in a given set of circumstances.	An entry of *yes* or *no* (or nothing) indicating whether the given process or procedure should be executed in the given circumstances. The appropriate process or procedure to be executed may be shown instead.
Rule trigger	A rule that automatically fires another rule in a given set of circumstances.	An entry of *yes* or *no* (or nothing) indicating whether the given rule should be fired in the given circumstances. The appropriate rule to be fired may be shown instead.

PART IV

What Is the Business Rule Approach?

Readings for IT Professionals

Overview

This part expands on the material presented in Parts I–III, with emphasis on the special features, needs, and opportunities of the business rule approach. Although this part is aimed primarily toward information technology (IT) professionals, technical details have been kept to a minimum so that a more general audience can understand the ideas presented here.

I have divided the discussion into two chapters, as follows:[1]

- Chapter 13 discusses additional ideas of the business rule approach, with emphasis on what you need to know to be successful in its application. In particular, this chapter examines the following fundamental principles.
  - Rule management: Rules can and should be managed in an organized manner.
  - The knowledge principle: What the company knows should be balanced with what it does.
  - Business-driven solutions: The business solution should be worked out completely before any system is designed—and for sure before any coding begins.

---

1. At certain points in the discussions that follow in this part, I mention elements of methodology or deliverables that pertain specifically to Business Rule Solutions, LLC. When I use *we* or *our* in these contexts, please note that I am referring to the Principals of Business Rule Solutions.

- Chapter 14 reviews fact models, with emphasis on critical success factors in their creation. It also examines how the need to support large numbers of rules shapes fact models in distinctive ways. Finally, it examines ways in which rules, in conjunction with generalized data models and database designs, can be used to support current business practices more effectively. As I explain in the chapter, this approach opens important new opportunities for building more adaptive business systems.

More Principles of the Business Rule Approach

A New View of Business Logic

Rule Management

Rules can and should be managed in an organized manner.

The Basic Principles of Rule Management

Databasing Your Rules

How many rules does your company have? A hundred? A thousand? Ten thousand? More? How easy is it to change any one of those rules? How easy is it to determine where the rule is implemented? How easy is it to find out why it was implemented in the first place?

Many companies today are starting to realize they have problems with rule management. Often, this perception did not start off that way. Initially, the perception might have fallen under some other label such as *change management, data quality, knowledge retention, communication gap,* or so on. Call it what you may, these companies are discovering that the business logic at the core of their day-to-day operations is not being managed in any consistent or coherent manner.

Databasing the Rules

The purpose of rule management is to provide the infrastructure necessary to correct that problem. Such a solution assumes, of course, that rules *can* be managed. But

179

why not? In one sense, the literal specification of rules is just data, and in general, we certainly already know how to manage data.

So the first and most basic principle in rule management is that your rules should be *databased*. In other words, you should store the rules in an automated facility or repository where they can be managed and readily accessed.

Then comes the question of what else to store besides just the rules themselves and what additional kinds of support are needed. The key lies with remembering that business rules represent *business* logic—not programming logic. The goal of rule management is to give business workers and/or business analysts the ability to manage and access their business logic directly. The focus should be on the kinds of challenges these business workers and business analysts face on a day-in-and-day-out basis.

Fundamental in this regard is vocabulary management. When rules number in the thousands—or even just in the hundreds—coordinating business terminology becomes essential. Imagine trying to understand and apply that much business logic without such coordination. In practice, rule management is not simply about coordinating rules but also about coordinating the underlying business vocabulary. It is hard to stress this point too much.

In thinking about the other needs of business workers and analysts, it turns out that many of their questions about rules are quite predictable. Frequently asked questions include those listed in Table 13–1. Although the importance of these questions is self-evident, most companies have never managed this kind of core knowledge in any coordinated or comprehensive manner.

Traceability

Another question crucial to managing rules is being able to address relationships *between* rules—that is, rule-to-rule connections. There are many ways in which rules can be interconnected, as the list presented in Table 13–2 suggests. Being able to trace these relationships easily and reliably is also crucial to rule management.

The items in this list of connections, as well as the typical questions in the earlier list, illustrate various forms of *traceability.* Comprehensive support for rule traceability is a key ingredient in successful rule management.

How can such support be achieved? *Databasing* your rules is one part of the solution. Equally important is providing appropriate access to them once stored. Predefined reports and queries provide many kinds of basic support

Table 13–1 Typical Questions Business Workers and Business Analysts Could Ask about Rules

To which areas of the business does a rule apply?

What work tasks does a rule guide?

Where is a rule implemented?

In what jurisdictions is a rule enforced?

What purpose does a rule serve?

What deliverables in a new system design need to address a rule?

When was a rule created?

When did a rule become effective?

Are there previous versions of a rule?

Is a rule still in effect, and if not, when was it discontinued?

Was a rule retired or replaced, and if so, why?

What influenced the creation or modification of a rule?

Who can answer particular kinds of questions about a rule?

Who has been involved with a rule over time, and in what way?

Where can more information about a rule be found?

in that regard. Beyond that, visualization techniques are very useful for presenting more complex or highly interrelated information.

In one way or another, I believe that every company will eventually discover the need for rule management. To support it, new techniques must be learned and new tools implemented. Fortunately, pioneering companies have already discovered what these techniques are, and good commercial tools have emerged to support them.[1] Rule management is a practical idea whose time is now!

Table 13–2 Kinds of Rule-to-Rule Connections

A rule is an exception to another rule.

A rule enables another rule.

A rule subsumes another rule.

A rule is semantically equivalent to another rule.

A rule is similar to another rule.

A rule is in conflict with another rule.

A rule supports another rule.

A rule is interpreted from another rule.

---

1. Business Rule Solutions, LLC, developed the first software tools for this area during the late 1990s. Refer to *http://www.BRSolutions.com* for current information.

The Knowledge Principle
What the company knows should be balanced with what it does.

What Is a Business Rule?

Separating the "Know" from the "Flow"

In a way, everybody knows what business rules are—they are what guide your business in running its day-to-day operations. Without business rules, you would always have to make decisions on the fly, choosing between alternatives on a case-by-case, ad hoc basis. Doing things that way would be *very* slow. It would likely produce wildly inconsistent results. I doubt it would earn very much trust from your customers.

In today's world, you cannot really operate that way—not for very long, anyway. So every organized business process has business rules. But what are they? What exactly do you use to "guide your business in running its day-to-day operations"?

In a moment, we will examine several definitions of *business rule*.[2] Before doing that, however, I should be clear about what business rules are *not*.

- **Business rules are *not* software.** Let me be a little more precise. Business rules are often *implemented* in software, but that is a different matter. In fact, application software is only one of several choices in that regard. Alternative implementation approaches include supporting them in manual procedures (not very efficient but sometimes necessary) or implementing them as rules using business logic technology[3] (a much better choice). The point is that business rules arise as an element of the *business*—as the name *business* rules suggests—not from any particular hardware/software platform that supports them.
- **Business rules are *not* process.** Roger T. Burlton[4] recently expressed the business rule message this way: "Separate the *know* from the *flow*." The implication is that the "know" part and the "flow" part are *different*.

---

2. Part V presents a formal definition of *business rule*.
3. By *business logic technology,* I mean *rule engines, decision management platforms, business logic servers,* and so on.
4. Roger Burlton has written extensively about business processes from the business perspective; see, for example, Burlton [2001].

Business rules represent the "know" part—the separate stuff that *guides* the "flow." Guidance means rules; hence the name *business rules*.

Separate the know *from the* flow.

—Roger T. Burlton

Take a look at the definitions of *business rule* listed in Table 13–3. All the definitions are valid; however, if you are interested in a historical view, the entries appear in chronological order and reflect some natural evolution over time. Several important observations are worth making about these definitions, as discussed in the related boxed item starting on page 184.

Table 13–3 Definitions of *Business Rule*

Source	Definition
"Business Rules: The Missing Link," by Daniel S. Appleton [1984][a]	". . . [A]n explicit statement of a constraint that exists within a business's ontology."[b] [p. 146]
Entity Modeling: Techniques and Application, by Ronald G. Ross [1987]	". . . [S]pecific rules (or business policies) that govern . . . behavior [of the enterprise] and distinguish it from others. . . . [T]hese rules govern changes in the status [state] of the enterprise. . . ." [p. 102]
The Business Rule Book (1st ed.), by Ronald G. Ross [1994]	". . . [A] discrete operational business policy or practice. A business rule may be considered a user requirement that is expressed in non-procedural and non-technical form (usually textual statements). . . . A business rule represents a statement about business behavior. . . ." [p. 496]
GUIDE Business Rules Project Report [1995]	". . . [A] statement that defines or constrains some aspect of the business . . . [which is] intended to assert business structure, or to control or influence the behavior of the business. [A business rule] cannot be broken down or decomposed further into more detailed business rules. . . . [I]f reduced any further, there would be loss of important information about the business." [pp. 4–5]
The Business Rule Book (2nd ed.), by Ronald G. Ross [1997]	"A term, fact (type) or rule, representing a predicate.. . . ." [p. 380]

continued

a. This citation is the earliest article featuring the term business rule I have been able to find.
b. Appleton's use of *ontology* seems prescient given the growing use of this term in the industry, especially concerning rules. *Ontology* is a bit arcane, however, so I will defer explaining it until Chapter 14.

Table 13-3 *Continued*

Source	Definition
Business Rules Group (formerly GUIDE Business Rules Project), 1998[c]	"A directive that is intended to influence or guide business behavior. Such directives exist in support of business policy, which is formulated in response to risks, threats or opportunities."[d]
Capturing Business Rules, by Ronald G. Ross and Gladys S. W. Lam [2000b]	"An atomic piece of re-usable business logic, specified declaratively."[e]
Managing Reference Data in Enterprise Databases, by Malcolm Chisholm [2001]	"A single statement that takes data or information that an organization possesses and derives other data or information from it, or uses it to trigger an action." [p. 365]
Business Rules Applied: Building Better Systems Using the Business Rule Approach, by Barbara von Halle [2002]	"... [C]onditions that govern a business event so that it occurs in such a way that is acceptable to the business."[f] [p. 28]
Business Rules and Information Systems, by Tony Morgan [2002]	"Basically, a business rule is a compact statement about an aspect of the business. . . . It's a constraint, in the sense that a business rule lays down what must or must not be the case. At any particular point, it should be possible to determine that the condition implied by the constraint is true in a logical sense; if not, remedial action is needed. This interpretation, which might be described as Boolean from a software perspective, is the main reason that the term *business logic* is so commonly used."[g] [pp. 5–6]

c. From a prepublication 1998 draft of "Organizing Business Strategy: The Standard Model for Business Rule Motivation" [Business Rules Group 2000].
d. This is the definition we prefer from a business perspective.
e. This is the definition we prefer from a system perspective. We also accept the GUIDE Project definition (1995).
f. Note: von Halle adopts the GUIDE Project definition (1995). However, this excerpt is an excellent and succinct characterization of business rule.
g. Note: Morgan also adopts the GUIDE Project definition (1995). This excerpt characterizes business rule very well from a system perspective.

Observations about the Definitions of *Business Rule*

Business versus system perspective: Although all the definitions are consistent in theme, if you look closely, you will see tension between a purely business perspective (see the Business Rules Group definition from 1998) versus a system perspective (see the Ross and Lam definition from 2000). The bottom line is that *both* perspectives are correct—just different in their viewpoints.

Terms, facts, and rules: A general consensus emerged among experts in the 1990s that there are three basic categories of business rules—*terms*, *facts*, and *rules*. (This important breakthrough is credited to the GUIDE Business Rules Project and was originally reported in its 1995 paper.) Literally, in the business rule approach, the "know" part always comes in the form of a term (concept), a fact, or a rule. A business rule is *never* anything else. By the way, terms are the most basic of the three categories because facts must build on terms, and rules must build on facts. That principle produces a very powerful building-block approach for the "know" part.

Fact models: Note the term *business structure* in the 1995 GUIDE Business Rules Project definition. This term refers to basic structure for the "know" part—literally, how terms relate to one another in the form of facts. As discussed in Part II and later in this part, a fact model is the best way to express such structure.

Suggestors: The 1995 GUIDE Business Rules Project definition includes both the word *control* and the word *influence* in reference to business behavior. If you think of rules only as hard and fast constraints (asserting strict control), you miss at least half the scope of business rules. Operational-level suggestions, guidelines, heuristics, and so on (that is, *suggestors*) are *also* business rules!

Atomic form: The word *atomic* appears explicitly or implicitly in several of the definitions. This reflects an important goal for business rules—to achieve the most granular level of specification possible. Why is that so important? Because it allows for *fine-grained* change in business practices.

Reusability: Note the terms *re-usable* and *declaratively* in the Ross and Lam 2000 definition. *Declarative* specifications are what you get when you express business logic in the form of terms, facts, and rules. This approach has crucial advantages, not the least of which is that your business logic becomes reusable across both processes (the "flow") and hardware/software platforms. As such, it becomes both highly reengineerable and highly redeployable. Think of this as *business rules in a suitcase*—just the thing for a business always on the go.

Business rules really mean establishing the "know" part of your business processes as a resource in its own right. This new resource brings with it both benefit and responsibility. The benefit lies in being able to change elements of the "know" part directly, which in turn means being able to change them *faster*. (What business does not want to be able to change faster these days?)

But there is a price for that—this new resource must be managed. Therein lies the responsibility. You must now come to grips with management of that "know" part—that is, with *rule management*

A final point is this. In real life, some of the "know" part has always been separated from the "flow" part in the sense that workers carry the "know" part around in their heads. Does such *tacit* knowledge represent business rules? In the theoretical sense, *yes*, but in the sense that they can really be managed, *no*. If you need any proof of that, just think what happens when the workers retire—or go to work for the competition!

For practical purposes, business rules are that portion of the "know" part written down—that is, encoded—for ready reuse (or revision) as needed. Here then follows an additional way to describe business rules.

 Business rules are literally the encoded knowledge of your business practices.

Business Rules and the "Flow"

Correcting Some Misconceptions about Business Rules

Not long ago, I received an e-mail from an IT professional. The e-mail contained serious misconceptions about business rules. These misconceptions go to the heart of the distinction between declarative versus procedural specifications (that is, "know" versus "flow"), in particular concerning *sequence*. First I reproduce the original e-mail in full, then I give my point-by-point responses.

Subject: Business Rules versus Sequence

The IT professional wrote . . .

The Ross approach to business rules . . . tends to classify business rules based on a bias toward coercing perfectly good imperative constructs into less comfortable declarative ones. Ross loses sight of the need for appropriate behavioral language in favor of a misguided attempt at a purely structural expression of a business system. For example, steps in a cake recipe might be simply . . .

1. Combine flour, water, milk, and eggs in a large bowl.

2. Mix until batter is consistent but not entirely free of lumps.

Instead, Ross would prefer . . .

- Batter is mixed.

- Flour, water, milk, and eggs are combined.

- Flour, water, milk, and eggs are ingredients.

- After mixing, ingredients become batter.

- Batter must be in a bowl.

- Batter must be consistent but must retain lumps.

- Mixing batter is performed after combining ingredients.

Ross abhors sequence. Sequence is to be asserted by means of elaborate nets of [specially typed rules]. This adds nothing to the maintainability or expressive power of a business system's definition. We already have a perfectly natural and convenient means of expressing sequence: *an ordered list.*

Point-by-Point Reply

My response . . .

>Ross abhors sequence.

>>>*Absolutely dead wrong!* Some of the most effective and pragmatic work in the business rule community has been done in the areas of workflow models (the business view of work) and procedures or scripts (the system view of work).

>>>We use rules (defined independently) to *control* the work. This is why the NFL has a rule book that is *separate* from the teams' play books. That's because today you might be running one set of plays, but tomorrow you will probably be running another. To use your analogy, today you might be making a cake, but tomorrow you might be making a pie.

> 1. Combine flour, water, milk, and eggs in a large bowl.

> 2. Mix until batter is consistent but not entirely free of lumps.

>>>This recipe represents a perfectly acceptable (albeit very simple) procedure or script. I have no problem with it. Now let's ask, what rules do we need? Potential rules to provide appropriate control might include the following . . .

- Milk must be fresh.
- Bowl must be large enough so that contents do not spill out when stirred.
- Batter may be considered "entirely free of lumps" only if there are no visible masses of congealed batter larger than 2 cm in diameter.

>>>These rules represent business knowledge that must be present when the procedure or script is performed. All work requires guidance and/or control—such guidance and control is what business rules are about. The business rule approach simply says not to embed these rules in the procedure or script directly.

>Instead, Ross would prefer:

> • Batter is mixed.

> • Flour, water, milk, and eggs are combined.

> • Flour, water, milk, and eggs are ingredients.

> • After mixing, ingredients become batter.

> • Batter must be in a bowl.

> • Batter must be consistent but must retain lumps.

> • Mixing batter is performed after combining ingredients.

>>> *No!* I want both a script to follow (your two-step recipe will do) and rules to guide me in doing the work. But most importantly, I want the script and the rules to be *separate*. So what you say I prefer above is actually the exact *opposite* of what I want—you've embedded the rules in the procedure. We do agree on one thing, however. The result is really messy!

Business Rules and the "Know"

Rules for Processes and Rules for Products/Services

Over the years, developers of expert-system applications have consistently focused on a fundamental aspect of business problems that most IT professionals fail to perceive. The reverse, however, is also true. Most developers of applications using traditional expert systems fail to perceive what IT professionals know almost intuitively. Consequently, almost all approaches to developing business systems fall woefully short in one respect or the other. Let me explain who is missing what and how the problem can be corrected.

Decision Points

Developers of expert-system applications have traditionally focused on *decision points* in the work environment. A decision point is where some critical decision (usually a complex one) must be made. Such a decision typically might have to do with one of the following kinds of tasks: classification, diagnosis, assessment, monitoring, prediction, assignment, allocation, and so on.

The rules governing such decisions are usually viewed as peculiar to and characteristic of the company's *product/service* offerings. These offerings invariably involve the company's special area(s) of expertise. Examples of such decisions include whether or not to:

- Approve an application for automobile insurance
- Pay a claim
- Buy a stock
- Declare an emergency
- Give an on-the-spot discount to a customer
- Assign a particular resource to a given request
- Diagnose a patient as having a particular disease
- Accept a reservation
- Indicate possible fraud

Such decision points, all rule-intensive, are of vital importance to the business. Capturing the relevant rule sets should therefore be a key component of a company's approach to developing its business systems.

Unfortunately, most approaches for system development used by IT professionals have never done this outright. Most such approaches are highly procedural and offer no direct support for capturing large numbers of rules in declarative form. By and large, IT professionals have not even grasped how significant this omission really is.

Work Avoidance

Turning now to developers of expert-system applications, what is typically missed in their approaches? The answer requires digging a bit deeper into two basic assumptions of traditional expert systems.

Expert-System Assumption 1. It is possible to define all relevant rules well enough for automated decision making to be effective.

There are, of course, some very difficult problems (for example, weather forecasting) where this assumption does not hold true today. In the typical business, on the other hand, a large number of important decision points in day-to-day operations come nowhere near that magnitude of complexity.

So this first assumption is basically correct for business systems. Indeed, if the business goals for a project include *disintermediation* (that is, eliminating the middleman, as in Web-based self-service applications), capturing and managing these decision-making rules is a must.

Expert-System Assumption 2. The cost and difficulty of gathering the appropriate data is a relatively trivial issue compared with the complexity of the rules.

This is a point about *business* systems—a huge one—that developers of expert-system applications historically got wrong. In a business context it can be *extremely* costly and difficult (and inefficient) to gather all the appropriate data simply to set things up for all the decision-making rules to fire.

Let me offer a simple example. An automobile insurance company might have the following business rule: *An application for car insurance may be approved only if the applicant is at least as old as the minimum driving age.* This rule, of course, might be only one of hundreds determining whether an application should be approved. Other rules might involve creditworthiness (which could involve an extensive credit check), previous driving history (which could require requesting records from the state), and so on. In other words, there is a lot of work (time and money) involved in gathering all the data required to support all the rules.

Consequently, one of the basic goals in designing business processes is what I call *work avoidance* (no pun intended). For example, if the applicant for automobile insurance is less than the minimum driving age, why perform the credit check and acquire the driving records (and so on)? If you can determine up front in the business process that the applicant is too young, all that other data-related work can be avoided.

Simply capturing all the decision-making rules is clearly not enough for effective support of business systems. In fact, capturing the rules is only half the problem. First you need to develop the *workflow* for the business process in order to fully explore all opportunities for *work avoidance*. Rules governing the business process (such as the minimum driving age rule above) must be tested as early in the workflow as possible. Waiting to test them at some downstream decision point is simply inefficient. This early-bird testing of business process rules is a basic principle of the business rule approach.

The Workflow Imperative: Early-Bird Testing of Rules

To avoid unnecessary work, rules should be tested as early as possible.

Business Process Rules versus Product/Service Rules

This insight sheds new light on the knowledge principle (*what the company knows should be balanced with what it does*). It comes down to these final points.

Two Kinds of Rules. To some extent, every company has both business process rules and decision-making rules (usually product/service rules). The "know" part really has two dimensions, both crucial. Examples of business process rules and product/service rules for three different organizations are given in the following boxed item.

Examples of Business Process Rules versus Product/Service Rules

Internal Revenue Service (IRS)

Business Process Rule	Product/Service Rule
Rule: *A processed tax return must indicate the IRS Center that reviewed it.*	**Rule:** *Calculated total income must be computed as tax return wages (line 1) plus tax return taxable-interest (line 2) plus tax return unemployment compensation (line 3).*

Ministry of Health

Business Process Rules	Product/Service Rules
Rule: *A claim must be assigned to an examiner if fraud is suspected.* **Rule:** *An on-site audit must be conducted for a service provider at least every five years.*	**Rule:** *A claim involving comprehensive visits or consultations by the same physician for the same patient must not be paid more than once within 180 days.* **Rule:** *A claim that requests payment for a service event that is a provision of health service type 'consultation' may be paid only if the service event results from a referral received from another service provider.*

continued

Ship Inspection Agency

Business Process Rules	**Product/Service Rules**
Rule: *A ship inspection work order must include at least one attendance date.*	**Rule:** *A ship area subject to corrosion must be inspected annually.*
Rule: *A ship must indicate a client who is financially responsible for inspections.*	**Rule:** *A salt water ballast tank must be inspected empty if the ship is more than five years old.*
Rule: *An inspection due for a ship must be considered suspended if the ship is laid up.*	**Rule:** *A barge must have an approved bilge system to pump from and drain all below-deck machinery spaces.*

Do the Business Process "Know" First. If a project will address both kinds of rules, workflow model(s) for the business process (and the associated business process rules) should generally be developed first. The reason is that decision-making tasks (and the associated product/service rules) are always embedded within a business process and therefore dependent on its basic sequence, specification, and vocabulary.

Do the Product/Service "Know" Too. Capturing the workflow models (the "flow") and the business process rules is by no means sufficient. To fully support the "know" part, the product/service rules must be captured in an appropriate manner too.

✦   ✦   ✦

Business-Driven Solutions

The business solution should be worked out completely before any system is designed—and for sure before any coding begins.

Why Business Rule Methodology Is Different

What It Means to Mean Business

Outwardly, the business rule approach produces many of the same deliverables as any other approach to building business systems—screens, processes, data, controls, and so on. In other words, the end result is almost sure to include some automated components. So why is the business rule approach any different from other system development methodologies? This section explains why.

The goal for development is to ensure a more adaptable *business*. This goal produces three imperatives.

Business Rule Systems Imperative 1: A Business Model

Application components must be seamlessly integrated into the business. Such integration requires a blueprint, a top-down business model covering the full business capacity within scope.

To say that a business rule project aims toward producing application software misses the point. The real objective is to produce a full business capacity that covers all the factors or abstractions[5] listed in Table 13–4.

Table 13–4   The Factors of a Full Business Capacity

Business Aspect	Business Component	Business Model Deliverable[a]	IT Component
Knowing	Terms and facts	Fact Model	Data
Transforming	Business processes	Business Process Models	Processes
Connecting	Business links	Business Connectivity Map	Machine links
Interacting	Roles and work products	Organizational Work Model	Human interfaces
Staging	Time frames and milestones	Business Milestones	States
Guiding	Business goals and tactics	Policy Charter	Rules

a. These are deliverables of Proteus, the business rule methodology developed by Business Rule Solutions, LLC.

5. Those readers familiar with John Zachman's Architecture Framework will realize that I am referring to its six columns, which address the interrogatives *what, how, where, who, when,* and *why,* respectively. For more information on Zachman's thinking, refer to Zachman [2002] and collected articles by Zachman found in the *Business Rules Journal,* available at *http://www.BRCommunity.com*.

To support this first imperative, a complete top-down business model should be developed involving key business-side workers and managers. By the way, *complete* here means the model addresses all the key business questions but *not* system or implementation questions.

With the right people and the right approach, this business model can be developed in a matter of weeks and requires relatively modest amounts of time from the business-side participants. And (this may come as a surprise), we find that these business-side participants almost always actually *enjoy* the process. I think that is simply because they find the process so relevant and valuable. To sum this point up in a word, we find they finally feel they can take *ownership*.[6]

Business Rule Systems Imperative 2: The Best Business Solution

The business needs the very best business solution possible. "Best" must be demonstrated, so a battle plan must be developed up front in which each key element of the solution is motivated from a business perspective.

A business capacity will be of little value if it addresses the wrong business goals. The key question is *why* a particular form of the business capacity is the right one for the company.

Traditional approaches for building application systems have not done a very good job of answering that key question. In the 1980s, information engineering, for example, sought to answer it by involving sponsors and key managers directly in producing deliverables. As you can imagine, this was very expensive and time-consuming. Worse, it did not even really work. Today, most projects are still managed based on cost. Money is important, of course—but it is not a substitute for knowing *why*.

The business rule approach offers a fresh approach. Briefly, the central idea is that achieving business goals[7] always involves a particular set of business risks and inherent conflicts and tradeoffs. Business tactics and core business rules are formulated to address these risks, conflicts, and tradeoffs.[8]

---

6. I use *ownership* here deliberately. *Owner* is the term John Zachman uses to describe the perspective of row 2 in his Framework, the row that has to do with developing an enterprise model (also known as a *business model*).

7. I do not mean *project* goals or *project* objectives, so to avoid confusion I will continue to say *business goal* rather than simply *goal*, as I also did in Part I.

8. For in-depth discussion, refer to Ross and Lam [2000a].

Rather than involving sponsors and key managers in data or process deliverables, the business rule approach gets those people directly focused on developing these crucial elements of the business solution. I will have more to say about the deliverable that makes this possible momentarily.

Business Rule Systems Imperative 3: High-Impact Sponsorship

Project sponsor(s) must have maximum leverage for controlling a project with a minimum investment of their time.

As mentioned above, a critical success factor for projects is to enable sponsors to manage projects by business benefit rather than primarily by cost. This is achieved by a coordinated focus on the *motivation* for the key elements of the business solution, including core business rules.

High-impact sponsorship has additional advantages, including the following.

- Sponsors can have a clear, concise, and *continuing* understanding of how the business goals are being transformed into a complete design for the desired business capacity, including (but not limited to) the automated components.
- Sponsors can detect easily and *early* in the project life cycle that the project is failing to meet the original business goals so they can take timely action as necessary.

What enables sponsors to monitor a project without lengthy participation in the development of deliverables? The answer is the *Policy Charter.*[9]

A Policy Charter outlines the business tactics proposed to meet the business goals. The business motivation for each element of these business tactics is established. This battle plan offers the sponsors a direct view of how the needs of the targeted business capacity are being addressed. It also permits the following.

- Assessment of business-side feasibility
- Examination of business risks and how they will be addressed
- Explanation of any divergence or shortfall that might have occurred in meeting the original business motivation

---

9. For more information, refer to Lam [1998]. For an enterprise-level approach, refer to the landmark work by the Business Rules Group [2000].

- Exploration of specific reengineering opportunities for the business process
- Acquisition of rapid and highly focused feedback

A page from one recent project's Policy Charter is presented in Figure 13–1. This segment (which represents about 15 percent of the entire deliverable) is presented in graphic form.[10] We find graphic presentation (as opposed to a purely textual format) enables better communication and discussion among business-side team members and sponsors.

This sample Policy Charter segment concerns a business capacity involving an insurance claim process whose reengineering featured automated handheld pads to estimate repair costs for damaged autos. The elements shown in the segment include business goals, tactics, risks, and core business rules linked in appropriate manner. Note the prominent role of core business rules in addressing business risks.

If any part of a draft Policy Charter is unacceptable, unworkable, or incomplete, sponsors can immediately take appropriate action with minimal loss of time and resources relative to the project as a whole. Such early intervention will be much less costly than during later phases of the project during which technical design, construction, and testing occur.

Our experience is that with the right people and the right approach, a Policy Charter can often be developed in a matter of days. Also, we find that sponsors almost always *enjoy* their participation in the process. We recognize this is partly because the process takes so little of their time. However, we again find it also comes down to a sense of *ownership*.

Analysis Paralysis

Preventing the Disease Behind the Symptoms

Many predators hunt based on movement. In fact, even with their keen eyesight, they cannot really see their prey unless the prey itself moves. Consequently, many hunted animals are programmed literally to *freeze with fear*. Not a bad thing to do if it saves your life!

Recently, we were asked to perform a postmortem review of a large project that had failed miserably at a major corporation. I will spare you all

---

10. Refer to *http://www.BRSolutions.com* for current information about products.

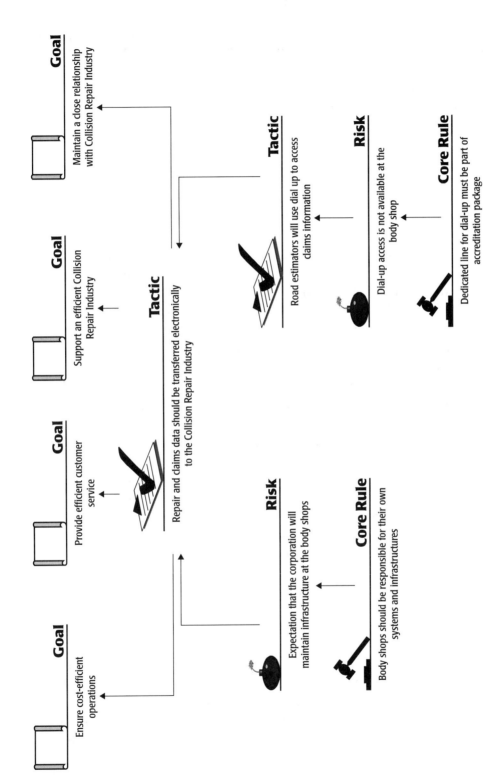

Figure 13–1 Sample Policy Charter (segment)

the unpleasant details—let's just say they started the coding phase way too early. The wounds to the business were deep, and in several ways, the company had begun to ooze red ink, its very lifeblood.

What went wrong? The diagnosis was relatively easy for us to make—no Policy Charter or other means to assess business motivation, and no true top-down business model.

They should have *frozen with fear* then and there. Instead, they jumped right on into development, loosely following a spiral "methodology" based on the mantra *analyze a little, design a little, code a little, test a little.* The company learned the hard way what that mantra means in practice—*lots of rework for lots of time!* (By the way, on other projects the company called such rework "maintenance." Sound familiar?)

Projects spiral out of control all too often. Unfortunately, there are no magic cures—just very expensive and time-consuming ones. Can the company really afford to squander its resources in this way? We think an ounce of prevention is worth a pound of cure.

Take a hard, early look at projects and learn to read the symptoms before it is too late to prevent the disease. Here are some possibilities.

- Maybe you do not really know what the business problem is. *In that case, how will you know if you are developing the right solution?*
- Maybe the business problem itself is hard. *Will thinking about it in a programming language (or in IT system models) make understanding it easier?*
- Maybe you are not getting the right answers from the right people. *Then, realistically, how good are your chances of success?*
- Maybe there are unresolved differences of opinion on the business side about what form the business solution should take. *If left to the programmers, do you think they can code their way to some satisfactory resolution?*
- Maybe future business directions are hard to predict. *Are designers and programmers in a position to make the best strategic choices?*

The next time you hear anyone say, "Watch out for analysis paralysis," take pause. Just freeze—it might save your company's life (or your own job). Somewhere close by there is probably a programmer poised to pounce on a keyboard. To stay on the safe path, think business model, Policy Charter, and business rules. Remember, every problem is first and foremost a *business* problem!

References

Appleton, Daniel S. 1984. "Business Rules: The Missing Link." *Datamation*, October 15, pp. 145–150.

Burlton, Roger T. 2001. *Business Process Management: Profiting from Success.* Indianapolis, IN: Sams Publishing.

Business Rules Group (Ronald G. Ross and Keri Anderson Healy, eds.). 2000. "Organizing Business Strategy: The Standard Model for Business Rule Motivation." Version 1, November 2000. Available at *http://www. BusinessRulesGroup.org.*

Chisholm, Malcolm. 2001. *Managing Reference Data in Enterprise Databases.* San Francisco, CA: Morgan Kaufmann.

GUIDE Business Rules Project Report. 1995. Third edition available in November 2002 as "Defining Business Rules—What Are They Really?", edited by David C. Hay and Keri Anderson Healy, Business Rules Group, July 2000, at *http:// www.BusinessRulesGroup.org.*

Lam, Gladys S. W. 1998. "Business Knowledge—Packaged in a Policy Charter." *DataToKnowledge Newsletter* (formerly *Data Base Newsletter*), May/June. Available at *http://www.BRCommunity.com.*

Morgan, Tony. 2002. *Business Rules and Information Systems.* Boston, MA: Addison-Wesley.

Ross, Ronald G. 1997. *The Business Rule Book* (2nd ed.). Houston, TX: Business Rule Solutions, LLC. Available *http://www.BRSolutions.com.*

———. 1994. *The Business Rule Book* (1st ed.). Boston, MA: Database Research Group.

———. 1987. *Entity Modeling: Techniques and Application.* Boston, MA: Database Research Group.

Ross, Ronald G., and Gladys S. W. Lam. 2000a. *The BRS Core Business Rule Practitioner's Guide: Using Business Rules in Developing Business Strategy.* Houston, TX: Business Rule Solutions, LLC. Available *http://www.BRSolutions.com.*

———. 2000b. *Capturing Business Rules.* Workbook for public seminar, presented in Boston, MA, June 19–21.

von Halle, Barbara. 2002. *Business Rules Applied: Building Better Systems Using the Business Rule Approach.* New York: Wiley Computer Publishing.

Zachman, John A. 2002. *The Zachman Framework: A Primer for Enterprise Engineering and Manufacturing* (electronic book). Available at *http://www.zachmaninternational.com.*

CHAPTER 14

More about Fact Models

Structuring the Basic Business Knowledge

Critical Success Factors for Fact Models

Organizing the Basic "Know" Part[1]

Fact models, a key deliverable in the business rule approach, were introduced in Part II. Refer to the boxed item, Again, What Is a Fact Model?, for a quick review.

Again, What Is a Fact Model?

A *fact model* structures basic knowledge about business practices from a business perspective. *Basic* means that the knowledge it represents cannot be derived or computed from any other knowledge. It that sense, a fact model is a crucial starting point for developing more advanced forms of business knowledge, including measures and rules.

In particular, a fact model focuses on assertions (called *facts*) involving core concepts of the business. In a fact model, concepts are represented by *terms*. Facts connect those terms in a manner that should reflect the real world. Both terms and facts in the fact model should be basic in the sense defined above.

---

1. This material is based on Ross and Lam [2000].

A fact model focuses on the "know" part of a business problem—that is, on how knowledge underlying business operations (the "flow") is organized. Literally, the fact model indicates what you need to *know* in order to *do* what you do.

A good fact model therefore tells you how to structure your basic thinking (or knowledge) about the business process based on a standard vocabulary. This ensures that you can communicate effectively about that knowledge with other project participants. It also allows you to exploit this standardized knowledge and vocabulary to express *other* types of requirements, especially rules—and to communicate about those effectively too.

A focus on structuring how business people can think and communicate about the business process has an important additional benefit. Inevitably, it helps bring into clear relief alternative ideas about how the business capacity itself can be best structured to satisfy business goals. When and by whom should such issues be resolved? As I have discussed, these are issues that should be resolved by *business-side* workers and managers *before* the project moves into system design or coding.

How do you know when you have done a good job on the fact model? The true test is below. By the way, *excruciating level of detail*[2] in this test means thorough business analysis—but not system design.

 Real-World Test for a High-Quality Fact Model

Once you have completed the fact model to an excruciating level of detail, you should be able to communicate with knowledgeable business workers about the basic business knowledge for the business process as if you had been in the business just as long as they have.

There should be only a single, consolidated fact model covering the entire scope of a problem domain. The goal is to unify basic business knowledge within that scope and to express each element of that basic business knowledge uniquely. This can be expressed as the following fundamental goal for fact models.

---

2. *Excruciating level of detail* is the term John Zachman [2002] uses for being very, very thorough but always staying carefully at the correct perspective for the given audience—in this case, the owners.

Fundamental Goal for Fact Models
One fact, one place, one name.

What is *not* important when you create a fact model is how you will organize any class diagram or design the database. Putting those things aside is often a challenge for IT professionals trained in those difficult disciplines.

Nonetheless, the key to success with the fact model is keeping the model focused squarely on the business perspective. All specifications (including the graphic model) should be aimed toward structuring how business people can think and communicate about the business capacity in an organized fashion. *Everything* in the fact model is about the business vocabulary needed to support such structure.

Defining Terms

Whenever possible, a native English[3] word or word phrase should be selected as the term of choice to represent a concept unless there is simply no such word in the language. Our experience is that this circumstance arises less often than might be imagined.

Moreover, instead of composing new definitions, a standard definition from *Webster's* (or another dictionary) should be selected and used for a term whenever possible. This not only saves work but also avoids arguments—it's hard to argue with standard definitions! If it is not possible to use a standard definition as is, the next choice is to extend or revise a dictionary definition as needed (carefully!). Only in the last resort should a new definition be composed from scratch.

Some approaches recommend that fundamental terms used in exactly their real-world sense (for example, *person, time,* and so on) need not be defined explicitly. This guideline can be followed with due caution, recognizing, however, that even native English words often have multiple meanings. For this reason, we prefer to make explicit the intended meaning of *all* terms, even when such meaning is simply taken verbatim from the dictionary.

If you are thinking that all this intense focus on terminology might create the need for a special skill on the project, you are right on track! Refer to the discussion in the boxed item, The Terminator.

---

3. Or whatever language is being used (for example, French, Mandarin, and so on).

The Terminator

In everyone's life, there is always *someone*—a teacher, a mother, a friend, a business colleague, whoever—who insists (maybe gently, maybe not) that things should be called by their right names. This is a person who always seems to have several words to choose from to put just the right spin on things. He or she forever has a dictionary at the ready and is never loath to use it no matter what the nature or objective of the discourse. Someone who excels at word games. Easily coins nicknames for new ideas. Knows that coining new terms is called *neology*.

Such people are the ones always called upon to do *wordsmithing* (usually not meant as a compliment). They are naturally good at turning a phrase. They think writing definitions is a really fun thing to do. As for grammar, where the rest of us see purgatory, they find poetry. They might have even been *liberal arts majors!*

Be that as it may, wordsmithing is a must-have skill for your business rule project. I mean fluency in *BusinessSpeak*, as opposed to *SystemSpeak* or *TechnoSpeak*. You need at least one team member who insists that things are always called by their right names and that proper definitions are always worked out and written down.

What you need is a *terminator*. That is what they have been called—with respect, I hope—on some of our business rule projects.[4]

Why is a terminator so fundamentally important? Remember the business rule mantra: *Rules build on facts, and facts build on terms.* Terms and their definitions are the foundation in the business rule approach. Build on a weak foundation, and your whole business logic becomes a house of cards.

The job does need a bit more dignified title than *terminator*, of course. Let me share a little dictionary research I did on this matter.

Ever heard of a *glossographer*? In case you are wondering, no, a glossographer is not someone who is good at glossing things over. I did not make up the term, either. It is a real term as well as an honorable profession (I presume).

---

4. To our knowledge, the first usage was by (and for) Karel Van Campenhout, a business-side subject matter expert who participated in a client project.

As it happens, one of the definitions of *gloss* is "a brief explanation . . . of a difficult or obscure word or expression."[5] A glossographer, then, is someone who writes down stuff like that. Unfortunately, another definition for *gloss* is "a false and often willfully misleading interpretation." That is not going to do!

What about *lexicographer*? This term means "the author or editor of a dictionary." A *lexicon* is "the vocabulary of a language, an individual speaker or group of speakers, or a subject." This sense is exactly right for what we need, but the word itself is somewhat obscure and a bit hard to say. Are there any other candidates?

The *New Oxford Dictionary of English* indicates *terminologist* to be a word in contemporary usage.[6] That label is a good one. So officially at least you should probably call your "terminator" a *terminologist*.

Relationships to Other Architectural Products in the Business Model

A fact model relates to other key deliverables in the business model for a business capacity in the following ways.

- *Concepts Catalog:* The collection of all terms and definitions for the "know" part of the business process is called a *Concepts Catalog*. Every term used for the fact model (and for any rule as well) should have a business definition in the Concepts Catalog. By the way, coordinating the Concepts Catalog is a fundamental part of rule management.
- *Policy Charter:* As described earlier, a Policy Charter is a battle plan identifying the key elements of the business solution (including core business rules). Each of these elements is implicitly based on basic knowledge that needs to be structured and standardized. Therefore, the Policy Charter is a rich source for terms (concepts) and facts that need to be included in the fact model.
- *Workflow models:* Workflow models outline the "flow" part of a business process. Performance of any given task produces knowledge (things that

---

5. This and other quoted definitions in this section come from *Merriam-Webster's Collegiate Dictionary*, 10th ed. (1999).
6. Thanks to Donald Chapin of Business Semantics, Ltd.

can be known) that should be represented by terms and facts in the fact model. Therefore, workflow models are another rich source for terms (concepts) and facts that need to be included in the fact model.

- *Rules:* A central deliverable in a business rule project is the Rule Book. Each rule will depend directly on the terms and facts developed in the fact model. Therefore, no term should appear in a rule that has not been defined in the Concepts Catalog. In addition, the fact model provides re-usable sentence patterns (the facts) for expressing the rules. As discussed in Part III, following these standard sentence patterns is essential for en-suring consistent expression and interpretation of the rules.

Again, Fact Model versus Data Model

Let's expand a bit on the distinctions made in Chapter 5 between fact models and data models.[7]

We view a fact model as part of the business model that a project should develop, whereas a data model is part of the system model it should develop. A fact model provides a business-based starting point—a blueprint—for subsequent development of a data model or database design. A good fact model can be easily transformed into a first-cut data model.

There are naturally significant differences in perspective, purpose, and success criteria between fact models and data models. In contrast to a fact model, a data model generally places emphasis on the following areas.

- *Delineating the data and its proper format to support system-level require-ments:* In a fact model, a box represents a term and the business concept for which it stands. In a data model, a box generally represents a collec-tion of attributes or fields that are structured to retain the appropriate data for storage and manipulation by applications.
- *Looking ahead toward the database environment and introducing features appropriate for database design in the given technical environment:* Exam-ples include normalization (or possibly denormalization), cardinality,

---

7. As mentioned in Part II, *class diagram* is more or less the corresponding term in object orientation. I certainly understand that important distinctions can be made between a data model and a class diagram—and even that these distinctions themselves can be con-troversial. However, this discussion is informal. For the sake of simplicity, I will simply say *data model* from this point on and assume you understand I also mean class diagrams of a corresponding nature.

associative entity types to support many-to-many relationship types, mandatory fields and relationships, and so on.

- *Addressing the complexities of time:* In general, fact models do not concern themselves with history. They simply identify what should be known about the basic business process at any given point in time. A data model, in contrast, must concern itself with the *points-over-time* aspect of data so the business (and its rules) can deal with the past (and the future). Modeling this points-over-time structure of data is one of the most important (and difficult) challenges in data modeling. I will return to this topic at the conclusion of this chapter.

None of the items above are appropriate for the fact model. Again, the primary audiences for the fact model and the data model are different. The primary audience for the fact model consists of business-side workers and managers (and business analysts), whereas the primary audience for the data model consists of system and database designers. It is very important to keep these distinctions in mind, especially since data models often use graphic conventions (boxes and box-to-box connections) that might appear similar to those used for fact models.

Getting to the Instance Level of the "Know" Part

A fact model and a data model also often have very different perspectives on the best handling of what is commonly known as *type codes*. Remember that the emphasis in fact models is on standardizing the business vocabulary and then capturing rules. The emphasis in a data model, in contrast, is often on achieving the most flexible data design possible—usually the best design for accommodating change.

The typical approach for data models therefore features special data objects or tables to handle type codes. The instances of such a data object or table represent valid type code values. This data object or table is related to any data object that is to be given one (or more) of those valid types. Creating a table for the codes in this fashion allows changes to the set of codes without impact on the database design. The data model itself, however, does not concern itself too much (if at all) with what the actual type code values might be.

Handling type codes in that manner is generally not adequate for fact models. In large measure, this is because standardized names for the *instances* of the type code are often highly relevant to product/service-type rules. Capturing and standardizing the underlying business terminology is critical.

This requires a special kind of model that focuses directly on predefining these instances. (We can stop using *type code* in the discussion at this point—it only causes confusion.) We call such models *instance models*. In all other respects, an instance model is basically like a fact model.

Consider the following examples.

- *Health care:* An instance model might be created to organize all recognized health services—for example, *Consultation, Office Visit, Hospital Admission, Surgery,* and so on.
- *Ship inspection:* An instance model might be created to organize all recognized parts of a ship—for example, *Bulkhead, Hatch Cover, Railing, Deck,* and so on.

In these examples and others like them, the business is likely to have hundreds of specialized instance-level terms and thousands of product/service rules that depend on them. Naming and categorizing these product/service terms—that is, building the appropriate instance models—is therefore crucial.

By the way, the encoding of what a company "knows" becomes so extensive at this point that the knowledge might deserve a special name. If so, that special name would probably be *ontology*. This term is defined in the related boxed item.

Definitions of Ontology[8]

1. [Philosophy] A systematic account of existence.
2. [Artificial Intelligence] (From philosophy) An explicit formal specification of how to represent the objects, concepts and other entities that are assumed to exist in some area of interest and the relationships that hold among them.
3. [Information Science] The hierarchical structuring of knowledge about things by subcategorizing them according to their essential (or at least relevant and/or cognitive) qualities. This is an extension of the previous senses of *ontology,* which has become common in discussions about the difficulty of maintaining subject indices.

---

8. From *The Free On-line Dictionary of Computing,* accessed in November 2002 at *http://www.foldoc.org/*; Denis Howe, editor.

Doing the Data Model Right for Business Rules

Using Rules to Reduce the Impact of Change

IT professionals with significant database experience generally agree that the hardest part of an operational business system to change or enhance is the database design itself. This fact is no less true for business systems developed using a business rule approach than for systems using more traditional techniques. The reason is that a database design represents *structure*. As discussed in Part II, structure is the most fundamental part of a business system—and therefore always the hardest part to change.

Change, of course, is a central fact of life for businesses today. Unfortunately, since businesses must sometimes change in fundamental ways to meet new business challenges, the potential impact for database designs can never be eliminated completely. A good data model, however, is one that reduces the need for future changes *to an absolute minimum.*

How can this objective be achieved? The answer is through rules. Rules are about control, not structure, so they can be changed or discontinued far more easily than the data model. This observation brings us to the following principle for data models in a rule-oriented environment.

Use Rules Based on Generalized Data Models to Manage Change

Anticipate change by generalizing the data model as much as is reasonable. Then support current business practices by using rules.

The following discussion briefly suggests several ways in which this principle can be applied. One caution before continuing: The operative word in this principle is *reasonable*, which here means generalized without loss of meaning or clarity. It also means a reasonable chance exists that some change might actually occur in the future. If the chances of a future change are remote, then applying the principle in that case is *not* reasonable.

Generalizing Relationships

The idea of generalizing relationships is best illustrated by an example. Suppose Company ABC expresses the following current business practice: *Credit clerk approves order.* Its data model shows credit clerk as a subtype of employee.

Figure 14–1 illustrates how this current business practice would be directly represented in the structure of the data model.[9]

Organizational roles and their responsibilities form one of the fastest-changing aspects of most businesses. With regard to approving orders at Company ABC, the following questions would therefore be in order.

- Why are credit clerks responsible for approving orders?
- Is the role of credit clerk likely to be a stable one?
- Why not permit other types of employees to approve orders in the future?
- Is it conceivable that any employee might be permitted to do so in the future?

Because of the potential for change in the current business practice, the safe approach would be to generalize the relationship *Credit clerk approves order* to *Employee approves order*. Figure 14–2 shows the revised data model. The current business practice (that is, only credit clerks approve orders) can be handled as a rule: *An order may be approved only by a credit clerk.* This rule can be dropped or redefined in the future as circumstances warrant.

Generalizing the relationship *approves* to the supertype *employee* permits greater flexibility to accommodate future changes. A change in the current business practice (as represented by the rule) will no longer affect the database design.

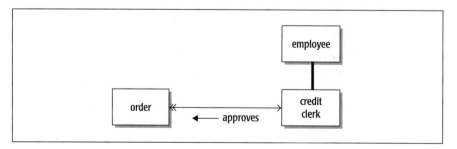

Figure 14–1   Current-practices data model (partial) for Company ABC

---

9. In this example and the ones that follow in this chapter, a double-headed arrow is used to represent a cardinality of *many,* and a single-headed arrow represents a cardinality of *one.* This choice of convention is unimportant with respect to the points made in the discussion.

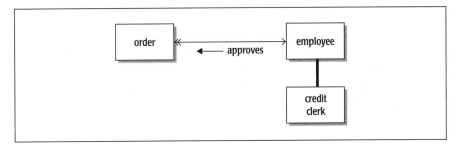

Figure 14–2 Generalized data model (partial) for Company ABC

Generalizing Cardinality

Rules offer similar flexibility in addressing the *cardinality* (also called *multiplicity*) of relationships. Again, the guideline is to design the data model for the most general case and to support current restrictions by using rules. For relationships, the most general case is a cardinality of *many* rather than a cardinality of *one*. An example illustrates.

Company XYZ currently permits an order to be shipped to only a single destination. This current business practice is reflected in Figure 14–3.

Company XYZ's customers, however, are beginning to request multidestination orders, and the database design might have to address this new requirement in the future. In anticipation of that possible change, the safe approach is to support the more general *many* case for the relationship *Order is shipped to destination*. Figure 14–4 illustrates the revised data model.

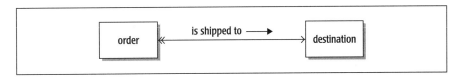

Figure 14–3 Current-practices data model (partial) for Company XYZ

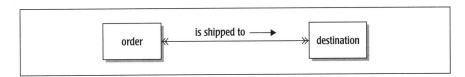

Figure 14–4 Generalized data model (partial) for Company XYZ

The cardinality of the relationship *is shipped to* has been indicated as *many* into *destination* to support the most general case. The following rule is expressed to support the current business practice limiting the relationship's cardinality to one: *An order must not be shipped to more than one destination.* Note that this rule is easily dropped (or altered) in the future, should the potential change in business policy actually occur. Such a change, however, will no longer affect the database design.

Generalizing Time

Fact models generally ignore the time dimension—that is, the past and the future—and simply express a "right now" perspective. Even for data models, ignoring time in expressing initial versions of relationships and cardinality is often expedient. Such models give point-in-time views of the business "know."

An example of a point-in-time view is the following: *An employee must not be assigned to more than one department.* This statement, of course, is actually a rule. It indicates that the appropriate cardinality for the relationship *Employee is assigned to department* is *one* into *department*. This is illustrated in Figure 14–5.

Clearly, point-in-time views are very limited. The cardinality of relationships over time is often not *one* but *many*. For example, the points-over-time view of the employee assignment relationship is probably as follows: *Over time, an employee may be assigned to many departments.* This revision clearly suggests a *many* cardinality, as Figure 14–6 illustrates.

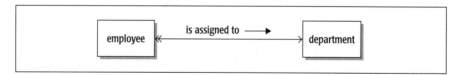

Figure 14–5   A point-in-time view of the employee assignment relationship

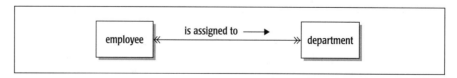

Figure 14–6   A points-over-time view of the employee assignment relationship

The actual situation for many points-over-time relationships, however, is often even more complicated. For example, the following might be true for the employee assignment relationship: *Over time, an employee may be assigned to the same department more than one time.*

The key to addressing this kind of complexity (which, by the way, is not at all unusual) is to recognize that specific kinds of events are occurring in the "flow" part of the business. These business events occur in a predictable, repetitive, and structured manner. The *result* of these events represents something we can know and therefore something that must be included in the "know" part of the system model.

In any given case, such recognition typically gives rise to a new term in the business vocabulary. In the example above, this new term might be *assignment* (of employees to departments). Up until now I have been using this term only informally.

Generalizing time in a data model means including data objects or tables to represent the results of such business events directly. The data model in Figure 14–7 illustrates this for *assignment*. It is important to remember, of course, that as included in this data model, *assignment* does not represent the actual activity but rather the knowledge that results from the activity.

Generalizing a data model by including such event-recording data objects or tables permits the expression of true points-over-time relationships. For example, it permits two or more assignments of an employee over time to be to the same department.

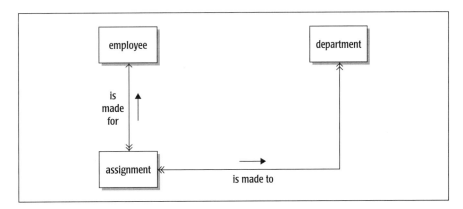

Figure 14–7 A generalized view of the employee assignment relationship

As always, current business practices should be expressed as rules. Such rules might include the following.

Rule: *An employee must not have more than one active assignment.*

Rule: *Successive assignments of an employee must not be to the same department.*

Note that either of these rules is easily dropped (or altered) in the future, should a change in the given business practice be warranted. As before, the database design is unaffected by such changes. Thus by generalizing time and expressing current business practices as rules, database designers can achieve maximum flexibility for future change.

More on the Lighter Side of Rules

Church Rules[10]

Announcement in a church bulletin for a national Prayer and Fasting Conference: "Note: The cost for attending the Fasting and Prayer conference includes meals."

"Ladies, don't forget the rummage sale. It's a chance to get rid of those things not worth keeping around the house. Don't forget your husbands."

"Don't let worry kill you off. Let the church help."

"At the evening service tonight, the sermon topic will be 'What Is Hell.' Come early and listen to our choir practice."

"Please place your donation in the envelope along with the deceased person you want remembered."

"Attend and you will hear an excellent speaker and heave a healthy lunch."

"This evening at 7 P.M. there will be a hymn sing in the park across from the Church. Bring a blanket and come prepared to sin."

"Low Self-Esteem Support Group will meet Thursday at 7 P.M. Please use the back door."

---

10. Editor's note: This material was forwarded to the author via e-mail. Original sources unknown.

"The eighth graders will be presenting Shakespeare's *Hamlet* in the Church basement Friday at 7 P.M. The Congregation is invited to attend this tragedy."

"Weight Watchers will meet at 7 P.M. at the First Presbyterian Church. Please use the large double doors at the side entrance."

"The Associate Minister unveiled the church's new tithing campaign slogan last Sunday. 'I upped my pledge. Up yours.'"

References

Ross Ronald G., and Gladys S. W. Lam. 2000. *The BRS Fact Modeling Practitioner's Guide: Developing the Business Basis for Data Models.* Houston, TX: Business Rule Solutions, LLC. Available at *http://www.BRSolutions.com.*

Zachman, John A. 2002. *The Zachman Framework: A Primer for Enterprise Engineering and Manufacturing* (electronic book). Available at *http://www.zachmaninternational.com.*

PART V

A Theory of Business Rules

A Tutorial on the Formal Basis for Business Rules and Business Rule Notation[1]

Overview

The discussion that follows provides a general tutorial on the theoretical foundation of business rules. It is aimed for those who seek a deeper, more universal understanding of business rules than is apparent in vendor software products, particular business rule methodologies, or individual business applications.

---

1. Version 8.

Acknowledgments for Part V:

Pedram Abrari and Mark J. Felder Allen, both of Corticon Technologies, Inc., provided significant contributions and continuing support in the development of this work.

My partner in Business Rule Solutions, LLC, Gladys S. W. Lam, has provided sound practical advice on numerous occasions.

Thanks are also due to Donald Chapin of Business Semantics, Ltd., and Keri Anderson Healy, Editor of the *Business Rules Journal* (http://www.BRCommunity.com), for their very helpful reviews of early drafts.

In several subsequent drafts, thanks are due to C. J. Date, who gave generously and graciously of his time and knowledge.

In addition, Michael Eulenberg, Terry Halpin of North Face Learning, Inc., Allan Kolber, and Markus Schacher of KnowGravity, Inc., provided numerous suggestions, clarifications, examples, and constructive criticisms.

To "Mary."

In this tutorial, we[2] offer specific, formal[3] answers to several of the "big questions" of the business rule approach, including the following.

- Is there a theoretical basis for business rules?
- How do the three fundamental kinds of business rules—*terms*, *facts*, and *rules*—relate to one another?
- Is there only one way to look at business rules, or are different views valid depending on one's perspective?
- What do business rules and logical deduction or inference have in common?
- How can business rules be represented in a theoretically sound manner?
- How can higher-order rules be supported?

These questions are answered using basic constructs of the[4] predicate calculus.[5] Predicate calculus is part of *formal logic*, which has a long and respected history.

The boxed item, Notes on Formal Logic and Predicate Calculus, presents some brief notes describing formal logic and predicate calculus. These notes are intended for those readers who are not familiar with these bodies of work or who need a quick refresher. Obviously, we are just scratching the surface—there is *far* more to predicate logic than these notes represent. Nonetheless, they provide sufficient background for our purposes in this tutorial.

---

2. The informal *we* used in this discussion and throughout Part V refers to the Principals of Business Rule Solutions, LLC.

3. Unless otherwise specified, I will use the word *formal* in this tutorial as in everyday usage. According to *Merriam-Webster's Collegiate Dictionary*, 10th ed. (1999, first definition), *formal* means "belonging to or constituting the form or essence of a thing." However, the theories discussed in this part (for example, the predicate calculus, relational model, and so on) are *formalizations* or *formal systems* of a special kind. (Refer to Appendix H.) Use of *formal* in those contexts (which is frequent) therefore has special status. Also, *formal logic* has a special meaning, as will be indicated.

4. There are other forms of calculus besides *predicate* calculus—for example, *propositional* calculus. The existence of multiple forms is why the definite article *the* is sometimes used in reference to *the predicate calculus* in discussions of formal logic. However, including *the* makes the text a bit unfriendly, so I will omit it from this point on in the discussion.

5. The terms *predicate logic* and *predicate calculus* are often used interchangeably in the literature. However, *predicate calculus* is a bit more accurate for our purposes in this tutorial.

Notes on Formal Logic and Predicate Calculus[6]

Logic or formal logic: ". . . [T]he science of formal principles of reasoning or correct inference" [Simpson 2000, p. 2]. "A science that deals with the principles and criteria of validity of inference and demonstration: the science of the formal principles of reasoning" [*Merriam-Webster's Collegiate Dictionary*, 1999, first definition].

Calculus: ". . . [A] general term that refers to any system of symbolic computation; in [predicate calculus], the kind of computation involved is the computation of the truth value—true or false—of certain formulas or expressions" [Date 2000, p. 772].

Predicate calculus: ". . . [A] general method or framework . . . for reasoning about any subject matter whatsoever" [Simpson, p. 2]. "The predicate calculus [also known as *first-order logic*] dates from the 1910's and 1920's.[7] It is basic for all subsequent logical research. It is a very general system of logic which accurately expresses a huge variety of assertions and modes of reasoning. . . . It is much more flexible than [Aristotelian logic]" [Simpson, p. 5].

Predicate: "Aristotelian logic begins with the familiar grammatical distinction between subject and predicate. A *subject* is typically an individual entity, for instance a man or a house or a city. It may also be a class of entities, for instance all men. A *predicate* is a property or attribute or mode of existence which a given subject may or may not possess.[8] For example, an individual man (the subject) may or may not be skillful (the predicate), and all men (the subject) may or may not be brothers (the predicate)" [Simpson, p. 3].

continued

---

6. For an excellent short introduction to the history and concepts of formal logic, see Simpson [2000]. For an in-depth treatment, refer to Nilsson [1998, pp. 215–358].
7. Predicate calculus, in turn, was based on a "remarkable" treatise, the Begriffsschrift ("concept script"), published in 1879 by the German philosopher Gottlob [Simpson, p. 5].
8. There are objections to this characterization of predicate. For example, C. J. Date indicates that he does not find it very helpful (private correspondence, November 11, 2001). However, I believe these difficulties probably arise from a difference in perspective, as I discuss later in the tutorial.

"... [I]n the predicate calculus [in contrast to Aristotelian logic], a subject is always an individual entity, never a class of entities. For example, an individual man can be treated as a subject, but the class of all men must betreated as a predicate.[9] . . . For example, if *M* is the predicate 'to be a man' and *a* is the individual 'Socrates,' then *Ma* denotes the assertion 'Socrates is a man'" [Simpson, p. 5].

"Some predicates require more than one argument. For example, if *B* is the predicate 'bigger than,' then *Bxy* denotes the assertion '*x* is bigger than *y*'. Thus *B* requires two arguments. . . . If we try to use *B* with only one argument, we obtain something like *Bx*, i.e., '*x* is bigger than'. This . . . is only a meaningless combination of symbols. In analogy with English grammar, we could say that *Bxy* is like a grammatically correct sentence, while *Bx* is merely a sentence fragment. Such fragments play no role in the predicate calculus" [Simpson, p. 5].

"The essential idea of the predicate calculus is that predicates are treated as atomic (black boxes). Logical formulas are comprised of predicates and individual variables or constants, along with logical operators (e.g., AND, OR, NOT, IF . . . THEN . . .), and logical quantifiers[10] (i.e., the universal quantifier 'all' [or FORALL] (best read as 'for each' or 'given any') and the existential quantifier 'some' [or EXISTS] (meaning 'there exists at least one')" [Halpin 2001].

First-order predicate calculus: "We are concerned [in this tutorial] only with the *first-order* predicate calculus, which basically means that (a) there are no 'predicate variables' (i.e., variables whose permitted values are predicates), and hence that (b) predicates cannot themselves be subjected to quantification [i.e., by means of the two logical quantifiers]" [Date 2000, p. 778].

---

9. We believe the point here is simply to emphasize the sharp distinction between instance and class in predicate calculus. It is certainly possible for a class to be the subject of a predicate. C. J. Date cites the following examples: "The class of all men is finite." "The class of all men has a total biomass of less than a million tons" (private correspondence, November 11, 2001).

10. The logical quantifiers are actually shorthands useful for finite problems.

> **Proposition:** "A proposition[11] in logic is something that evaluates to either true or false, unequivocally. For instance, 'illiam Shakespeare wrote *Pride and Prejudice*' is a proposition (a false one as it happens)" [Date 2000, p. 13].
>
> **Validity:** "... [A] piece of formally correct reasoning is not scientifically valid unless it is based on a true and primary starting point [i.e., true and primary business rules].... [A]ny decisions about what is true and primary do not pertain to logic but rather to the specific subject matter under consideration" [Simpson, p. 2].
>
> "[Propositions presented to the system] can be checked for consistency within the world of [other propositions known to be true], but cannot be fully verified as mirroring reality in the external world. In the end, that is the responsibility of the person stating the fact" [Chapin 2001].
>
> "*The system can't enforce* truth, *only* consistency.... Sadly, truth and consistency aren't the same thing! ... **Correct** implies **consistent** (but not the other way around), and **inconsistent** implies **incorrect** (but not the other way around)" [Date 2001, original emphasis].

This part of the book shows how the fundamental ideas of business rules are directly grounded in the basic constructs of predicate calculus. The material is organized into four chapters, as follows:

- Chapter 15 presents basic ideas, including the crucial idea of perspective.
- Chapter 16 examines the formulation of rules in depth.
- Chapter 17 examines predicates and facts in depth.
- Chapter 18 provides a theoretical basis for higher-order rules.

To keep this part as readable as possible for a broad audience, including those who have never been exposed to predicate calculus, I made the deliberate decision not to introduce or use its notation. However, there is one important exception—a basic and relatively compact notation is needed to illustrate and discuss business rules.

Conventional notation for rules in formal logic is used for this purpose. This notation is extended for certain special needs, particularly for

---

11. A proposition can be viewed as a special or degenerate case of a predicate. For example, C. J. Date indicates, "A predicate has a set of arguments. A proposition is what you get if that set happens to be empty" (private correspondence, November 11, 2001).

representing facts and higher-order rules. These extensions result in a scheme called *R-Notation*.[12] This extended notation is introduced in Chapters 16 and 17 as we go along.

Higher-order rules are called *Pattern-R* rules in our approach. The typing scheme for these higher-order rules was originally developed and presented in *The Business Rule Book* [Ross 1997].[13] We believe *Pattern-R* rules hold promise for significant productivity improvements in business rule specification.

References

Chapin, Donald. 2001. Private correspondence, May 15.

Date, C. J. 2001. "Constraints and Predicates: A Brief Tutorial (Part 3)." *Business Rules Journal*, 2(12). Accessed in August 2002 at *http://www.BRCommunity.com/a2001/b065c.html*.

————. 2000. *An Introduction to Database Systems* (7th ed.). Boston, MA: Addison-Wesley.

Date, C. J., and Hugh Darwen. 2000. *Foundation for Future Database Systems: The Third Manifesto* (2nd ed.). Boston, MA: Addison-Wesley.

Halpin, Terry. 2001. Private correspondence, July 18.

Nilsson, Nils J. 1998. *Artificial Intelligence: A New Synthesis*. San Francisco, CA: Morgan Kaufmann.

Ross, Ronald G. 1997. *The Business Rule Book* (2nd ed.). Houston, TX: Business Rule Solutions, LLC. Available at *http://www.BRSolutions.com*.

Simpson, Stephen G. 2000. "Logic and Mathematics." Available at *http://www.math.psu.edu/simpson/*.

---

12. It could be easily assumed that the *R* in *R-Notation* simply stands for *Ross*, but that is not the case. Use of the *R* in the various names that appear in this part (for example, *R-Notation* and *Pattern-R*) emerged more or less by accident during the development of this work as various contributors and reviewers communicated with me and with each other. I take the *R* to stand for *rules*, and perhaps also for *relational*. With regard to the latter, our work draws heavily from relational theory—especially the recent work of C. J. Date and Hugh Darwen [2000]. Also, both our work and relational theory are based on the same theoretical foundations—namely, predicate calculus and set theory. (Part V addresses predicate calculus directly but not set theory.)

13. This work provides numerous atomic and derived rule types, which collectively are called *Pattern-R* rule types in this part of the book.

CHAPTER 15

Three Perspectives on Business Rules

A Framework for Formal Discussion

The Three Perspectives

The business rule approach follows three major tracks, as outlined below.

1. *The business track:* Here it is an approach to creating and managing a business or business process.
2. *The system track:* Here it is an approach to developing an appropriate knowledge and/or information system to support such a business or business process. (Such a system usually involves significant automation.)
3. *The technical track:* Here it is an approach to designing a suitable implementation such a system.

There are therefore three distinct perspectives on business rules, each valid and each targeting a different audience.[1] These audiences have distinct needs and agendas, as follows.

- *The business manager's perspective:* This audience faces the challenge of creating and managing a business or business process. As seen from the other two

---

1. Followers of John Zachman will recognize these perspectives as corresponding to rows 2, 3, and 4 respectively, of his Enterprise Architecture Framework. Refer to Zachman [2002] and collected articles by Zachman found in the *Business Rules Journal*, available in November 2002 at *http://www.BRCommunity.com*.

perspectives, the business manager's perspective represents a layperson's view of system designs and IT technology. At this perspective,[2] the focus is on developing business vocabulary and business logic (that is, capturing business rules).

- *The system developer's perspective:* This audience faces the challenge of developing a sound system design. At the system developer's perspective, the focus is on rigorous specification of business rules relative to the systematic representation of information and/or knowledge. This activity involves analysis and transformation of business rules captured at the business manager's perspective.
- *The technical designer's perspective:* This audience faces the challenge of developing a suitable implementation design for the automated components of the system design. At the technical designer's perspective, the focus is on optimal implementation of business rules under the given choice(s) of IT technology.

The business rule approach is business-driven *by design*—that is, on purpose. We therefore consider the first of the above perspectives to be preeminent. If there were no business problems to solve, the second perspective and then the third perspective would not even be needed.

We believe the three major tracks of the business rule approach can be organized so that they align with one another quite closely. One additional purpose of this tutorial is to demonstrate how such alignment is achieved. Such alignment, we believe, will serve to enhance support for the business manager's perspective—which, again, we believe is preeminent.

---

2. In discussions using Zachman's Enterprise Architecture Framework, practitioners often couch statements in the following way: "at row 2," "at row 3," and so on. In this tutorial, such reference to rows might be confusing to many readers, so I have avoided it throughout. Nonetheless, I do use *at*, rather than the more proper *from*, when referencing any given perspective—for example, "*at* the business manager's perspective," "*at* the system developer's perspective," and so on. I ask for the reader's indulgence on this point.

> ### Special Note about the Technical Designer's Perspective
>
> The business manager's perspective and the system developer's perspective are intentionally independent of any specific implementation technology. At these perspectives, the discussion in this tutorial can stand on its own.
>
> The technical designer's perspective, in contrast, is technology-dependent. Any discussion at this perspective must therefore be framed in the context of a particular technology.
>
> We have elected the relational model to provide our technology context in this regard since it has had such a pervasive influence on database thinking. In particular, we find the approach of Date and Darwen [2000] to be an attractive one, and thus I comment on that approach as warranted in this tutorial.

A Word about Terms

The earlier notes about formal logic indicated the importance of distinguishing between individual things, or *instances*, and *classes*. An example of an individual thing or instance might be a particular person—for example, the person named "Mary." An example of a class of instances might be the set of all people.

Throughout this tutorial, I focus on the kinds of *terms* that can be used in formal expressions of rules, predicates, and propositions. I will give the precise definition of *term* in that context later. In general, however, the names given to either instances or classes can be terms. Where it is important to distinguish in individual cases, I will say *instance term* or *class term*.

At the system developer's perspective, this distinction in terms is relatively straightforward. A class term generally might be taken to represent what system developers see as an *entity type* or *business object*. I will refrain from using these latter terms, however, since they play no role in formal theory.

At the technical designer's perspective, the picture is more complicated. Here we are further removed from the business manager's perspective, where the terms originally arise (or *should* arise, anyway). For that reason, the issue requires closer analysis, which is given in Chapter 16 and in Appendix B.

A Word about Types

Type is unfortunately used to mean at least two quite different things in the IT world.

- Data modelers generally use the term in a way that is equivalent to *class* as described above. For example, a data modeler might speak of the employee *type*.
- Usage in the context of programming languages usually means the type (or data type) that values must have to be suitable for a variable. For example, a programmer might speak of a variable of *type* integer.

Note that the former usage is typically at the system developer's perspective, whereas the latter usage is typically at the technical designer's perspective. The conflict in the two meanings can be managed so long as any usage is carefully framed as being for one purpose or the other.

A more serious problem occurs when the former usage occurs at the technical designer's perspective. Here, the two meanings collide in troublesome ways. This problem is especially noteworthy for theoretical work whose goal is to unite databases, rules, and programming—a fundamentally important area for support of business rules. (See Appendix B for additional discussion.) That area, however, is largely beyond the scope of this tutorial.

To keep things simple, I will therefore carefully qualify any usage I make of the term *type* in this tutorial.

Special Terminology

In looking at business rules from the viewpoint of formal logic, other significant problems arise in terminology. Terms commonly used in the IT community—especially *data* and *database*—can be easily misleading in that context. For the most part, this problem stems from the simple fact that commercial products offered to date for database management have provided virtually no support for rules.

For that reason, I will generally avoid the terms *data* and *database* in this discussion in favor of ones with less baggage, as follows. The reasons for particular choices will become apparent in due course.

- *Factbase:* The store that holds persistent "data"[3] of the enterprise. The contents of the factbase are believed to be accurate and true. For this reason, the contents are called *facts.* [4]
- *Rulebase:* The store that contains the business rules for a factbase. This store roughly contains *metadata,* but with emphasis on rules and their current operational status and evaluation. These rules will have been specified in a declarative manner. (See Appendix I for discussion of what *declarative* means with respect to rules.)
- *Logicbase:* The store that contains both a factbase and its associated rulebase. The current content of the logicbase comprehensively defines *state* for the targeted area of the business—or at least those parts of it that can be automated. In other words, the logicbase should be viewed as *the* authoritative and exclusive source of information describing the cumulative effect of business operations up to the current point in time.[5]
- *Business logic server:* The runtime system software responsible for the logicbase—that is, for managing the factbase and executing the rules in the rulebase.[6] A business logic server might also be called a *rule engine, rule processing server,* or *decision management platform.* The boxed item, Rule Independence and the Business Logic Server, emphasizes the importance of business logic servers.

Several observations should be made about the terms above.

- The distinction between *factbase* and *rulebase* emphasizes that the evaluation of rules (and in particular, any information that needs to be retained *between* evaluations) should be handled separately from the persistent "data" itself. This separation ensures the highest possible degree of flexibility (tolerance of change) in the rules over time.

---

3. "Data" will always appear in quotation marks in this tutorial since whenever it is used from this point on, I actually mean *facts* (except as noted).
4. By convention, these facts are taken to be true propositions in the sense of predicate calculus.
5. Such information can, of course, include schedules for business activities that have not yet actually occurred.
6. Depending on the architecture of the business logic server, associated software facilities might include a rules compiler.

Rule Independence and the Business Logic Server

Giving a business logic server exclusive responsibility for executing the rules is highly desirable. Ultimately, the only way to ensure the integrity (that is, correctness)[7] of the logicbase is by *isolating* the rules from application processes.

Consider what might happen if the business logic server did not have exclusive responsibility for the rules: "... otherwise different users (and/or different applications) might erroneously have different notions of correctness. For example, A might believe the maximum salary is 100K while B believes it is 80K. Then A could update the [factbase] in such a way as to make it incorrect as far as B is concerned, and B might then proceed on a false assumption—*viz.*, that all salaries in the [factbase] were less than or equal to 80K" [Date 2001].

At a more technical level, suppose some outside process assigns a value of false to a variable in the logicbase while a rule "thinks" the variable should be true, or a process assigns true while a rule "thinks" it should be false. Quite simply, the business logic server will use faulty logic in reasoning.

Furthermore, the rationale for the change would be embedded in the process rather than externalized (that is, made visible) by the explicit rules. This externalization of (business) logic from processes is a fundamental goal of the business rule approach. By this means, the (business) logic is more accessible, more readily understood, and more easily changed. We call this *Rule Independence.*

- The terms *logicbase* and *business logic server* emphasize the need to view persistent "data" and rules *together* when considering business rules from the perspective of formal logic.[8] They are also meant to place emphasis on *business* logic—which of course is what business rules are all about. Unfortunately, the terms *database* and *database management system* (DBMS) do not carry that same sense, at least as commonly used in cur-

---

7. *Consistency* is actually a more precise term here. The business logic server cannot *really* know if the logicbase is correct with respect to the external real world it purports to reflect.
8. A classic work covering this area is Widom and Ceri [1996].

rent IT practice (no rules).[9] Neither do the terms *inference engine* and *expert system*, albeit for the opposite reason (no persistent "data").

- In expert systems, *expert system shell* corresponds very roughly to a business logic server. Unfortunately, *expert system shell* generally carries the following sense: "... short-term memory that contains specific data about the actual problem under study" [Crevier 1993, p. 156]. "Short-term memory" is clearly inconsistent with the business logic server's responsibility for managing the factbase.

- Expert systems, artificial intelligence (AI), and certain other disciplines[10] often use the term *knowledgebase*. Although *knowledgebase* can be defined in many ways (that is part of the problem!), at least for expert systems and AI it can be generally characterized as follows: "In its simplest form ... a list of IF ... THEN ... rules [each of] which specifies what to do, or what conclusions to draw, under a set of well-defined circumstances" [Crevier, p. 156]. A minor concern is this emphasis on the IF ... THEN ... syntax. (Refer to Appendix D.) A more serious concern is that research into AI is far more ambitious—and difficult—than this "simplest form." We prefer to focus on the immediate problem of organizing and managing operational business logic—not other possible forms of knowledge. For this reason, we prefer the more cautious (and possibly more accurate) term *rulebase*.

References

Crevier, Daniel. 1993. *AI: The Tumultuous History of the Search for Artificial Intelligence.* New York: BasicBooks.

Date, C. J. 2001. Private correspondence, November 19.

———. 2000. *What Not How: The Business Rule Approach to Application Development.* Boston, MA: Addison-Wesley.

---

9. C. J. Date [2000, p. 113] writes, "... this is a place where the SQL vendors *really* let us down. ... [There are] several ways in which the SQL vendors let us down, but this one is perhaps the biggest; indeed, it underlies many of the others."

10. For example, automated tools supporting enterprise architecture.

Date, C. J., and Hugh Darwen. 2000. *Foundation for Future Database Systems: The Third Manifesto* (2nd ed.). Boston, MA: Addison-Wesley.

Widom, Jennifer, and Stefano Ceri (eds). 1996. *Active Database Systems: Triggers and Rules for Advanced Database Processing.* San Francisco, CA: Morgan Kaufmann.

Zachman, John A. 2002. *The Zachman Framework: A Primer for Enterprise Engineering and Manufacturing* (electronic book). Available at *http:// www.zachmaninternational.com.*

CHAPTER 16

The Theoretical Foundation of Rules

About Formal Constraints

The Formal Definition of *Rule*

At a theoretical level, rules are based directly on predicate calculus. More specifically, they are the IF-THEN connective of predicate calculus (also known as the *implication connective* or *logical implication*). The general form of the IF-THEN connective appears below. Definitions for the terms we need to explore this connective are given in the boxed item, More Notes on Terminology.

IF p THEN q

Note the following about this form.

- p and q must be Boolean expressions—that is, they must evaluate to either true or false.
- p is called the *antecedent*.
- q is called the *consequent*.
- This example can also be read as follows: "p implies q."

More Notes on Terminology

Truth value: A value of either true or false.

Boolean: A truth value.[1]

continued

---

1. *Boolean* as a noun is taken to mean a value of either true or false, in the same way that *integer* is usually taken to mean an integer *value*.

Truth-valued variable: A variable capable of holding a Boolean—that is, a variable of type Boolean. Truth-valued variables are also known as *Boolean variables.*

Logical operator: A nonarithmetic operation that can be performed on truth-valued variables. The three basic operators are AND, OR, and NOT. All other logical operators can be expressed in terms of these three.

Logical expression: An expression that evaluates to a truth value.[2] For example, a logical expression might be formed by using the logical connectives OR and/or AND. Logical expressions are also known as *Boolean expressions, truth-valued expressions,* and *conditional expressions.*

Premise: An antecedent is sometimes called a *premise.* However, the term *premise* is often used in discussion of metarules (rules about rules), which we take to be its proper (reserved) usage. An example of such a metarule is the following: (p AND q) implies p, which simply says "p is a logical consequence of (p AND q)." The premise in this example is (p AND q).

Conclusion: A consequent is sometimes called a *conclusion.* The same comment as above, however, also applies to the term *conclusion.* The conclusion in the given metarule example above is the portion of the expression after the "implies"—that is, p.

In predicate calculus, the expression IF p THEN q is *exactly* equivalent to the following logical expression, which might actually be easier to interpret correctly. (There is more here than meets the eye!)

$$OR\ ((NOT\ p), q)$$

The syntax is unimportant here. This expression could also be written ((NOT p) OR q).

---

2. In contrast, a *proposition* in logic is something that evaluates to either true or false, *categorically.*

This expression is precisely (and completely) the formal definition of a rule.[3] What the expression says in everyday English is simply that "Either p is not true or q is true."[4] So when can p be true? It can be true *only if* q is true. In other words, the truth of q is *required* for p to be true. If q is not true, then p *cannot* be true. Here is an example to illustrate.

> p: "it is raining"
>
> q: "streets are wet"
>
> Rule: OR ((NOT "it is raining"), "streets are wet")
>
> Question: When can "it is raining" be true?
>
> Answer: Only if "streets are wet" is true.

If "streets are wet" is *not* true, then according to the rule, the expression (NOT "it is raining") must be true. The only way that (NOT "it is raining") can be true is if "it is raining" is *false*.

Several additional points should be made here.

- First, q can be true even if p is *not* true. Nothing in the expression OR ((NOT p), q) prohibits that. In other words, just because q is true does not mean that p is necessarily true. For instance, in the example above, q ("streets are wet") can be true even if p ("it is raining") is *not* true.
- It is important to remember that the expression OR ((NOT p), q) as a whole is itself also a Boolean expression—in other words, given a set of arguments (that is, specific values for p and q), the rule as a whole evaluates to either true or false. (This evaluation is in addition to the Boolean expressions p, NOT p, and q.) The complete truth table for rules and related explanations are given in Appendix A, which also explains related subtleties.
- This example illustrates that the IF . . . THEN . . . syntax is not essential for expression of the rules. The boxed item, The IF-THEN Connective versus the IF . . . THEN . . . Syntax for Rule Statements, examines the relationship between logical implication and IF-THEN syntax.

---

3. Refer to Appendix C for discussion of where computation and derivation "rules" fit.
4. The expression is also satisfied if *both* of the following are true: (a) p is not true and (b) q is true.

The IF-THEN Connective versus the IF . . . THEN . . . Syntax for Rule Statements

We use the term *rule statement* for the expression of a rule in everyday English at the business manager's perspective.[5] Such rule statements can be given using IF . . . THEN . . . syntax. An example is "*If* a person is female and of age, *then* that person is a woman."

Note carefully that the IF-THEN connective is *not* the same thing as the IF . . . THEN . . . syntax for expressing rule statements. The IF-THEN connective is simply an alternative form in predicate calculus for the logical expression OR ((NOT p), q).

Also note carefully that the IF-THEN connective *in no way mandates* use of the IF . . . THEN . . . syntax for expressing rule statements. The issue of syntax is altogether distinct. Refer to Appendix D for additional discussion.

If a given logical implication (that is, rule) is *required* to be true,[6] then that logical implication is said to be a *constraint*.[7] For example, suppose we define the earlier expression as a constraint: OR ((NOT p), q). The sense of this constraint in everyday English is: "p *must* imply q." In other words, q *must* be true when p is true.

A logical implication (that is, rule) need not necessarily be required to be true. (Here, the meaning of *rule* differs in formal theory from its everyday sense.) If we do not require it to be true, then in effect we are merely expressing some test or posing a query about the current state or *condition* of the logicbase.

---

5. Obviously, since *rule statement* as I use it here refers to the expression of a rule at the business manager's perspective, there is no correlation to *statement* as commonly used in the context of application programming languages. In the latter context, *statement* often means something imperative (that is, a command). *Rule statement*, in contrast, carries the everyday sense of *rule*—a guideline or constraint for (business) behavior.

6. This requirement might be supported in any of several ways. In one approach, the rule would temporarily evaluate to false, and the business logic server would take appropriate action (for example, returning the factbase to a previous state) to ensure that the rule evaluates to true upon subsequent reevaluation.

7. Or *integrity constraint,* which is the term used in *The Business Rule Book* [Ross 1997].

Again consider the rule OR ((NOT p), q). Defined as a test or query rather than a constraint, the sense of the expression in everyday English becomes "*Does* p imply q?" As this illustrates, we are now in effect simply asking a true-false question (that is, posing a query) that the logicbase presumably can answer.

The focus of the first three chapters of this tutorial is on the use of logical implications as constraints rather than as tests or queries. Note, however, that their use as tests or queries is important for expressing higher-order rules, as discussed later in Chapter 18. Higher-order rules typically involve complex patterns that would be difficult to express otherwise. A logical implication used as a test or query in expressing higher-order rules is called a *condition*.[8] Refer to Appendix C for discussion of constraints versus conditions.

More on Terms

In formal and informal discussions of rule theory, *term* is the word most frequently used[9] to refer to each individually named element in any given rule (for example, p, q, and so on). It is not by accident that this use correlates with the use of *term* in the business rule approach.

In expressing rules (and, indeed, for predicate calculus in general), formal theory prescribes that a term must be exactly one of the following three kinds:[10]

1. The name of an *individual thing.* The thing so named might be a particular person, place, item, concept, and so on—for example, "Mary," "Memphis," "gold," true, 5, and so on.[11]

---

8. *Condition* is the term used in *The Business Rule Book* [Ross 1997].
9. See Date [2000a, p. 778]. However, Date prefers *placeholder* or *parameter* to *term* in the context of rules (private correspondence, November 19, 2001). See also the following references: Halpin [2001, pp. 63–64] and Charniak and McDermott [1985, p. 15].
10. This restriction applies to any term used in well-formed formulas (WFFs) of predicate calculus. See Date [2000a, p. 778] and Charniak and McDermott [1985, pp. 15 and 321].
11. For discussion purposes in this part of the book, I use quotation marks to indicate alphabetic names (for example, "Mary," "gold," and so on). This convention helps distinguish them from the names of variables, which I will indicate without quotation marks (for example, XYZ, Employee, salary, and so on).

2. The name of a *variable* capable of holding a value. For example, variables defined to hold the values above might be named person, city, metal, of-age, and rank, respectively.

3. The name of a *function* capable of producing a value. Examples include ADD, SQUARE ROOT, and so on.

As this list indicates, *all* terms are names of one kind or another. There is much confusion over this point. For example, many texts simply indicate that terms can be values, variables, or functions.

Upon reflection, however, it is obvious that variables and functions cannot be terms *per se.* For example, "x" is the *name* of a variable that can hold a value—not the actual variable itself. And "+" (or ADD) is the *name* of the function that performs addition—not the actual function. For more about function names in the business rule approach, refer to the boxed item, A Note about Function-Type Terms.

In the case of terms that denote individual things, it is also obvious that the names of people, places, and items are not the *actual* people, places, or items. For example, the literal "Mary" is not the real flesh-and-blood person. The literal "Memphis" is not the actual place in Tennessee. The literal "gold" is not the real metal.

The case of terms that denote concepts or ideas, however, is more difficult. When someone says "true," is this the actual idea or simply the name of the idea? When someone says "5," is that the actual number or the name of the concept five?

The answer becomes clear when you realize that the same concept or idea can be denoted by different literals. For example, the *idea* of true can be denoted by "T" (as opposed to "F") or "on" (as opposed to "off") or "1" (as opposed to "0"). The *concept* of five can be denoted by "5" or "5.0" or "cinco" (in Spanish) or "V" (in Roman numerals). Clearly, all these literals are the names of some underlying concept or idea.[12]

   All terms are names.

---

12. C. J. Date [2000b, p. 73] refers to this underlying concept or idea as the *value.*

A Note about Function-Type Terms

As mentioned above, the names of functions are viewed by the predicate calculus as terms when included in a Boolean expression.[13] Such a function might or might not be a truth-valued function, but it must, like all functions, return a single value for any given set of arguments. Non-truth-valued functions are permitted for convenience to allow inclusion of computations (for example, add or "+", subtract or "−", or any other mathematical function).

Such non-truth-valued functions clearly represent *processes*. Since they produce values merely for evaluation within logical functions of the given rule(s), their names (for example, "add" or "+", "subtract" or "-", and so on) are generally *not* considered to be terms in the business rule approach.[14]

Terminology: Instances and Classes, Values and Variables

At the system developer's perspective, the name of an individual thing corresponds directly to an individual instance, and the name of a variable corresponds directly to a class. We mean *instance* and *class* in the straightforward sense of predicate calculus as discussed earlier. For example, "Monday" is an instance; *weekday* is a class.

A critical point is the following. At the technical designer's perspective, a variable must be capable of actually holding an instance—or, more accurately, a *value*—in some physical sense. How the variable (or class) provides this capability is a key concern. Literally, the variable or class must be some kind of container.[15] Refer to Appendix B for additional discussion.

---

13. When included in a Boolean expression in this manner, the function-type term actually refers to the function *invocation*, rather than simply to the function per se. C. J. Date argues that "exactly the same is true for names of values and names of variables—in each case, the name really stands for a certain invocation [of an appropriate kind of function]" (private correspondence, November, 19, 2001). This distinction, however, is not central to the focus of this tutorial.

14. The names of the *results* produced by such functions are a different matter. Refer to Appendix C.

15. We prefer black-box containers, but that is a different question.

At the system developer's perspective, however, we believe there is *no need whatsoever* to consider how variables provide such capability. Furthermore, we believe it is crucial to be very clear and consistent about this important difference. To minimize the possibility of confusion for that perspective, I will therefore use neither *value* and *variable* nor *instance* and *class*. Instead, I will use *instance term* (for the name of an individual thing) and *class term* (for the name of a variable) in order to stay as close as possible to the true sense of predicate calculus.

Rule Notation

In addition to terms, specifying rules also requires appropriate notation. In the following discussion, I present the notation we prefer at the system developer's perspective. Our preferences are based to a significant extent on what we find most useful for treatment of higher-order rules, which are discussed in Chapter 18.

I also explain how the notation might be read in everyday English. Such rule statements often use the IF . . . THEN . . . syntax. Note that we have certain strong reservations about the use of this syntax in capturing and expressing business rules. These reservations are discussed in Appendix D.

There are a variety of ways in which rules (logical implications) can be formally expressed; however, at the system developer's perspective[16] we prefer the following traditional symbol. This symbol is basic to R-Notation.

$$\rightarrow$$

This arrow symbol ($\rightarrow$) denotes a logical implication (rule) involving specified terms (none shown here). The arrow itself is always taken (by convention) to mean "implies." Refer to the boxed item, Creating Rules, for discussion of this symbol in the context of business logic servers.

---

16. RuleSpeak provides guidelines for specification of rules at the business manager's perspective. (Refer to Part III.) Rule specification language for the technical designer's perspective is beyond the scope of this tutorial. In any event, such language might be invisible to system developers if the notation they use in their own perspective is sufficiently rigorous—which we believe it can be.

Creating Rules

A business logic server might also view the arrow symbol ($\rightarrow$) as the name (or label) for a system *process* that might also be called CREATE RULE (or ASSERT RULE). This special process merits closer scrutiny, which requires reviewing how the execution of processes in general differs from the "execution" of rules.

A fundamental distinction between processes and rules is that *users* generally control when processes are to execute.[17] This control is accomplished by sequencing the processes or by running a program that executes the processes in the appropriate order.

A business logic server, in contrast, controls[18] when rules are to "execute" (that is, be evaluated). In other words, the business logic server causes rules to "execute" automatically when it deems changes in the state of the logicbase make that appropriate. This support is implied in saying that rules are *declarative.* (Refer to Appendix I.)

When should a given rule first "execute"? Logically at least, to ensure absolutely no chance of inconsistency in the logicbase, every rule should be first "executed" *as soon as it is presented to the system.*[19] To say this differently, the creation of a rule is itself a change in state that should cause the business logic server to reevaluate the logicbase to (re)ensure comprehensive integrity. (What happens physically might be a very different matter, of course.)

In that sense, declaring a rule must be viewed as implying the first "execution" of the rule. The logical coupling of declaring a rule and first "executing" the rule is a deeper part of what it means for rules to be *declarative* (as opposed to procedural).

Now we must add the antecedent(s) and the consequent of the rule.[20] The former is/are placed on the left-hand side of the arrow, and the latter on the right-hand side of the arrow. For the sake of simplicity, the former are

---

17. Unless some trigger—a kind of rule—has been specified.
18. Not all rule engines currently control this as thoroughly as is possible or desirable.
19. Unless some future effective date is specified that is meaningful to the business.
20. The antecedent(s) and consequent can be thought of as denoting the "input" to the invisible process underlying the rule.

therefore often called *left-hand terms*[21] (LHTs), and the latter are often called *right-hand terms*[22] (RHTs). The following example illustrates:

$$S \rightarrow U$$

The term S is on the left-hand side of the arrow and is therefore the LHT. The term U is on the right-hand side of the arrow and is therefore the RHT. This rule should be read "S implies U" or "The antecedent, S, implies the consequent, U." Expressed in IF . . . THEN . . . syntax it becomes "If S, then U." As with any rule, it could also be expressed in the form OR ((NOT S), U).

Here is another example:

$$\text{sun-above-horizon} \rightarrow \text{daytime}$$

The term sun-above-horizon is on the left-hand side of the arrow and is therefore the LHT. The term daytime is on the right-hand side of the arrow and is therefore the RHT. This rule should be read "Sun-above-horizon implies daytime" or "The antecedent, sun-above-horizon, implies the consequent, daytime." Expressed in IF . . . THEN . . . syntax it becomes "If sun-above-horizon, then daytime." As with any rule, it could also be expressed in the form OR ((NOT sun-above-horizon), daytime). What this rule "means" to the business logic server is examined in the following boxed item.

What Terms "Mean" to the Business Logic Server

When expressing a rule such as $S \rightarrow U$, it is important to remember that the business logic server does not really "understand" what the terms S (or sun-above-horizon) and U (or daytime) mean. To the system, they are simply strings of characters without intrinsic meaning. We could just as well use something like "sgjdfkkei" and "fdeoifdjfb"—as long as *we* remember what they mean.

---

21. *Anchor* is the equivalent term used in *The Business Rule Book* [Ross 1997]. *Anchor* works better for higher-order rules, which are discussed in Chapter 18.
22. *Correspondent* is the equivalent term used in *The Business Rule Book* [Ross 1997]. *Correspondent* works better for higher-order rules, which are discussed in Chapter 18.

Every rule must have at least one LHT and exactly one RHT.[23] (For more on the one-RHT issue, refer to the boxed item below.) For now, we will consider cases involving only a single LHT; the multiple LHT case is discussed later.

> ### The Atomic Form of Rules and the One-RHT Restriction
>
> Some experts contend that rules must be translatable to Horn clauses (named after the logician Alfred Horn), which disallow ORs among RHTs.[24] However, it should be mentioned that this is the subject of considerable research and debate, and in some approaches, rules with ORs among their RHTs are considered to be information-bearing and are exploited as such.[25] In any event, I will not directly address rules with ORs among their RHTs in this tutorial.
>
> Any rule with ANDs among its RHTs is interpreted to represent an equivalent number of *individual* rules, each with only one RHT and all with the very same LHT(s). The former rules is not in atomic form.
>
> By convention, if a rule is shown simply with a list of RHTs (no explicit ANDs), *implicit* ANDs among them are assumed. Although this shorthand form is generally not recommended (because such a rule is not in atomic form), the shorthand is sometimes useful for the sake of economy or emphasis.

As mentioned before, we must indicate whether we intend a rule to be a constraint or merely to ask a true-false question (that is, to be a test or query). This designation requires a *rule type indicator*. Constraints are indicated as follows:

$$S^T \rightarrow U$$

---

23. If no LHT is given or no RHT is given, the antecedent or consequent defaults to true. Then "p →" and "→ p" are both the same as "p" (C. J. Date, private correspondence, November 19, 2001).

24. For more discussion, refer to Elmasri and Navathe [1994, pp. 734–735].

25. Note that the issue of ORs among RHTs causes far more difficulty for projectors (especially inference-type rules) than for rejectors. (Refer to Appendix C for explanation of these two terms.)

A rule type indicator—the superscripted T (for true) at the left of the arrow—defines this rule to be a constraint. As before, the rule should be read "S implies U." The IF . . . THEN . . . syntax is "If S, then U."

The truth value of any LHT or the RHT can be negated, as the following example illustrates:

$$S \overset{T}{\to} NOT\ U$$

The rule type indicator again indicates that this rule is a constraint.[26] The rule should now be read "S implies *not* U." The IF . . . THEN . . . syntax is "If S, then *not* U."

Here is another example:

$$\text{sun-above-horizon} \overset{T}{\to} NOT\ \text{nighttime}$$

The rule type indicator again indicates that this rule is a constraint. The rule should now be read "Sun-above-horizon implies *not* nighttime." The IF . . . THEN . . . syntax is "If sun-above-horizon, then *not* nighttime."

If a logical implication is used as a test or query, rather than as a constraint, it is expressed as follows:

$$S \overset{?}{\to} U$$

The rule type indicator now shows a superscripted ?. This indicates that the truth value of the rule is not required to be true but rather must be determined and could in fact be false. In other words, this rule indicates a logical implication used as a test or a query rather than as a constraint. The rule should now be read as a question: "Does S imply U?" The IF . . . THEN . . . syntax is "If S, then U?"

A convenient alternative form for logical implications used as tests or queries is the following. This alternative form helps emphasize the questioning nature of such usage.

$$S \to U?$$

---

26. Remember that the truth value of a constraint can never be false—thus false (or F) is never an option for its rule type indicator, even if the rule involves negation.

This rule (logical implication) is assumed to be a test or query.[27]

A rule without a question mark or other rule type indicator is always assumed to be a constraint, rather than a test or query. For example, the following rule is assumed to be a constraint:

$$S \rightarrow U$$

In our experience with real-life business problems involving hundreds or thousands of rules, the large majority of rules do not have natural names, and no name is ever required for them. For convenience, however, rules can be given one or more names. Naming a rule is especially useful when one rule needs to refer to another—for example, in cases of rules that express exceptions. Here are two examples of naming rules:

$$R1: S \rightarrow U$$

This rule has been named *R1*. The rule (actually its truth value) can now be referenced by that name.

$$\text{Rule-for-daytime1: sun-above-horizon} \rightarrow \text{daytime}$$

This rule has been named *Rule-for-daytime1*. The rule (actually its truth value) can now be referenced by that name should the need arise, just like any other named logical expression.

As mentioned earlier, a rule is not limited to a single LHT. Any logical connective (for example, AND, OR,[28] and even logical implication itself) can be used to construct more complex expressions.[29] Any such expressions, including those formed by NOT, are called *left-hand expressions* (LHEs) for convenience. (An LHE is also permitted to consist of only a single LHT.)

---

27. C. J. Date points out, "The answer to the question is *empirical*. If you get a 'yes' you can still only say something like 'the current state of the [factbase] *is not inconsistent with the hypothesis that* S implies U.' For example, does 'being an employee' imply 'being under 50 years old'? The answer is no, but the [factbase] might currently happen to suggest that the answer is yes" (private correspondence, November 19, 2001, original emphasis).

28. Like the rule symbol, these are actually the names for (Boolean) functions, which must be supported by some (automatic) computational process. Refer to Appendix G for additional discussion with respect to higher-order rules.

29. The truth-valued comparative operators GT, GE, EQ, NE, LE, and LT can also be used, but these need not be illustrated since their use is straightforward.

Some examples are given below. All of these examples are constraints, but corresponding examples of tests or queries could also be expressed.

S AND U AND W → Z

This example uses the logical operator AND twice to build a more complex LHE for the rule.[30] The rule should be read "S and U and W implies Z." It could also be written as follows: OR ((NOT (S AND U AND W)), Z). Expressed in IF . . . THEN . . . syntax it becomes "If S and U and W, then Z." The implication is that *all three* LHTs must be true in order for this rule to consider Z to be true. In other words, any one of S, U, or W alone (or any pairs thereof) being true does *not* imply Z to be true. The importance of this point will become apparent shortly.

motor-on AND brake-off AND in-gear → car-can-go

This example uses the logical operator AND twice to build a more complex LHE for the rule. The rule should be read "Motor-on and brake-off and in-gear implies car-can-go." It could also be written as follows: OR ((NOT (motor-on AND brake-off AND in-gear)), car-can-go). Expressed in IF . . . THEN . . . syntax it becomes "If motor-on and brake-off and in-gear, then car-can-go." The implication is that *all three* LHTs must be true in order for this rule to consider car-can-go to be true. In other words, any one of motor-on, brake-off, or in-gear alone (or any pairs thereof) being true does *not* imply car-can-go to be true.

Here are two examples on using ORs.

S OR U OR W → Z

This example uses the logical operator OR twice to build a more complex LHE for the rule.[31] The rule should be read "S or U or W implies Z." Expressed in IF . . . THEN . . . syntax it becomes "If S or U or W, then Z." The implication is that this rule will consider Z to be true if any *one* (or more) of the three LHTs are true.

it-is-raining OR melting-ice OR flood-stage → streets-are-wet

---

30. We assume the precedence or priority of the AND operator is higher than that of logical implication, so the AND operator is evaluated before the logical implication.
31. We assume the precedence or priority of the OR operator is higher than that of logical implication, so the OR operator is evaluated before the logical implication.

This example uses the logical operator OR twice to build a more complex LHE for the rule. The rule should be read "It-is-raining or melting-ice or flood-stage implies streets-are-wet." Expressed in IF ... THEN ... syntax it becomes "If it-is-raining or melting-ice or flood-stage, then streets-are-wet." The implication is that this rule will consider streets-are-wet to be true if any *one* (or more) of the three LHTs are true. Refer to the related boxed item for discussion of the relationship between ORs in LHTs and atomic rule form using this multi-OR, streets-are-wet rule as an example.

The Atomic Form of Rules: ORs in LHTs

The multi-OR, streets-are-wet rule, with adjacent LHTs separated by ORs, can actually be expressed in more *atomic* form as three distinct rules, each with one of the three LHTs and all with streets-are-wet as the RHT, as follows:

R1: it-is-raining→ streets-are-wet

R2: melting-ice → streets-are-wet

R3: flood-stage → streets-are-wet

This observation raises interesting questions about when such splitting or *reduction* of rules with ORed LHTs should be undertaken. Our view is that the answer depends on the perspective at which the rule is specified. We find it is *not* desirable for rules expressed at the business manager's perspective. It is also generally not desirable for rules expressed at the system developer's perspective—at least when using higher-order rule types.

At the technical designer's perspective, reduction of rules to their most atomic form, at least internally to the rule-processing server, might be highly desirable.[32] *Or maybe not!* The answer might very well depend on the particular implementation scheme. In any event, such reduction raises questions beyond the scope of this tutorial.

 Formally, a rule is in atomic form only if both of the following are true:

- The rule has no ORs among its LHTs.
- The rule has no ANDs among its RHTs.

---

32. If a rule is reduced in this fashion, optimization might be required, recognizing common sub-expressions (C. J. Date, private correspondence, November 19, 2001).

ANDs and ORs can be mixed in the same rule. Parentheses might be necessary to ensure the proper order of evaluation, as shown in the next example.

$$(S \text{ AND } U) \text{ OR } W \rightarrow Z$$

This rule should be read "S and U (together), or W (alone), implies Z."[33]

As indicated previously, NOTs can also be used as appropriate.

$$S \text{ OR } (\text{NOT } U) \rightarrow W$$

This rule should be read "S or not U implies W."[34] This rule example bears closer examination. See anything interesting about the LHE? Refer to the boxed item, Using Rules in Specifying Other Rules.

Using Rules in Specifying Other Rules

Upon closer inspection, the NOT example (given again below) is quite interesting.

$$S \text{ OR } (\text{NOT } U) \rightarrow W$$

Note that the LHE for this rule, S OR (NOT U), can be rewritten in the form (OR (NOT U), S), which you might now recognize as the form for a logical implication (rule). Indeed, the above expression can be rewritten as follows:

$$(U \rightarrow S?) \rightarrow W$$

This revision of the former version shows a logical implication (rule) as the LHE. Note that the new logical implication (rule) is indicated as a test or query rather than as a constraint. This designation is appropriate since that logical implication is not required to be true. In other words, there is nothing *inevitably* true about the original LHE, S OR (NOT U).

---

33. This rule could be broken into two more atomic rules.
34. This rule could also be broken into two more atomic rules.

> Using logical implications as embedded tests or queries in the manner above is not particularly useful for rules expressed at such a basic level. It becomes far more useful, however, in expressing higher-order rules where the emphasis is on patterns. Indeed, this is a central idea in *The Business Rule Book* [Ross 1997].

Constraints: Rejection versus Inference

As earlier discussion explained, a constraint is simply a rule (logical implication) that must always be true. (*Always* here means, more precisely, "must always be true given instance terms for the class terms it mentions."[35]) A crucial question, however, has not yet been addressed: *What action should the business logic server take when a constraint needs to be enforced?* This circumstance happens specifically when any new state requested (by a user or application) for the logicbase is such that the LHE of a constraint would be true, but its RHE would be false.

There are two and only two choices when this circumstance occurs, as discussed below. (Refer to Appendix C for additional discussion.) See the boxed item, The Meanings of *Constraint*, for the discussion of the relationship between these two choices and the term *constraint*.

1. *Rejection:* The constraint can be instructed (by the specifier) to reject the new state—that is, to undo the results of whatever action tried to produce it. Such a constraint is called a *rejector*.

   Consider a simple rejector such as *An employee must have a name.* If any user or application attempts an action that would leave an employee without a name (as represented in the factbase), the business logic server would cause that action to be rejected (that is, to fail).

2. *Inference:* The constraint can be instructed (by the specifier) to indicate the RHE as now being true. In this case there is never any rejection of user or application actions. Instead, when the requested state of the logicbase is such that the LHE of a constraint is true but its RHE is false, the

---

35. The next chapter discusses predicates. We view a constraint to be a predicate. Like any predicate, a constraint cannot be either true or false until it is instantiated.

business logic server simply infers that the RHE has now become true. By this means, the constraint is said to enable inference or logical deduction by the business logic server.

Consider the following simple inference-type rule statement (not in RuleSpeak form to facilitate discussion): *Anyone who is female and of age should be considered a woman.* If any user or application takes an action such that the factbase indicates both *female* and *of age* are true, the business logic server will automatically *infer* that *woman* is true.[36] This example is worked out more fully later in this chapter.

The Meanings of *Constraint*

Constraint clearly has a different sense in inferencing or logical deduction than the sense typical for environments where traditional database products have been used. For the latter environments, *constraint* typically is taken to mean that any event should be rejected that would leave the database in an inconsistent state. Inferencing-type rules are also constraints, but for them, there is *no* rejection. Just the opposite: new truths are derived from existing truths.

Does this mean that there is a fundamental difference between *constraint* for inferencing or logical deduction and for database environments? The answer is *yes and no.*

At the most fundamental level, the answer is *no.* In both cases, constraints are formally rules (logical implications) that must be true. Recognizing this deep equivalence is critical since it means that both kinds spring from common theoretical roots.

At a higher level, the answer is *yes.* In business logic servers, the two kinds must exist side by side so this important distinction *must* be recognized. (Refer to Appendix C for additional discussion.)

This recognition has not been so important in the past. In practice, there has been virtually no overlap in software tools for inferencing (for example, expert systems) and software tools for managing "databases" (that is, database management systems). As this tutorial emphasizes, however, that separation *must* now end.

---

36. Actually, if the truth values of *any* two of the variables are known, the business logic server can infer the truth value of the third (C. J. Date, private correspondence, November 19, 2001).

The woman rule above shows that inference-type rules require the business logic server to make an assessment of the logicbase and possibly change the value of the rule's RHE. Often, such action logically cascades into more assessments, since one rule's RHE is often another rule's LHE. Such activity is commonly known as *inferencing* or *logical deduction.* [37]

The following simple example (using R-Notation for the rules) illustrates this. In Chapter 17, after discussing predicates and facts (which are not used below), we will revisit this same example.

Constraint statement at the business manager's perspective: *Anyone who is female and of age should be considered a woman.*

True-false question: Is Mary a woman?

Constraints:

female AND of age → woman

"Mary" → female

"Mary" → of age

Female, of age, and *woman* are Boolean variables. "Mary" is a name for a real-world person. For the sake of simplicity, let's assume that any literal can be taken to imply true. Note that in essence the latter two rules are merely giving the business logic server some starting-point "data"[38] to work from. This "data" could be expressed better as facts—but that would require predicates, which have not yet been discussed![39]

Answer: Yes (true)

By logical deduction, *female* and *of age* are evaluated (inferred) to be true (by the business logic server). Then, in turn, *woman* is evaluated (inferred) to be true. Therefore, the answer to the question is yes—"Mary" is indeed a

---

37. In the literature of logic-based databases, a distinction is therefore made between a *deductive axiom* (something found to be true through inferencing) and a *ground axiom* (something taken to be true as a given). See Date [2000a, p. 784]. The same distinction applies in the relational model. Although the terminology is different, the concepts are the same (C. J. Date, private correspondence, November 19, 2001).

38. That is, ground axioms.

39. This system will not work when "data" about a second person, male or female, is introduced (unless the user or application discards the "Mary" "data" first). This shortcoming is one reason why treatment of facts and predicates is so fundamentally important.

woman. Refer to Appendix J for a step-by-step explanation. For discussion of support for inferencing by business logic servers, refer to the boxed item, Forward Chaining versus Backward Chaining.

Forward Chaining versus Backward Chaining

Inferencing or logical deduction as illustrated by the "Mary" example can be done in any of several ways, including the following.

- As above, starting from "Mary" and working through the other rules to see if *woman* can be reached (that is, proves true). This approach is sometimes called *forward-chaining* or *data-driven reasoning*.
- Starting from *woman* and working back through the other rules to see if they support that inference. This approach is sometimes called *backward-chaining* or *goal-driven reasoning*.[40]

The choice of which chaining technique the business logic server should employ for any particular case of inferencing should be completely hidden from all users and applications. This separation of logical expression of inference-type rules from their mechanical (that is, physical) implementation is a crucial feature for business logic servers.

We view this separation as one of two fundamental dimensions for Rule Independence. The more obvious dimension, as suggested earlier, is separation (or isolation) of rules from the *user's* procedural logic. Now we identify a second dimension—separation (or isolation) of business rules from the *implementer's* logic. (By *implementer's logic* I mean the evaluation logic of the business logic server.)

Behind the scenes (that is, invisible to users), of course, the choice of which inferencing approach is best to use for particular circumstances can be handed to system administrators who have an understanding of the characteristics of the logicbase and of the tools or algorithms available to optimize its evaluation. General heuristics are available for choosing the optimal approach in such selection.

---

40. C. J. Date [2000a, p. 775] indicates that logically this means trying to prove the contrapositive—in other words, instead of trying to prove p implies q, trying to prove that NOT q implies NOT p.

Ideally, the business logic server should have multiple algorithms at its disposal and should be sufficiently intelligent to choose the best one for any given case. In general terms, of course, this itself is a rule-oriented problem— and the business logic server should be able to use its *own* rule-processing capabilities to address it. Perhaps it could even continuously reengineer its own rules through trial and error to enhance them over time, becoming in effect a machine capable of learning from its own experience. We must, of course, view such capability as a long-term future objective.

 The second meaning of Rule Independence: The expression of business rules should be completely isolated from the implementer's logic—that is, from the evaluation logic of the business logic server, including forward chaining and backward chaining.

References

Charniak, Eugene, and Drew McDermott. 1985. *Introduction to Artificial Intelligence.* Reading, MA: Addison-Wesley.

Date, C. J. 2000a. *An Introduction to Database Systems* (7th ed.). Boston, MA: Addison-Wesley.

————. 2000b. *What Not How: The Business Rule Approach to Application Development.* Boston, MA: Addison-Wesley.

Elmasri, Ramez, and Shamkant B. Navathe. 1994. *Fundamentals of Database Systems* (2nd ed.). Redwood City, CA: Benjamin/Cummings.

Halpin, Terry. 2001. *Information Modeling and Relational Databases.* San Francisco, CA: Morgan Kaufmann.

Ross, Ronald G. 1997. *The Business Rule Book* (2nd ed.). Houston, TX: Business Rule Solutions, LLC. Available at *http://www.BRSolutions.com.*

CHAPTER 17

The Theoretical Foundation of Facts

About Predicates

Predicates and Facts

Thus far in Part V we have examined rules and terms. Let us now focus on *facts*. As evidenced by the core business rule principle *Rules build on facts, and facts build on terms*, the role of facts is fundamental. The boxed item, What Is a Fact?, takes a closer look at what facts represent.

> **What Is a Fact?**
>
> The everyday English definition of *fact* includes the following meanings[1]:
>
> - A thing done
> - The quality of being actual
> - Something that has actual existence
> - An actual occurrence
> - A piece of information presented as having objective reality

---

1. From *Merriam-Webster's Collegiate Dictionary*, 10th ed. (1999).

> The use of *fact* in this tutorial does not diverge from these meanings. However, we maintain that the answer to the question "What is a fact?" depends on your perspective. We will come back to this important issue later, after reviewing relevant ideas of predicate calculus.

The central idea in predicate calculus—*predicates*—provide the formal basis for facts in the business rule approach.[2]

To understand the concept of predicates, we believe it is very important to distinguish between the three audiences discussed earlier (see Chapter 15). Corresponding to these three perspectives are three parallel interpretations of *predicate*, each correct and necessary, we believe, in its own way. Let us now examine each of these in turn.

Predicate at the Business Manager's Perspective

At the business manager's perspective, *predicate* follows the everyday definition of the word, as follows: "The part of a sentence or clause that expresses what is said of the subject and that usually consists of a verb with or without objects, complements, or adverbial modifiers."[3] Incidentally, in one way or another, this orientation toward sentences is characteristic of *predicate* at the other two perspectives as well, as we will see later. First, here is an example:

"An employee works in a department."

The subject of this sentence (a fact, or more precisely, a fact *statement*[4]) is "employee." The predicate, which asserts something about that subject, is "works in a department." This predicate also includes an object, "department." See the related boxed item for a note on subjects and objects.

---

2. The term *fact* is often used in formal and informal discussions of *predicate* in the literature of artificial intelligence and expert systems. Refer to Charniak and McDermott [1985, pp. 13, 20, 337].

3. From *Merriam-Webster's Collegiate Dictionary*, 10th ed. (1999).

4. For convenience, I will often use the word *fact* instead of the more correct *fact statement* in the discussion that follows. The distinction is that the same fact can be given by statements in different forms and/or by statements in different languages (for example, French, Mandarin, and so on). In other words, there can be many different *fact statements* for exactly the same *fact*.

> **About Subjects and Objects**
>
> The kind of sentences we are interested in here always have clear subjects and usually have objects. This pattern is not always strictly followed, of course, in everyday speech. For example, we might hear utterances such as such as "Let's go with it!," or "Any coffee left?," or "Here is a good one." For our purposes, we are not interested in utterances of these kinds.
>
> It is *very* important not to read too much into *subject* and *object* at this perspective. We are *not* talking about "data" things or objects as IT professionals might understand them. Rather, the subjects and objects should be viewed as representing *real* people, places, things, concepts, and so on, of the business.

An essential step in capturing business rules from businesspeople is identifying and defining all such potential subjects (and objects) within the relevant scope. Those potential subjects and objects are the *terms* at this perspective. By means of definitions and declarative statements such as the above, businesspeople are encouraged to convey how these terms (or more precisely, the underlying concepts) interrelate.

These interrelationships represent fundamental *facts* about the business. At this perspective, a fact is simply an assertion about one or more terms. It represents something that can be known about the business at the operational level, which is essential to support what the business does. See the boxed item, Another Look at Expressing Rules, for how these assertions relate to rules.

A fact is assumed true at the business manager's perspective if the businesspeople *agree* that it is true. If they disagree about an assertion being true, then for our purposes it is *not* a fact—at least until such time that the disagreement is resolved, if ever.

> **Another Look at Expressing Rules**
>
> At the business manager's perspective, it is natural and relatively easy to express rules as predicates in the sense above. For example, we might say, "An employee *must* work in a department." For this reason, RuleSpeak emphasizes
>
> *continued*

carefully choosing a *subject* for every rule statement.[5] (Refer to Part III for additional discussion.)

Also, the business rule approach highlights the idea that rules always build directly on facts. In RuleSpeak this means simply adding a rule word (that is, *must, only,* or *should*) to one or more fact statements. (Refer to Part III for in-depth discussion.) The rule statement above, *An employee must work in a department,* provides a trivial example. In this case, the rule word *must* is added to the fact "An employee works in a department" to form the rule.

It follows that since all facts have subjects at the business manager's perspective, all rules naturally will as well. Note that this observation runs counter to use of the IF . . . THEN . . . syntax for expressing rules at the business manager's perspective. (Refer to Appendix D for additional discussion.)

Predicate at the System Developer's Perspective

At the system developer's perspective, predicates and facts are viewed in the following way. The starting point should be some fact given at the business manager's perspective.[6] The name of the fact (that is, predicate) is created by removing the subject and all objects, if any,[7] from the fact. For an additional view of predicates, see the boxed item, Halpin on Predicates.

Let us return to the example used earlier.

"An employee works in a department."

This fact makes an assertion about the two terms "employee" and "department." The name of the fact (that is, the predicate) is formed by removing the subject ("employee") and the object ("department") as well as the article ("An"), producing simply ". . . works in. . . ."[8]

---

5. This subject actually can be a term (as in the given example), a fact, or another rule. An example of a fact as a subject is the following: *The person who manages a department must not be an employee working in that department.* The subject of this rule is the fact "Person manages department."

6. In general, it *should* be if the logicbase is developed in top-down fashion.

7. And all articles, such as *a, an, the,* and so on.

8. This approach does not preclude this same name ". . . works in . . ." from being used as the name for some other predicate. For example, in the same logicbase we might also have the fact "Employee works in shift." Obviously some means for distinguishing the predicate names at the metalevel is required.

Halpin on Predicates

Terry Halpin defines predicate as follows: "... basically a sentence with object-holes in it. To complete the sentence, the object-holes or placeholders are filled in by object-terms" [Halpin 2001, pp. 63–64]. Our view of predicate at the system developer's perspective is consistent with this definition.

For the example "... works in ...", each object-hole is represented by an ellipsis (...). The object-terms necessary to fill in the object-holes and thus complete the sentence (that is, give the full predicate), are "employee" and "department," respectively.

Again, it is important not to read too much into *object-term*. Halpin defines *object* in this usage as follows: "[a] thing of interest. An object may be either an entity or a value" [Halpin 2001, p. 714].[9] This corresponds closely to the use of *term* in the business rule approach. (Refer to Appendix E for related definitions.)

As this discussion indicates, a fact at the system developer's perspective represents an assertion about one or more terms.[10] It is important that the fact be worded as clearly and precisely as possible, not only to avoid ambiguities but also to provide an increasingly precise wording template for any rules based on that fact.

Such tight correlation between facts and rules becomes especially important as the number of rules grows and their complexity increases. Incidentally, this is an additional problem that RuleSpeak addresses.

Are all facts proper predicates? The answer is no. Predicate calculus requires every predicate to include at least one class term. If a fact does *not* include at least one class term—that is, if it includes only instance terms—then predicate calculus calls the fact a *proposition*.[11] An example might be the fact "Mary works in the payroll department."

---

9. Halpin also writes, "A term is a lexical expression—it may reference another object (if the object is an entity) or simply reference itself (if the object is a value)" (private correspondence, September 9, 2001).

10. Halpin [2001, pp. 60–92] uses the term *fact* extensively in his approach. Refer to Appendix E for his definition of *fact* and of other related terms.

11. Or, sometimes, a *degenerate predicate*.

Facts that include only instance terms are *not* prohibited in the business rule approach. Indeed, they are sometimes necessary for specifying rules at the system developer's perspective. We will return to this point later.

Predicate at the Technical Designer's Perspective

As always for the technical designer's perspective, the prescribed approach—in this case regarding predicates—depends on the choice of technology. Again, we find the approach of Date and Darwen [2000] in *Foundation for Future Database Systems: The Third Manifesto* to be an attractive one, worthy of closer examination. Refer to the boxed item, Terminology of *The Third Manifesto*, for a quick overview of their terminology. After that, let us more closely explore the essential elements of their approach that pertain to this discussion.

Terminology of *The Third Manifesto*

In the Date and Darwen [2000] approach, a relation as a whole should be viewed as a value. This value must be held in an appropriate variable—specifically, a named container capable of holding relation-type values. They call such a variable a *relation variable*, abbreviated in their work as *relvar*.

The value (that is, relation) held in a relvar includes a heading, which provides the name and type (named, of course) of each column. (*Type* is used here in the sense of *data type* as in programming languages.) These names are the actual terms in the sense of predicate calculus. (Refer to Appendix B for additional discussion and examples.)

At the business manager's and system developer's perspectives, the relationship of *predicate* with sentences has been explicit and relatively obvious. At the technical designer's perspective, it becomes implicit and not at all obvious.

In particular, all fact names (that is, verb wordings) are removed from the system developer's version of the predicate such that the predicate now becomes entirely "objectified." This "objectification" organizes the information in a manner well suited for the automated environment.

To illustrate *predicate* effectively at this perspective, we need to expand the above example somewhat, as shown below.[12]

"An employee has an identifier, also has a name, works in a department, and earns a salary."

This fact is clearly composite (and probably incomplete). It has been written in this nonatomic form simply for clarity. Date [2000, p. 256] would call such statements informal or *external* predicates, meaning they are "understood by users, but not by the system."

If we are implementing in a relational environment, we could create the following relvar to hold these facts. Only the heading for the relvar is shown (along with the relvar name). This heading, along with any relevant constraints that might have been specified (there are none in this example[13]), is what Date calls the relvar's formal or *internal* predicate. (See the boxed item, The Golden Rule, for an important note on constraints in this context.) Date indicates that the internal predicate "is understood by both users *and* the system" [Date 2000, p. 256].

EMP

EMP# : EMP#	ENAME : NAME	DEPT# : DEPT#	SALARY : MONEY

Note the following comments.

- The name of this relvar is "EMP," an abbreviation for "employee."
- There are four attributes or columns in this relvar. (The second name in each pair of names is the domain or type on which the attribute is defined.) The names of each of these four attributes or columns can be taken as terms known to the system.
- The order of these terms (or more precisely, attribute-and-type pairs) is *not* significant. In other words, there is no inherent meaning to the order in which the columns of the relvar appear. This is a by-product of the "objectification" of the predicate.

---

12. This example is based on Date [2000, p. 66].
13. We could easily add some constraints—for example: (a) EMP.SALARY < 100K; (b) {EMP.DEPT#} subset of {DEPT.DEPT#}; (c) employee numbers unique; and so on (C. J. Date, private correspondence, November, 19, 2001).

- Presumably, there is another relvar (not shown) corresponding to "department." The values of DEPT# would refer to rows (tuples) of that other relvar.
- Collectively, the four name pairs are called the *heading* of the relvar. This heading, along with any relevant constraints that might have been specified (there are none in this example[14]), is the relvar's *internal* predicate.

The Golden Rule[15]

Although I am not illustrating constraints in this example, it is *very* important to recognize that constraints are also considered part of the relvar's predicate. This fact leads to The Golden Rule for relvars: *"No update operation must ever be allowed to leave any relvar in a state that violates its own [internal] predicate."*

Incidentally, The Golden Rule applies to all relvars—including *logical views*—a fact of significant consequence for inferencing and deduction. An example showing how logical views relate to inferencing and deduction is given later in this chapter.

Date also extends these notions to the logicbase as a whole. He defines a *database predicate* as the "logical AND of all database and relvar constraints that apply to the database in question." The extended version of The Golden Rule consequently includes this: *". . . no update operation[16] is allowed to leave the database in a state that violates its own predicate."*

Note that in the relvar's internal predicate, the verb phrases in the original fact statement (external predicate) have disappeared—that is, "employee *has an* identifier," "employee *has a* name," "employee *works in* department," and "employee *earns* salary" have all become *implicit*. They have become objectified in the sense that they are represented by terms rather than by verb phrases.

---

14. As noted before, some constraints could be easily added.

15. The discussion of The Golden Rule in this context is based on Date [2000, pp. 254–256]. Quotations in this boxed item are from p. 256 of that work.

16. *Operation* is more accurate than the term *transaction*, which appears in the original text (C. J. Date, private correspondence, November, 19, 2001). *Operation* appears in Date [2001].

Nonetheless, it is important to recognize that even though objectified in this fashion, the internal predicate's implicit sense of "sentences" is still very real. Here is what Date has to say about the above example, which is actually his own [Date 2000, p. 66, original emphasis]:

In a nutshell, therefore:

- *Types* are the (sets of) things we can talk about;
- *Relations* are (sets of) things we say about the things we can talk about.

(There is a nice analogy here that might help you appreciate and remember these important points: *Types are to relations as nouns are to sentences.*) Thus [in the relation above] the things we can talk about are employee numbers, names, department numbers, and money values, and the things we say are true utterances of the form "The employee with the specified employee number has the specified name, works in the specified department, and earns the specified salary."

By convention, the rows (tuples) in a relvar at a given time are taken to correspond to "true facts" (or, more precisely, propositions that evaluate to true at that time).[17] For example, suppose a row with the following values were found in the EMP relvar: employee number, "1065"; employee name, "P. Jones"; department, "HR"; and salary, "65,000". This row can be taken to mean that the following fact is true: "The employee with employee number '1065' has the name 'P. Jones,' works in the 'HR' department, and earns the salary '$65,000.'"

This point of view leads to a very different perception of "data" and "databases" than most people currently have, but one that aligns perfectly with the business rule approach. Date sums this point up nicely as follows.

There is another (and important) way of thinking about what data and databases really are. The word *data* derives from the Latin for "to give"; thus, data is really *given facts*, from which additional facts can be inferred" [Date, 2000, p. 13, original emphasis].[18]

---

17. It is important to remember that a row (tuple) must have satisfied the relevant internal predicate (including relevant constraints) to be included in the relvar in the first place.
18. The term *fact* is often used in discussion of *deductive* database systems. For more information, refer to Date [2000, p. 787] and Elmasri and Navathe [1994, pp. 730, 736].

The formal definition for predicate in the technical designer's view, however, is actually broader than that. Date's definition is as follows: A predicate is "a *truth-valued function*—i.e., a function that, given appropriate arguments for its parameters, returns either *true* or *false*" [Date 2000, p. 777, original emphasis].

Facts: Type versus Instance

As discussed above at each of the three perspectives, a fact always corresponds directly or indirectly to a declarative sentence in English, which asserts something about its terms. Here is an example:

"The customer Acme Supply places order a601."

This sentence makes an assertion, "places," about the terms "customer Acme Supply" and "order a601." Assuming this sentence is true, it can be considered literally to be a fact.

Certain terms in this sentence, specifically "Acme Supply" and "a601," presumably stand for or represent actual things in the real world. These names are instance terms. Certain other terms, "customer" and "order," appear to stand for or represent classes of like things to which the former things belong, respectively. These names are class terms. (Refer to the boxed item, A Note on Representing Class Terms, regarding related conventions for this discussion.)

> **A Note on Representing Class Terms**
>
> At this point, I will start using names with an initial capital letter for class terms that might be viewed as *business objects* or *entity types* at the system developer's perspective. However, I stress that this carries no innate meaning for either formal logic or machines. The convention is merely used here as a way to focus attention on the core kinds of things in the business.

Let us then rewrite the original sentence so that it mentions only instance terms or only class terms. We thereby produce two sentences, as follows:

Sentence 1: "Acme Supply places a601."

Sentence 2: "Customer places Order."

Sentence 1 contains only instance terms. Sentence 2 contains only class terms.[19]

Based on this instance versus class differentiation in terms, we can call the former sentence[20] (assuming it is true) a *fact instance*, and the latter sentence a *fact type*. Refer to the related boxed item for a note about the choice of terminology here.

- *Fact instance:* A fact instance contains only instance terms, no class terms. Sentence 1 above, "Acme Supply places a601," is a fact instance. It requires no further resolution because each of the terms (that is, "Acme Supply" and "a601") denotes an instance rather than a class.
- *Fact type:* A fact type always contains at least one class term.[21] Sentence 2, "Customer places Order," is a fact type because it contains two class terms, Customer and Order. It cannot be evaluated until appropriate instance terms are substituted for these two class terms. One such substitution for the two class terms, of course, could be "Acme Supply" and "a601," respectively. Given this substitution, or *instantiation* of the predicate, the truth of the expression now *can* be ascertained.

A Note on Terminology: *Fact Instance* and *Fact Type*

At the system developer's perspective, practitioners usually mean *fact type* when talking about "facts." At the technical designer's perspective, practitioners usually mean *fact instance* when talking about "facts." This inconsistency produces unfortunate confusion. I will avoid any ambiguity by always explicitly saying either *fact instance* or *fact type* from now on when it makes a difference in the given context.

In this book I do not offer any recommendation about what term should be used for *fact instance* at the technical designer's perspective. Date and

continued

---

19. In predicate calculus, the terms Customer and Order denote *free variables* in the context of sentence 2. Since they are not variables in the familiar sense of programming languages, C. J. Date suggests that *parameter* is a better term for them (C. J. Date, private correspondence, November, 19, 2001).
20. In predicate calculus, this would be viewed as a proposition.
21. But by definition, never a function, rule, and so on in the business rule approach.

Darwen [2000] demonstrate formally that a factbase can be constructed at an atomic level from only values, variables, and types—*instance* is extraneous. In other words, *instance* has no useful definition that is not the same as either value or variable.[22]

In this discussion I have chosen *fact type* over alternatives (for example, *fact template* or *fact pattern*) for the sake of common usage. However, as discussed earlier, I recognize that the use of *type* invites ambiguity. *Type* (as in *data type*) has a specific meaning in programming languages[23]—and what I mean by fact type does *not* conform to that definition.

Other possibilities considered but discarded for *fact type* include *relationship instance* and *relationship type*. These terms have proven much less comfortable to the business community than to IT professionals. I think *fact*, with its correct, commonsense connotation, is much better in this regard.

The complete set of all "true" fact instances that have been presented and accepted at a point in time is what we call a *factbase*. Any fact instance in such a factbase is called a *base fact*.

The distinction between *fact instance* and *base fact* should be noted carefully. These terms are not synonymous. A fact instance can be either a base fact (one given in the factbase) or a derived fact. A *derived fact* is inferred by the action of one or more inference rules from other fact instances.[24]

The equivalent distinction can be made between *base fact type* and *derived fact type*.[25] A *derived fact type* is any fact type specified as the RHE of an *inference rule*.[26]

---

22. Based on C. J. Date, private correspondence, August 24, 2001. Putting it even more strongly, Date later said, ". . . the term is *worse* than useless, because it leads to confusion" (C. J. Date, private correspondence, November, 19, 2001, original emphasis).
23. Including database theory, such as in Date and Darwen [2000].
24. For the most part, this discussion is concerned with *base facts* rather than *derived facts*. Therefore, for convenience, from this point on in the discussion I will simply say *fact* whenever I really mean *base fact*.
25. Refer to Ross [1997, pp. 108–109] for discussion of derived fact types.
26. For the most part, this discussion is concerned with *base fact types* rather than *derived fact types*. Therefore, for convenience, from this point on in the discussion I will simply say *fact type* whenever I really mean *base fact type*.

We call the complete set of base fact types that have been presented and accepted a *fact model*.[27] At the technical designer's perspective, such a fact model corresponds to a database schema or definition. In that sense, a factbase corresponds directly to what most people think of as a "database."

As this discussion indicates, the business rule approach suggests that a much more productive way to think about "data" (and "database" and "database design")—especially at the business manager's perspective—can be achieved by replacing the term *data* with the term *fact*.[28] *Facts* suggests that the database should be correct—unfortunately, *data* does not carry the same weight in that regard. We believe that integrity (that is, correctness, or at least consistency) is *the* issue in "database"—after all, *what good is the "data" if it is not correct?*[29]

The Existence Principle

Included in the notes on predicate calculus given at the beginning of Part V were the following observations.

> Some predicates require more than one argument. For example, if *B* is the predicate 'bigger than,' then *Bxy* denotes the assertion '*x* is bigger than *y*'. Thus *B* requires two arguments. . . . If we try to use *B* with only one argument, we obtain something like *Bx*, i.e., '*x* is bigger than'. This . . . is only a meaningless combination of symbols. In analogy with English grammar, we could say that *Bxy* is like a grammatically correct sentence, while *Bx* is merely a sentence fragment. Such fragments play no role in the predicate calculus [Simpson 2000, p. 5].

---

27. A fact model should address all relevant business questions, including the naming of predefined instances. As discussed in Part IV, development of such terminology often requires an extension to the fact model called an *instance model*. At the technical designer's perspective, such instances can become permissible values defined for *domains* (or types) as in Date and Darwen [2000].

28. With respect to "data models," our problem is not with *graphic* models—indeed, graphic models can be quite useful for fact modeling—but rather with the emphasis on "data."

29. As mentioned earlier, *consistent* is actually a more precise term here. The business logic server cannot really know if the logicbase is *correct* with respect to the external real world it purports to reflect. Also, note that 100 percent correctness could often be very expensive as a real-life business matter and therefore not the optimal tradeoff at the business manager's perspective. For example, consider what it would take to keep a large sales prospects address database 100 percent correct! (Example provided by Allan Kolber, private correspondence, August 24, 2001.)

We can now understand more clearly what these observations mean, again using the example above to illustrate.

Fact type: "Customer places Order."

Statement 1: "Acme Supply places a601."

Statement 1 represents a grammatically correct sentence. Instance terms for both of the class terms, Customer and Order, have been given.

Statement 2: "Best Supply Ltd. places."

Statement 2 does not represent a grammatically correct sentence. An instance term for only one of the class terms, Customer, has been given. As such, the statement is merely a "sentence fragment" and *must* be rejected.

The business rule approach depends on this basic assumption of predicate calculus. As described earlier, in the business rule approach, facts build on terms (and rules build on facts). It follows then that in giving base facts, not only must instance terms be provided for each of the class terms but that these instance terms must be valid ones as well. In other words, *these instance terms must exist in their own right.*[30] We call this the *Existence Principle.*

The Existence Principle

The following must be true about every fact: Given its fact type, each instance term for each class term must exist in its own right.

In the example given as statement 1 above, the Existence Principle requires that both "Acme Supply" and "a601" exist in their own right. If they do not, the fact instance must be rejected under the business rule approach.[31]

---

30. Remember that we are talking here only about base facts. There is a well-known example that illustrates that this observation might not be true for derived facts: "The present King of France is bald." Assume a statement in predicate calculus of the form "For all x, if x is the King of France, then x is bald." This statement evaluates to true, even though France has no King at the present time. Note, however, that the fact type "x is bald" is the RHE of the given inference rule and therefore is a derived fact.

31. What happens at the technical designer's perspective might be a different matter. For example, the technical designer might specify that for a given class term in a given fact type, an instance of the term should be created automatically when any fact is given that specifies an instance term that does not already exist. The operational effect would satisfy the Existence Principle.

The Existence Principle can be expressed more formally in the following way. A fact type always implies one or more rules (logical implications) about the terms it involves. This is illustrated in the following example:

Fact type: "Customer places Order."

Rule 1: *Customer places Order → Customer*

Rule 2: *Customer places Order → Order*

The first rule should be read "Any instance of the fact 'Customer places Order' implies that Customer exists." The second rule should be read "Any instance of the fact 'Customer places Order' implies that Order exists." For database professionals, these observations will have a familiar ring to them. Refer to the boxed item, About Referential Integrity.

About Referential Integrity

Some readers have probably recognized that this discussion pertains directly to what is traditionally called *referential integrity* in relational database design. Unfortunately, referential integrity has often been downplayed as a feature in commercial database management system (DBMS) products or not understood or used even when available.

This discussion emphasizes that such "data" integrity arises directly from the semantics of the factbase itself and is in no sense optional. Business logic servers *must* provide this fundamental and innate kind of business rule support.

For additional discussion about the issue of semantics in relational theory, including referential integrity, see Appendix F.

For the sake of emphasis, let us now combine the two rules above into a single rule with two RHTs (or, more precisely, RHEs in this case). The combined form includes a comma to indicate AND (a shorthand commonly used in this way). This combined (nonatomic) rule does not change the meaning of the original two rules in any way.

Combined rule: *Customer places Order → Customer, Order*

This rule indicates that every base fact for the fact type "Customer places Order" (the LHE) must include valid instance terms for each of the RHTs,

Customer and Order. In other words, a "places" base fact may exist only if *both* the Customer and the Order exist.

Included in the notes on predicate calculus given at the beginning of this tutorial was also the following observation:

> ... [I]n the predicate calculus [in contrast to Aristotelian logic], a subject is always an individual entity, never a class of entities. For example, an individual man can be treated as a subject, but the class of all men must be treated as a predicate. ... For example, if *M* is the predicate "to be a man" and *a* is the individual "Socrates," then *Ma* denotes the assertion "Socrates is a man" [Simpson 2000, p. 5].

Let us apply this restriction to the example above. We start with the following sentences:

Fact type: "Customer places Order."

Base fact: "Acme Supply places a601."

The class term Customer represents the set of all customers, including "Acme Supply." The class term Order represents the set of all orders, including "a601." According to predicate calculus (as above), both of these class terms *themselves* must also be treated as predicates. The names of these predicates could be (again as above) "to be a customer" and "to be an order," respectively. In keeping with our emphasis on sentences, however, we would prefer "Customer is" or "Customer exists," and "Order is" or "Order exists," respectively.

We can summarize as follows:

- In predicate calculus, what we think of as class terms are actually themselves predicates.
- A class term's predicate can be expressed as a sentence in the form "... is" or "... exists."
- The Existence Principle says that any instance term referenced in any base fact must also be an instantiation of its own predicate.[32]

---

32. Since it has satisfied its own predicate, by convention it can also be taken to be a "true fact."

- A final point: As above, we see that all terms, as well as all facts, are predicates.[33] In predicate calculus, *rules* are also predicates. A rule's predicate is simply one that adds the additional sense of *must* (or *only if* or *should*) to one or more underlying fact types (that is, to other predicates). Therefore, we can say that *all business rules are predicates.*

  All business rules are predicates.

A Brief Introduction to R-Notation for Facts

R-Notation proves convenient for specification of facts,[34] as illustrated below. (Refer to the boxed item, About Using R-Notation for Facts, for an important clarification.) This representation is aimed at the system developer's perspective. It is especially useful in building expressions for rules having higher-order rule types, as discussed in Chapter 18.

Fact: Customer ^{places} $\leftrightarrow$ Order

The *bidirectional arrow*[35] between the two terms, along with the superscripted predicate name ("places"), indicates that this expression is a fact. The use of the bidirectional arrow is also a reminder that instantiations of the predicate (base facts) require valid instance terms for each of the specified class terms, as required by the Existence Principle.[36]

All facts with two terms are potentially reversible[37]—that is, they can be "turned around." In other words, the second term can be indicated as the subject without changing the meaning of the fact. Of course, a different form of the verb phrase, or even a different choice of verb, is usually required for the revised form to read properly.

---

33. We must allow for degenerate predicates to cover fact instances.

34. Remember that *fact* at the system developer's perspective is usually taken to mean *fact type*, so I follow that usage in this discussion.

35. We recognize that bidirectional arrows are sometimes used in formal logic to represent *if and only if* (iff). However, we do not foresee that usage as being needed by (or even familiar to) the three primary audiences addressed in Part V.

36. Some system developers like to use role names when expressing facts. We suggest that these optional role names be put in brackets, as follows:
term-A[role name-1] $^{\text{predicate name}}$ $\leftrightarrow$ [role name-2]term-B.
A classic example is the following: flight[arriving flight] $^{\text{arrives at}}$ $\leftrightarrow$ [arrival city]city.

37. In data modeling and entity-relationship approaches, "relationship (types)" are said to be inherently *bidirectional.*

About Using R-Notation for Facts

I use R-Notation for facts in this discussion primarily to assist in explaining the-oretical issues, especially higher-order rules as discussed in Chapter 18. Inciden-tally, its use in that context clearly illustrates the powerful core principle of the business rule approach: *Rules always build on facts (and facts always build on terms).*

When reviewing the examples that follow here and in Chapter 18, please remember that we are attempting to do in a static, tutorial mode what could be extremely powerful and effective in a point-and-click environment.

For example, "Customer places Order" could be reversed and reworded as follows: "Order is placed by Customer." Note that there is no fundamental change in meaning.

Reversed-form fact: Order $\overset{\text{is placed by}}{\longleftrightarrow}$ Customer

This form of the fact is equivalent in meaning[38] to the original expression.

The following unified notation can be used to emphasize the inherent equivalence of the two versions.

Fact: Customer $\overset{\text{places}}{\longleftrightarrow} \overset{\text{is placed by}}{}$ Order

This example illustrates the optional additional inverse naming of the fact. From left to right, it reads "Customer places Order." From right to left it reads "Order is placed by Customer."

A fact, of course, can involve any number of terms, not just two. Refer to Appendix K for discussion and examples.

The examples above focused on *user-defined* facts. Several useful *pre-defined* or *built-in* fact types are also offered in R-Notation for facts. Refer to Appendix L for discussion.

---

38. That is, *semantically equivalent.*

R-Notation for facts can also be used to express tests or to ask questions. Such usage is often relevant when expressing higher-order rules. As before, we use the "?" symbol for this purpose.

Example: "Acme Supply"$^{INST} \leftrightarrow$ Customer?

The inclusion of the "?" symbol indicates that this expression is a question or test. A built-in fact type INST (*is instantiation of*) is indicated. This expression can be read "Is Acme Supply an instance of Customer?"

Inferencing and Deduction Revisited: Using Predicates

To conclude this 2discussion of predicates and facts, let us revisit the example of inferencing or logical deduction given at the end of Chapter 16. In particular, I now introduce the predicate Person and also the predicate Woman, which were not used in the earlier version.

The example is given at the technical designer's perspective. It also illustrates how inferencing or logical deduction is approached by Date and Darwen [2000].

PERSON

PERSON-NAME : NAME	FEMALE : BOOLEAN	OF-AGE : BOOLEAN

The heading for the relvar named Person represents the appropriate new predicate. This predicate can be instantiated with values (that is, "data") representing "Mary." Note that for the sake of simplicity, the attributes[39] *female* and *of-age* retain type Boolean in this version of the example. Although only three attributes or columns are shown in the heading, others of course could be added.

WOMAN

WOMAN-NAME : NAME

The heading for the relvar named Woman represents the appropriate new predicate. Although only one attribute or column is shown, others (perhaps

---

39. More precisely, Date views them as *parameters* (C. J. Date, private correspondence, November 19, 2001).

from Person) could of course be added to the example. This relvar is probably a logical view, but we will get to that point in a moment.

> Constraint statement at the business manager's perspective: *A person who is female and of age must be considered a woman.*
>
> Constraint[40]: (Person → female AND of-age?) → Woman

This two-part expression involves (1) a test using a logical implication to determine whether a given Person is both female and of age, and (2) a constraint, to indicate that such a person must be considered a Woman. Given this kind of constraint, Date and Darwen would consider Woman to be a *logical view* in the relational sense. In their approach, a logical view is considered to be a predicate whose instantiations are derived.

> The instantiation in which we are interested is for "Mary."
>
> Instantiation: Person {name = "Mary", female = true, of-age = true}

PERSON

PERSON-NAME : NAME	FEMALE : BOOLEAN	OF-AGE : BOOLEAN
Mary	true	true

> The appropriate row for "Mary" has been inserted into the relvar.
>
> The business logic server then makes the logical deduction and automatically populates the logical view Woman with "Mary."[41]

---

40. For simplicity, I give this constraint in R-Notation. The actual syntax of this constraint in predicate calculus might be as follows. (Note: *x* is a *bound variable* in the sense of predicate calculus.)

$$\text{Person } \{ \text{person-name} = x, \text{female} = \text{true}, \text{of-age} = \text{true} \} \rightarrow$$
$$\text{Woman } \{ \text{woman-name} = x \}$$

(Courtesy of Pedram Abrari, private correspondence, August 31, 2001.)

41. Logically, the instantiation of logical view Woman is immediate. Such instantiation must also satisfy all constraints given for Woman, if any. (None are given in this example.) When *physical* population of the relvar might occur, if ever, is a different matter. For example, such population might occur only when the logical view is actually put to use in some query. "Physical materialization of views is always to be avoided if possible" (C. J. Date, private correspondence, November 19, 2001).

WOMAN

WOMAN-NAME : NAME
Mary

True-false question at the business manager's perspective: Is Mary a woman? [42]

Query: Is-Mary-a-Woman: "Mary" ^{INST} $\leftrightarrow$ Woman?

Result: Is-Mary-a-Woman = true

This example is meant to show the logical—not necessarily physical—mechanisms of inference or logical deduction in the relational context. As this example illustrates, logical views play a crucial role. A logical view is nothing more than a predicate whose instantiations are derived through one or more rules of inference. There is considerable elegance in this approach.

Finally, as for the earlier version of this inferencing example in Chapter 16, although constraints are definitely present in this revised version, there is no sense of events being rejected to maintain integrity. As before, just the opposite is the case—these constraints ascertain *new* truths from existing ones. For additional discussion, refer to Appendix C.

References

Charniak, Eugene, and Drew McDermott. 1985. *Introduction to Artificial Intelligence*. Reading, MA: Addison-Wesley.

Date, C. J. 2001. "Constraints and Predicates: A Brief Tutorial (Part 2)." *Business Rules Journal* 2(9). Available at *http://www.BRCommunity.com/ a2001/b065b.html*.

————. 2000. *An Introduction to Database Systems* (7th ed.). Boston, MA: Addison-Wesley.

Date, C. J., and Hugh Darwen. 2000. *Foundation for Future Database Systems: The Third Manifesto* (2nd ed.). Boston, MA: Addison-Wesley.

---

42. For simplicity, I again use R-Notation here.

Elmasri, Ramez, and Shamkant B. Navathe. 1994. *Fundamentals of Database Systems* (2nd ed.). Redwood City, CA: Benjamin/Cummings.

Halpin, Terry. 2001. *Information Modeling and Relational Databases.* San Francisco, CA: Morgan Kaufmann.

Ross, Ronald G. 1997. *The Business Rule Book* (2nd ed.). Houston, TX: Business Rule Solutions, LLC. Available at *http://www.BRSolutions.com.*

Simpson, Stephen G. 2000. "Logic and Mathematics." Available at *http://www.math.psu.edu/simpson/.*

CHAPTER 18

Higher-Order Rules

Pattern-R Rule Types

The Definition of Pattern-R Rule Types

A rule (logical implication) based on a higher-order rule type has a higher level of expressive power than the rules discussed thus far. This higher level of expressive power arises because these rules incorporate not only a truth-valued function but a special "built-in" computational function, called the *yield-value function*, as well.

We call such higher-order rule types *Pattern-R rule types*. These rule types are discussed and illustrated in *The Business Rule Book* [Ross 1997].

Pattern-R rule types represent convenient shorthand expressions. Commonplace examples of Pattern-R rule types include *mandatory, mutually exclusive, unique, cyclic, frozen, timed,* and so on. Pattern-R rule types are aimed toward the system developer's perspective.

Each of these rule types represents some pattern that is found repeatedly among the rules typically specified for factbases—hence the name *Pattern-R*. There are numerous such patterns—indeed, *The Business Rule Book* identifies dozens more.

In many cases—probably most—specifying rules based on patterns will prove much more productive than doing so using the lower-level, *unpatterned* rules. We believe the potential usefulness of pattern-based rule specification is self-evident, especially for rejectors. C. J. Date comments on this point as follows.

> Recognizing frequently occurring patterns and building knowledge regarding them into "the system" effectively raises the level of abstraction. Among other things, it saves writing and simplifies thinking (like macros). A good example is "unique identification": This property *can* be expressed in a general constraint language, but the KEY shorthand is so much more convenient (not to mention the fact that it's probably capable of more efficient implementation).[1]

A Pattern-R rule type must be assembled directly from more basic components, including R-Notation rules and yield-value functions[2] of specified kinds. Such assembly, of course, is completely hidden to system developers when specifying actual Pattern-R rules. For their convenience, it is anticipated that the business logic server should offer many preassembled Pattern-R rule types.

All Pattern-R rules, by definition, are able to compute *something* apart from truth value. Sometimes this computation is for something simple, but usually it is for something more complex. Another way of saying this is that all Pattern-R rules must have some kind of computed yield value (the result of the yield-value function) *in addition to* the normal truth value. This fundamental (and powerful) feature is what distinguishes Pattern-R rules from "regular" rules [Ross 1997, pp. 3, 15–16, 35–37].

At the technology developer's perspective, a Pattern-R rule is defined formally as follows.[3]

- *Pattern-R rule:* An indivisible, two-part unit of business logic in the form of a rule (logical implication) of a known type.
- *Pattern-R rule type:* The type of a Pattern-R rule comprises both a logical function (that is, a truth-valued function) and a yield-value function

---

1. C. J. Date, private correspondence, November 19, 2001.
2. The computational function given as a yield-value function can be arbitrarily complex.
3. The correspondents(s) mentioned in the definition can also be executable operations (processes or procedures), but that takes us outside the realm of predicate calculus, so we will not discuss it here.

(which is not truth-valued). The logical function produces a set of truth values that is based on evaluating the results of the yield-value function. This yield-value function is evaluated for each specific occurrence of a reference point (called the *anchor*) and the anchor's associated correspondents. The anchor and correspondent(s) can be terms, facts, and/or other Pattern-R rules, as appropriate for the given rule.

The name of any Pattern-R rule type is the name given to its truth-valued function.[4] Thus names such as *mandatory, mutually exclusive, unique, cyclic, frozen, timed*, and so on are actually the names of truth-valued functions that have been included in the respective assemblies of these Pattern-R rule types.

Naturally, it is desirable to exploit existing operators, both logical and nonlogical, when establishing basic (that is, *atomic*) higher-order rule types. Such use of existing operators raises interesting questions, which are explored in Appendix G.

Pattern-R rules can be specified by using the same basic form as in R-Notation for rules given in Chapter 16. Since Pattern-R rules are higher-order, of course, we must also specify their types.[5] The following two examples illustrate. At the end of this chapter, we will look more closely at the assembly of the two Pattern-R rules used in these examples.

Examples of Pattern-R Rules

Example 1: The Monitor Rule[6]

Consider the following true-false question at the business manager's perspective:

> Question: Does a monitor attend two or fewer patients in critical condition?

---

4. We believe this truth-valued function can be viewed as a predicate, but that is not central to the definition.

5. From this point on, I will call all untyped rules *lower-order rules.*

6. This example is adapted with permission from *The Business Rule Book* [Ross 1997, p. 64].

The Pattern-R rule for this expression (unassisted by any graphic model[7]) would be given as follows.

Given: Patient $^{\text{is attended by}}\leftrightarrow{}^{\text{attends}}$ Monitor

Critical-Condition-Patient $^{\text{ISA}}\leftrightarrow$ Patient

Then: Monitor $^{\text{LIM, U, 2}}\rightarrow$ Critical-Condition-Patient?

Note several things about this example.

- The "givens" provide the relevant fact basis for the rule. The second fact uses the built-in fact type ISA, which means *is a category of* (or *is a subset of* or *is a subtype of*). (Refer to Appendix L for additional explanation.)
- The Pattern-R rule type for this rule is *limited*, abbreviated LIM, as indicated by the rule type indicator.
- Based on the Pattern-R rule type LIM, the rule will count (or if a constraint, *limit*) the number of fact instances for Critical-Condition-Patient (the correspondent) for any given instance of Monitor (the anchor).
- The "U" (for *upper*) and "2" are qualifiers for the rule, giving the appropriate threshold for the evaluation.
- For a given instance of Monitor, the condition (true-false question) will produce true if the number of Critical-Condition-Patients attended is two or fewer; otherwise it will produce false.

Note that this example represents a condition (as indicated by the "?") rather than a constraint. It could very easily be made into a constraint by simply removing the "?" as follows.

Constraint: Monitor $^{\text{LIM, U, 2}}\rightarrow$ Critical-Condition-Patient

Now the rule is a constraint. The rule statement at the business manager's perspective would be as follows: *A monitor must not attend more than two patients in critical condition.*

---

7. The "given" fact types in the example—that is, "attends" and the "ISA"—would probably be implicit if specification of the rule were built in a point-and-click manner based on some model (for example, a graphic fact model or data model).

Example 2: The Union Rule[8]

Consider the following true-false question at the business manager's perspective:

Question: Does a group include only nonunion employees exclusively or union employees exclusively?

The Pattern-R rule for this expression (unassisted by any model[9]) would be given as follows:

Given: Group $^{\text{includes}} \longleftrightarrow$ Employee

Non-Union-Employee $^{\text{ISA}} \longleftrightarrow$ Employee

Union-Employee $^{\text{ISA}} \longleftrightarrow$ Employee

Then: Group $^{\text{ME}} \longrightarrow$ Non-Union-Employee, Union-Employee?

This expression conveys many things.

- The "givens" provide the relevant *fact* basis for the rule. The second and third facts use the built-in fact type ISA, which means *is a category of* (or *is a subset of* or *is a subtype of*). (Refer to Appendix L for additional explanation.)
- The Pattern-R rule type for this rule is *mutually exclusive*, abbreviated ME, as indicated by the rule type indicator.
- Based on the Pattern-R rule type ME, the rule will evaluate whether each instance of Group (the anchor) "possesses" at least one instance for each of the two correspondents, Non-Union-Employee and Union-Employee.
- For a given instance of Group, the condition (true-false question) will produce true if the Group does *not* include both Non-Union-Employees and Union-Employees; otherwise it will produce false.

---

8. This example is adapted with permission from *The Business Rule Book* [Ross 1997, p. 92]. This example is presented as a constraint in that book; however, I will treat it first as a condition in this examination.

9. As before, the "given" fact types in the example—that is, "includes" and the two "ISAs"—would probably be implicit if specification of the rule were built in a point-and-click manner based on some model (for example, a graphic fact model or data model).

Note that this example represents a condition (as indicated by the "?") rather than a constraint. It could very easily be made into a constraint by simply removing the "?" as follows:

Constraint: Group $^{ME}\rightarrow$ Non-Union-Employee, Union-Employee

Now the rule is a constraint. The rule statement at the business manager's perspective would be as follows: *A group must not include more than one of the following:*

- *Non-Union-Employees*
- *Union-Employees*

The Assembly of Pattern-R Rule Types

As described earlier, the assembly[10] of any Pattern-R rule type involves two closely associated functions—a yield-value function and a truth-valued function.[11] Such assembly follows the general outline described below. (See the boxed item for an important note.) Each of the described functions uses normal notation for functions of the general form: $w = f(x, y \ldots)$.

Is This Assembly a Formalization of the Pattern-R Language?

To get right to the point, the answer is *no*. For a more comprehensive answer, refer to Appendix H.

Part 1: The Yield-Value Function

$$YV = yvfn_{(rule\ type)}(anchor, correspondent(s))$$

where $yvfn_{(rule\ type)}$ is the yield-value function dictated by the given Pattern-R rule type. Note the following comments on this function.

- The anchor of a Pattern-R rule corresponds *exactly* to the antecedent (that is, left-hand expression) of the rule if it were expressed in R-Notation for lower-order rules.

---

10. Again, it is important to remember that such assembly is completely hidden from users, including system developers in everyday use.

11. A *derived* Pattern-R rule type is defined on the basis of other (eventually atomic) Pattern-R rule types. So in that sense a Pattern-R rule type can have a *composite* logical function.

- The correspondent(s) of a Pattern-R rule would *generally* become the consequent (that is, the right-hand term) of the rule if it were expressed in R-Notation for lower-order rules. The parallel is not exact, however, since the correspondents must also satisfy the needs (parameters) of the rule's yield-value function.[12]
- YV is the name of a variable capable of holding the results (that is, yield values) of the yield-value function. As required for any function, this yield-value function must not produce more than one yield value for any given instance of the anchor. Refer to the related boxed item for additional discussion about the yield value.

> **More about the Yield Value**
>
> Yield values [Ross 1997, pp. 35–37] produced by a Pattern-R rule are held in a variable, which for convenience we call YV. This variable has a *type* (or data type) in the programming sense of that term. YV should be optionally visible to authorized users of the factbase, in which case it appears simply as a (read-only) derived attribute. The actual yield values might or might not be persistent—this choice, however, should be hidden by the business logic server from all everyday users.

Part 2: The Truth-Valued Function

$$TV = \text{tvfn}_{(\text{rule type})}(YV)$$

where $\text{tvfn}_{(\text{rule type})}$ is the truth-valued function as dictated by the Pattern-R rule type. Note the following comments on this function.

- The name given to the truth-valued function is the name of the Pattern-R rule type.[13]

---

12. A metarule for every Pattern-R rule is the following. For each instance of a rule's anchor (antecedent), at least one of the following must exist: yield value or at least one instance of any correspondent. This restriction ensures there is always a consequent.
13. Although not central to our arguments, we believe the *type* in Pattern-R rule *type* should also be viewed in the programming sense. *Type* in that sense requires (a) specification of a set of values and/or rules for how values of the type are formed, and (b) a set of operations whose implementations are hidden (encapsulated) appropriate to the type. For a Pattern-R rule type, this means the following, respectively: (a) a set of "atomic" rule types and a set of rules for producing derived rule types from them, and (b) yield-value function(s) that support evaluation of rules that have a given rule type.

- Truth-valued functions, of course, come in two varieties: constraints (which must produce true) and conditions[14] (which can produce either true or false). To simplify matters, a selection has not been indicated in this assembly, but it is easy to specify either variety (see Chapter 16). Recall the rule type indicators "T" and "?" used in R-Notation for rules.
- TV is the name of a Boolean variable used for the truth values produced by the truth-valued function.
- A truth-valued function *must* produce either true or false[15]—its result can never be indeterminate. If the result of the rule's yield-value function is indeterminate (that is, there is no yield value for a given instance of the rule's anchor), the truth-valued function can nonetheless produce true (for that instance) since indeterminate is the *correct* answer for the yield-value function. Refer to the boxed item, Examples of Indeterminate Results from Yield-Value Functions.

Examples of Indeterminate Results from Yield-Value Functions

The logical function of a Pattern-R rule must produce either true or false for each instance of its anchor. If the rule is a constraint, of course, it *must* produce true. What if the result of the yield-value function is indeterminate? Consider the following two sample cases:

Case 1: A Pattern-R rule requires division in its yield-value function. Suppose that for a specific instance of the anchor, this requires it to divide by zero. The rule can still produce true, since indeterminate is the *correct* answer for its yield-value function.

---

14. I really mean *higher-order conditions* since any condition used in defining higher-order rules will also have a higher-order rule type. For convenience, I will drop *higher-order* when referring to them in this discussion.

15. Note that the anchor of a condition can be another condition. In such case, the truth value of the former condition is the logical AND of the anchor's truth value *and* the result of its own truth-valued function. Informally, this simply means the test results for such conditions are cumulative, as is appropriate. Suppose this were not the case and the result of the truth-valued function of the former condition stood on its own. If the truth value of the anchor is false, the former condition—according to the rules of logical implication—would always be true (no matter what its own truth-valued function produced). That result would clearly be inappropriate.

> Case 2: A Pattern-R rule requires evaluation of each value in a series of values to determine whether it is ascending in value from the previous one. Consider the first value in the series. The rule can still produce true for that value, since indeterminate is the *correct* answer for its yield-value function in that case.[16]

In the remainder of this chapter, I outline the assembly of the two Pattern-R rule types used in the earlier two examples of Pattern-R rules.

Assembly of Example 1: The Monitor Rule

In reviewing the formal assembly for the Monitor Rule given earlier, we would find the following. Part 1, the yield-value function, is addressed first.

$$\text{count-of-critical-condition-patients} =$$
$$\text{yvfn}_{(LIM)} \, (\text{Monitor, Critical-Condition-Patient})^{[17]}$$

where $\text{yvfn}_{(LIM)}$ counts (as dictated by Pattern-R rule type LIM) the number of Critical-Condition-Patients (producing the result as the rule's yield value, in count-of-critical-condition-patients) for each instance of the rule's anchor, Monitor.

Now the truth-valued function is addressed.

$$\text{TV} = \text{tvfn}_{(LIM)}(\text{count-of-critical-condition-patients})$$

where $\text{tvfn}_{(LIM)}$, the truth-valued function, produces true or false for each yield value (in count-of-critical-condition-patients) as dictated by the Pattern-R rule type, LIM, and the given qualification ("upper limit of 2"). The specific test in this example is as follows.

$$\text{count-of-critical-condition-patients LE 2}$$

---

16. See Ross [1997, p. 136, #545 and #547] for further examples.
17. The "given" fact types in the example—that is, "attends" and the "ISA"—are also arguments for this specification. However, these can again be assumed to be implicit if specification of the rule were based on some model (for example, a graphic fact model or data model). For that reason they are not included here.

Assembly of Example 2: The Union Rule

In reviewing the formal assembly for the Union Rule given earlier, we would find the following. Part 1, the yield-value function, is addressed first.

$$\text{count-of-correspondents-possessed} =$$
$$\text{yvfn}_{(ME)}(\text{Group, Non-Union-Employee, Union-Employee})^{18}$$

where $\text{yvfn}_{(ME)}$ determines (as dictated by Pattern-R rule type ME) the number of correspondents having at least one instance for each instance of the rule's anchor, Group. This result (which will be 0, 1, or 2 for any given instance of the anchor) will be produced as the rule's yield value in count-of-correspondents-possessed.

Now the truth-valued function is addressed.

$$TV = \text{tvfn}_{(ME)}(\text{count-of-correspondents-possessed})$$

where $\text{tvfn}_{(ME)}$, the truth-valued function, produces true or false for each yield value (that is, in count-of-correspondents-possessed) as dictated by the Pattern-R rule type, ME, and the implicit qualification ("upper limit of 1"). The specific test in this example is as follows:

$$\text{count-of-correspondents-possessed LE 1}$$

Reference

Ross, Ronald G. 1997. *The Business Rule Book* (2nd ed.). Houston, TX: Business Rule Solutions, LLC. Available at *http://www.BRSolutions.com*.

---

18. The "given" fact types in the example—that is, "includes" and the two "ISAs"—are also arguments for this specification. However, these can again be assumed to be implicit if specification of the rule were based on some model (for example, a graphic fact model or data model). For that reason they are not included here.

Part V Appendices

APPENDIX A: EVALUATING THE TRUTH VALUE OF A RULE

In predicate calculus, any rule (logical implication) can be expressed in the form IF p THEN q. This form is exactly equivalent to the logical expression OR ((NOT p), q). Table A–1 shows the truth table for evaluating such an expression.

The truth table indicates the result of evaluating a rule (this result is given in the column on the right) for each possible combination of p and q values (given in the two columns on the left). A row-by-row analysis of these results is instructive.

- *Row 1:* If p and q are both true, then the expression as a whole evaluates to true. We can say "p implies q." This result is reasonably straightforward—it conforms to use of the term *implies* in ordinary English.
- *Row 2:* Here p is true, but q is false. Consequently, the expression as a whole evaluates to false. We can say that "p does *not* imply q."[1] This result

Table A–1 Truth Table for Rules (Logical Implications)

p	q	NOT p	OR ((NOT p), q)
T	T	F	T
T	F	F	F
F	T	T	T
F	F	T	T

---

1. This statement is not the same as "p implies (NOT q)," of course.

is also reasonably straightforward—it too conforms to use of the term *implies* in ordinary English. Note that this result is *not allowed* if the rule is defined as a constraint. In other words, as a constraint, the rule would *prohibit* an evaluation to false—which in turn means that q can never be false if p is true. Informally, this probably corresponds to how most people think of a rule.

- *Rows 3 and 4:* In both these rows, p is false, yet the expression as a whole evaluates to true. This bizarre result flies in the face of common sense.[2]

  The reason, informally, is that we tend to read too much into the word *implies*. Specifically, we often associate the idea of *causation* to the IF . . . THEN . . . form. For example, we might say something like "If you will sign that petition, then I will sign it too." What that statement really means is that your action will influence or *cause* me to act or think in a certain manner. Although this usage of IF . . . THEN . . . is common in real life, it is *not* appropriate in predicate calculus. In formal logic, IF . . . THEN . . . never suggests causation or influence. Instead, it is always evaluated merely as a truth-valued expression. (For this reason, the phrases *the expression evaluates to* or *the logical expression is satisfied* are preferred over the potentially confusing *implies*.)

Charniak and McDermott [1985, p. 17] provide an excellent discussion of this issue as follows:

> Once one has accepted that the predicate calculus **if** does not express causality, it is not hard to convince oneself that the truth table must be filled out the way it is. For example, consider the [meta]rule that (**if** f t) [must be evaluated as] true. Suppose we were told that if anyone gets caught in the rain, then that person will be wet.
>
> (**if** *(anyone is caught in the rain) (that person is wet)*)
>
> One day we note that Dave is wet, but he was not caught in the rain (suppose he was sprayed with a hose). In this case we have (**if** f t). But clearly our experience with Dave does not invalidate our rule, so in this case the if-then rule must still be true. So (**if** f t) [evaluates to] true.

---

2. For additional discussion, refer to Tarski [1995, pp. 23–28] and Halpin and Girle [1981, pp. 49–52].

References

Charniak, Eugene, and Drew McDermott. 1985. *Introduction to Artificial Intelligence.* Reading, MA: Addison-Wesley.

Halpin, Terry, and Roderic Girle. 1981. Deductive Logic (2nd ed.). Brisbane, Australia: Logiqpress.

Tarski, Alfred. 1995. *Introduction to Logic and to the Methodology of Deductive Sciences* (2nd ed.). New York: Dover Publications. (Originally published in 1946 by Oxford University Press, New York.)

APPENDIX B: TERMS AT THE TECHNICAL DESIGNER'S VIEW

Variable in programming languages does not have the same connotation as *variable* in formal logic. For this reason, the question "What is a term?" cannot be answered as directly at the technical designer's perspective as at the other two perspectives.

In an automated system, a variable is basically a container capable of holding a value (possibly complex). This container must be given an identifier or name for reference purposes. This identifier or name could be meaningless (for example, "123456") which, of course, is sufficient for machines.

Technical designers often give such containers more meaningful names so the containers can be identified more readily (by the technical designers and possibly other users). For example, we might define a container *current-temperature* that holds only a single simple value (the current temperature).

Is *current-temperature* a term in the sense of predicate calculus? The answer is *no* if we mean the implementation container itself. The answer is *yes* if we remove any consideration of the implementation container and think only about the value it contains.

Now let's consider a more complex variable—in particular, a relvar as in Date and Darwen [2000]. Suppose we define a relvar called Employee. The columns of this relvar include emp-id, emp-name, SSN, emp-salary, and so on. Date and Darwen [pp. 16–17] call this set of column names the *heading* of the relvar and show that it represents the relvar's predicate.[1] (See Appendix F.) The names in this set are clearly terms in the sense of predicate calculus.

What about Employee? Is it a term?

---

1. Note that the relvar's internal predicate also includes any relevant constraints that might have been specified.

As before, the answer is *no* if we mean the implementation container itself. The answer is *yes* if we remove any consideration of the implementation container. In that case it can be argued that Employee is the *name* of the predicate and therefore does represent a term in the sense of predicate calculus.

To continue this analysis, Date and Darwen explain that each column in a relvar should be defined on some domain, which in their view is considered exactly equivalent to a type (or data type) in programming languages.[2] For example, emp-salary might be defined on the type currency-amount.

In the Date and Darwen view, however, the name of such a domain or type should *not* be viewed as a variable (container). Rather it should be viewed as a named "... **set of values**—*all possible* values of the type in question ... along with ... the valid **operators** that can legally be applied to values of that type. ..."[3] [Date 2000, p. 112, original emphasis]. The set of values can be given by list or by rule(s); possible (storage) representations can also be given.

In any event, such types should appear where appropriate in the heading of a relation, which makes them part of the relvar's predicate. (See Appendix F.) Because of that, the names of the types or domains are also terms in the sense of predicate calculus.

References

Date, C. J. 2000. *An Introduction to Database Systems* (7th ed.). Boston, MA: Addison-Wesley.

Date, C. J., and Hugh Darwen. 2000. *Foundation for Future Database Systems: The Third Manifesto* (2nd ed.). Boston, MA: Addison-Wesley.

---

2. Refer to Date [2000, p. 112] and Date and Darwen [2000, pp. 502–503].
3. That is, a set of operations whose algorithms are hidden (encapsulated) appropriate to the type.

APPENDIX C: THE FUNDAMENTAL KINDS OF RULES

This appendix reviews the three basic possibilities for the specification of any rule (that is, logical implication): *rejector, projector,* and *producer.* Every rule, whether lower-order or higher-order,[1] can be of one and only one of these three kinds. This appendix also examines where functions fit into this scheme.

Three Categories of Rules

The three kinds of rules are described briefly below.

- *Rejector:* A rule can be specified as a constraint that tends to[2] reject violations to maintain integrity.
- *Projector:* A rule can be specified as a constraint that tends to[3] perform inferencing or logical deduction[4] to maintain integrity. Projectors

---

1. That is, whether untyped or typed as explained in Chapter 18.
2. I say *tends to* because whether or not outright rejection occurs can also depend on the enforcement level chosen. Instead of strictly rejecting any violating event, for example, some other response might be deemed appropriate (for example, simply giving a warning or alert). Also, time may be a factor. Consider the following rejector: *A student must be enrolled in at least five courses within five days of the start of registration.* What should happen if a student is *not* enrolled in five courses by that time? Since time cannot be "rejected," some other course of action needs be indicated.
3. Here again, I say *tends to* because whether or not the actual projection occurs can also depend on the enforcement level chosen for the projector. For example, if the actual projection would result in a conflict, strict enforcement might not be indicated. However, this issue is a complex one and beyond the scope of this tutorial to address fully.
4. There are important types of higher-order projectors other than just inference-type constraints. Refer to Ross [1997, pp. 26–28]. For example, one type of higher-order projector, an *executive* (also known as a *trigger*), can be used to execute processes and procedures. This discussion does not directly consider these higher-order rule types.

essentially do just the opposite of rejectors. Projectors never reject "violating" events[5] but rather always accept them and cause new truths (or if higher-order, possibly other kinds of information) to be asserted automatically as a result. In other words, such rules can *project* an event into some new event(s) automatically.

- *Producer:* A rule (logical implication) can be specified as a test or query that can evaluate to either true or false. (For higher-order rules, as discussed in Chapter 18, such a test or query is called a *condition.*) In such case, events are never rejected or projected; only the truth value of the rule itself changes.[6] Producers are always specified only for the information they themselves produce.

These three variations are examined below in more detail using the following simple expression concerning employees. The expression has been given in IF . . . THEN . . . syntax to help make the comparison a bit more straightforward. The question mark in parentheses is a reminder that the expression can also be used as a query.

Expression: *If manager, then salaried employee(?).*

Defined as a constraint (as either a rejector or a projector), this expression could be read at the business manager's perspective as the following rule: *Each manager must be a salaried employee.*

Rejector

If the rule is defined as a rejector, the business logic server must "watch for" events producing potential violations. Such violations could occur, for example, if either of the following assertions were to be presented to the system:

- An assertion that an employee is to be a manager, but the employee is not found to be currently salaried.
- An assertion that an employee is no longer to be salaried, but the employee is found to be currently a manager.

---

5. By *violating events* I mean events that would produce changes to base facts resulting in the violation of some rule.

6. And also the rule's yield value, if a higher-order rule.

Projector

If the rule is defined as one that performs inferencing or logical deduction to ensure integrity (that is, as an inference-type projector), the business logic server must "watch for" the appropriate circumstances to do so. For example, when an assertion is made that an employee is a manager, the business logic server must automatically indicate that the employee is currently salaried (if not already so indicated). Since *salaried* has been inferred or derived according to the rule, the business logic server should disallow any direct assertion (by a user or an application) that a manager is *not* salaried (that is, that *salaried* is false).

Producer

Defined as a test or query, the expression (still actually a logical implication) could be read at the business manager's perspective as an implicit true-false question, as follows: *Are all managers salaried employees?* (With the proper qualification, it might also be read as follows: *Is any* given *manager a salaried employee?*).

Evaluating such a test or query does not involve either rejecting or projecting events. Rather, the business logic server simply needs to evaluate the current state of the factbase in order to *produce* an appropriate true-or-false answer. This true-or-false answer is given by the Boolean value of the logical implication itself.

In everyday English, *rule* is often assumed to carry the sense of *constraint*—that is, that something *must* be true or enforced. In formal logic, however, *rule* (that is, logical implication) does not necessarily carry that sense. The expression of a logical implication acts as a constraint *only* if we define it that way. Otherwise it is a merely a test or query. (Again, for higher-order rules such a test or query is called a *condition*.)

To say this another way, logical implications are like AND, OR, or NOT in that we can use them to specify tests or ask questions (pose queries) about the logicbase. This capacity to *produce* information or knowledge is important in at least two ways.

- It permits us to ask certain kinds of interesting questions. To use an example from Chapter 16, we might ask, "Does 'streets are wet' imply 'it is raining'?"
- It allows us to support higher-order constraints that are conditional, permitting expression of complex patterns—or, more accurately, patterns upon patterns—in the factbase.

Functions

Logical implications used as tests or queries are just one kind of producer. Producers in general are always simply *functions*.

Apart from logical implications used as tests or queries, a function must involve a named result to be of interest in the business rule approach.[7] Although the formula for the function is *not* a rule in the strict sense (that is, it is not a logical implication), the name of the result is a *term*—a legitimate and important kind of business rule.

For a logical (truth-valued) function, the result is a *derived term*; for any other kind of functions, the result is a *computed term*. An example for each of these respective cases follows.

Example of a producer involving a derived term:
high-risk = over-budget OR under-staffed

High-risk is a derived term based on the given formula. Its value can be either true or false (only).

Example of a producer involving a computed term:
total-amount-owed = SUM(line-item-charge) + sales-tax
+ delivery-charge

Total-amount-owed is a computed term based on the given formula. Note that the value of total-amount-owed will not be Boolean.

The formula for a function should always be specified in a declarative manner and should embody the precise definition for the associated term. These formulas or definitions should be managed carefully—as should all business rules.

Reference

Ross, Ronald G. 1997. *The Business Rule Book* (2nd ed.). Houston, TX: Business Rule Solutions, LLC. Available at *http://www.BRSolutions.com*.

---

7. The result of a logical implication used as test or query can also be named—just like the result of any other logical function. In practice, however, such names are usually not needed.

APPENDIX D: ABOUT THE
IF . . . THEN . . . SYNTAX

IF . . . THEN . . . syntax is used in Part V to explain examples wherever help-ful. Contrary to what some believe, however, the IF . . . THEN . . . syntax is *not* inevitable for expressing rules at the business manager's perspective (and quite possibly at one or both of the other two perspectives as well).[1] In par-ticular, the IF . . . THEN . . . syntax is often not convenient for expressing re-jectors, which play an important role in the business rule approach.

Consider the sample expression used in Appendix C: *If manager, then salaried employee(?)*. The best way to express this as a constraint is clearly as given there: *Each manager must be a salaried employee.*[2]

Emphasis on using IF . . . THEN . . . syntax in certain circles of the IT community probably arose from discussions of formal logic as applied to projector-type constraints (that is, rules aimed toward inferencing or logical deduction), most likely at the system developer's or technical designer's per-spective. In any event, retrofitting the IF . . . THEN . . . syntax to the business manager's perspective is inappropriate.

---

1. For good discussions of theoretical difficulties with the IF . . . THEN . . . syntax as used in everyday English sentences, refer to Tarski [1995, pp. 23–28] and Halpin and Girle [1981, pp. 49–52].

2. The underlying expression in predicate calculus for the rule makes use of IF . . . THEN . . . ($\rightarrow$) as follows: Forall x (Manager $x \rightarrow$ SalariedEmployee x) (Terry Halpin, private correspondence, September 9, 2001).

References

Halpin, Terry, and Roderic Girle. 1981. Deductive Logic (2nd ed.). Brisbane, Australia: Logiqpress.

Tarski, Alfred. 1995. *Introduction to Logic and to the Methodology of Deductive Sciences* (2nd ed.). New York: Dover Publications. (Originally published in 1946 by Oxford University Press, New York.)

APPENDIX E: HALPIN'S DEFINITIONS FOR *FACT* AND RELATED TERMS[1]

Fact (elementary): Assertion that an object has a property, or that one or more objects participate in a relationship, where the fact cannot be split into simpler facts with the same object types without information loss.

Object: Thing of interest. An object may be an entity or a value.

Entity: Object that is referenced by relating it to other objects (e.g., the Country that has CountryCode 'AU').[2]

Relationship: Property or association involving one or more objects.

Association: Relationship type, usually involving at least two roles.

Role: Part played by an object in a relationship.

---

1. Reprinted with permission from Halpin, Terry. 2001. *Information Modeling and Relational Databases.* San Francisco, CA: Morgan Kaufmann, glossary entries on pp. 713–715.
2. This definition is interesting. It illustrates how the system developer's perspective differs from the business manager's perspective. At the business manager's perspective, paraphrasing John Zachman, when terms are used (for example, *employee*), they are meant to refer to the "real flesh-and-blood things." At the system developer's perspective, in contrast, the focus is on building *representations* of real-world things, as Halpin's definition suggests. C. J. Date comments as follows: At the system developer's perspective, terms "denote *surrogates* or *models* or *representatives* of those real things inside the system; the system as a whole can be regarded as a 'model of reality.'" (C. J. Date, private correspondence, November 19, 2001).

APPENDIX F: SEMANTICS IN THE RELATIONAL MODEL

Consider a relvar MMQ with the following heading:

MMQ

Major_P# : P#	Minor_P# : P#	QTY : QTY

P# and the second QTY are types or domains.
Date and Darwen [2000, p. 146] indicate, "The predicate here is:

Part MAJOR_P# (a value of type P#) contains quantity QTY (a value of type QTY) of part MINOR_P# (a value of type P# again).

(Note, therefore, that the predicate is, informally, **what the relation means**.)" [emphasis theirs].

Suppose we now instantiate the predicate (insert a row into the relvar) using the following values: {P2, P4, 7}. Date and Darwen [2000, p. 146] indicate, "The proposition (or predicate instantiation) here is:

Part P2 contains quantity 7 of part P4."

What would happen if one, two, or all three of the three terms in this proposition were missing?

Quite simply, the "proposition" would not be a proposition. "A 'tuple' that contains a null is not a tuple—and a 'domain' that contains a null is not a domain, and a 'relation' that contains a null is not a relation, either" [Date 2001].

How about inserting "unknown" for a missing term—for example, for the *quantity* value if it were missing in the expression above? "The statement

'Part P1 contains an unknown quantity of part P2' *is* a proposition, but it's not an instantiation of the predicate given!—rather, it's an instantiation of the predicate 'Part P*x* contains an unknown quantity of P*y*'" [Date 2001].

One final point is this. Note that Date and Darwen [2000, p. 146] use the word "informally" above when they say, "...the predicate is, informally, **what the relation means**." This characterization is presumably because the business logic server does not understand in any real sense what the predicate *means*.

However, this is certainly *not* true at the business manager's perspective, where development of business rules must begin. The meaning is *highly* relevant for that audience (even if informal) and hence at the system developer's perspective as well.

References

Date, C. J. 2001. Private correspondence, November 19.

Date, C. J., and Hugh Darwen. 2000. *Foundation for Future Database Systems: The Third Manifesto* (2nd ed.). Boston, MA: Addison-Wesley.

APPENDIX G: BASIC OPERATORS AND HIGHER-ORDER RULE TYPES

Higher-order rule types such as *mandatory, mutually exclusive, unique, cyclic, frozen, timed,* and so on are of obvious use to logicbase designers. They can also be easily demonstrated to satisfy the two-function criteria prescribed in Chapter 18 for higher-order rule types. Many other patterns in typical fact-bases can as well.

Certain more commonplace or basic operators deserve special attention. As you examine these operators below, keep in mind that all Pattern-R rules *must* include a truth-valued function as one of their two functions.

OR, AND, and NOT

OR, AND, and NOT are logical functions. Given appropriate arguments for their parameters, each returns either true or false. Are they suitable candidates to serve as higher-order rule types? The answer is *no* for various reasons.

NOT. NOT is always applied to a single Boolean variable or expression. All rules, on the other hand (including higher-order rules), involve at least two terms.[1] Therefore, NOT can be used for qualification in higher-order rules, but not as a higher-order rule type per se.

AND and OR. AND and OR are unsuitable in native form for a different reason. Obviously, specification of higher-order rules does require ANDs

---

1. NOT is a *monadic* operator, whereas logical implication (like AND and OR) is *dyadic.*

and ORs of conditions. The problem, however, is broader than simple ANDs and ORs might suggest. The Business Rule Book [Ross 1997, pp. 77–104] proposes an entire family of "mutual" rule types to provide generalized support for patterns of this kind. This rule type family includes the special cases of mutually exclusive, mutually inclusive, and mutually prohibited—and a generalized *mutual* rule type supporting any specified number of conditions.

The Quantifiers of Predicate Calculus

The two logical quantifiers—EXISTS and FORALL—are fundamental to predicate calculus. EXISTS provides a test for "at least one" or "there exists at least one." FORALL provides a test for "all" (or "for each" or "given any"). These tests are likewise essential for higher-order rule types.

However, the need for testing quantities in higher-order rules is broader than simply "at least one" or "all." Relevant quantities or limits can also fall anywhere in between "one" and "all" (and often do).

The Business Rule Book [Ross 1997, pp. 47–75] proposes a family of rule types called *Instance Verifiers* that provide generalized support for patterns that involve counting instances. Incidentally, a special case in this rule family is *mandatory*, which involves testing for "at least one."

Comparative Operators

The comparative operators—for example, *greater than* (>), *equal to* (=), *less than* (<), and so on—are logical functions, which satisfies the first criterion of the definition for Pattern-R rules.[2]

---

2. Whether or not these comparative operators are predicates is not central to these arguments. Here are relevant comments on the question.

C. J. Date [2000, p. 777] indicates that these logical operators can be viewed as predicates: ". . . '>(x,y)'—more conveniently written 'x>y'—is a predicate with two parameters, x and y; it returns *true* if the argument corresponding to x is greater than the argument corresponding to y and *false* otherwise."

Terry Halpin [2001] indicates "These [logical operators] may be treated as dyadic predicates. In practice however, they are normally treated as scalar operators (e.g., arithmetic or character-string operators) rather than logical operators, since their terms are not logical expressions (even though their result is Boolean)."

The second criterion requires an underlying computation (the yield-value function) to support evaluation of the truth-valued function. For the comparative evaluators there would obviously have to be a "built-in" computation that the machine performs (for example, a subtraction between the values given as arguments for the parameters) to support evaluation of the truth-valued function. So even if such a yield-value function is a given, the comparative operators nonetheless qualify "as is" as (useful) Pattern-R rule types.[3]

Arithmetic Operators

Arithmetic functions, for example, SUM, SUBTRACT, AVERAGE, and so on, obviously satisfy the computational criterion for higher-order rule types. They do not natively involve a truth-valued function, but their inherent computation function could certainly be used as the basis for one. In theory then, any arithmetic function could be defined as a higher-order rule type. In practice, these might be deemed of limited practical use since (barring machine failures) such rules would never produce false.

References

Date, C. J. 2000. *An Introduction to Database Systems* (7th ed.). Boston, MA: Addison-Wesley.

Halpin, Terry. 2001. Private correspondence, September 9.

Ross, Ronald G. 1997. *The Business Rule Book* (2nd ed.). Houston, TX: Business Rule Solutions, LLC. Available at *http://www.BRSolutions.com.*

---

3. These comparative operators constitute one of the atomic Pattern-R rule type families given in Ross [1997, pp. 151–164].

APPENDIX H: FORMALIZATION OF THE PATTERN-R APPROACH

Formalization of any system requires several things, as follows [Hofstadter 1980, p. 41].[1]

- *Axioms*—that is, the givens.
- *Rules of production*—that is, the rules you must follow in creating derived results (called *theorems*) from the axioms (and/or other theorems).
- *Decision procedure*—that is, instructions indicating how to decide whether a proposed theorem is a valid one.

Does the assembly template for Pattern-R rule types satisfy these criteria? *No.* Essentially, the assembly template merely "opens up the covers" of Pattern-R rule types and shows what is inside.

Opening up the covers is not actually necessary for the atomic rule types given in *The Business Rule Book* [Ross 1997] since these are the *axioms* of the Pattern-R system. (Of course it is interesting for implementation purposes, but that is a different matter.)

It must be remembered, however, that the set of rule types in the Pattern-R system is open-ended or extensible. Opening up the covers *is* necessary in showing how *derived* rule types (the theorems) are produced. Therefore, the assembly template can be viewed as providing *rules of production* for derived rule types. Missing, however, in both this tutorial and *The Business Rule Book* is a decision procedure for deciding whether a proposed derived rule type is valid or not.[2]

---

1. Refer to Simpson [2000, p. 10] for a somewhat different view.
2. Developing such a decision procedure is the subject of current research.

Does that complete the answer to this question about formalization? *Not yet.* There is actually a second (and simpler) level at which the question must also be addressed. This level involves everyday specification of Pattern-R rules by system developers.

At this level, both atomic rule types and provably valid derived rule types constitute the axioms of the Pattern-R system. *The Business Rule Book* offers several dozen of these. The rules of production are the grammatical rules about using these rule types correctly. These rules of production are also comprehensively documented in the book. In addition, more than 500 theorems (correct examples of their application) are given and discussed. However, again missing is a decision procedure,[3] so the system cannot be said to be formal at this level either.

References

Hofstadter, Douglas R. 1980. *Godel, Escher and Bach: An Eternal Golden Braid.* New York: Vintage Books.

Ross, Ronald G. 1997. *The Business Rule Book* (2nd ed.). Houston, TX: Business Rule Solutions, LLC. Available at *http://www.BRSolutions.com.*

Simpson, Stephen G. 2000. "Logic and Mathematics." Available at *http:// www.math.psu.edu/simpson/.*

---

3. This decision procedure exists but has not been published.

APPENDIX I: WHAT DOES *DECLARATIVE* MEAN

Any logicbase generally includes many rules—in fact, often a very large number. Fundamentally, the order or sequence in which all these rules are evaluated should make no difference whatsoever to the results eventually achieved.[1]

A more accurate way to say this is the following: The *system developers* or *technical designers* who specify the rules need not be concerned with sequence. The business logic server itself will automatically determine the proper sequence (if any) for evaluating the rules based on natural dependencies among the rules themselves.

For example, suppose a rule indicates *A discount of 15 percent must be given to a customer order if the order is for a good customer and the total amount of the order is over $1,000.* Suppose there are other rules for determining whether a customer is good and for computing the total amount of the order. Clearly, these other rules must be evaluated before the discount rule can be applied (if appropriate). However, because the rules are declarative—that is, because the business logic server *itself* can determine the appropriate order of evaluation—the user can present the rules in any order and still get the same results in the end.[2]

---

1. User friendliness might be a different issue in some cases.
2. That is, after all the rules have been presented.

In other words, the final state of the logicbase should be exactly the same for *any* sequence of presentation. This outcome is very unlike the case for processes and procedures, where the importance of explicit sequence is paramount. This *sequence independence* is the fundamental reason why rules should be considered declarative rather than procedural.

 A set of rules is declaritive if their sequence of presentation to the business logic server makes no difference to the results produced for them.

APPENDIX J: THE "MARY" INFERENCING EXAMPLE STEP-BY-STEP

This discussion works through the "Mary" inferencing example presented in Chapter 16 step-by-step using the following: (a) no facts or predicates, (b) Boolean variables, and (c) forward chaining.

Each rule is also presented in the form OR ((NOT p), q) to assist the reader in the proper evaluations. It is important to remember (as always) that each rule as a whole is a Boolean expression.

R1: "Mary" → female

This expression can also be written as:

OR ((NOT "Mary"), female)

"Mary" is an instance term and must be taken as a given (that is, as true). The expression as a whole, R1, is indicated (by default) to be a constraint and therefore true. As a result, the rule-processing server sets the Boolean variable *female* to true.

R2: "Mary" → of-age

This expression can also be written as:

OR ((NOT "Mary"), of-age)

"Mary" is an instance term and must be taken as a given (that is, as true). The expression as a whole, R2, is indicated (by default) to be a constraint and therefore true. As a result, the rule-processing server sets the Boolean variable *of-age* to true.

R3: female AND of-age → woman

This expression can also be written as:

OR ((NOT female and of-age), woman)

Resulting from the earlier evaluations, female and of-age are both known to be true. The expression as a whole, R3, is indicated (by default) to be a constraint and therefore true. As a result, the rule-processing server sets the Boolean variable *woman* to true.

APPENDIX K: MORE ON R-NOTATION FOR FACTS

Facts Involving More Than Two terms

A fact can involve more than two terms, as the following example illustrates.

"Teacher advises Student in Course."

In this example, the fact, "...advises...in...", involves three terms: Teacher, Student, and Course.

This example is written in R-Notation for facts as follows. By convention, only the first term in the fact is shown on the left side of the bidirectional arrow; the remaining terms are always shown on the right side. This approach serves as a reminder that the fact represents a sentence, and a sentence can have only one subject.

$$\text{Teacher}^{\text{ advises}\ldots\text{in}} \leftrightarrow \text{Student, Course}$$

Note that the order of terms in the fact is significant (as always for facts specified at the system developer perspective) so that the terms "fit" into it correctly.

This fact, like all facts, must obey the Existence Principle. The rule implied by the fact under the Existence Principle is given as follows:

$$\ldots\text{advises}\ldots\text{in}\ldots \rightarrow \text{Teacher, Student, Course}$$

Any fact, including those involving more than two terms, can often be rephrased without changing the meaning. This typically involves a change in the order of the terms. For example, "Teacher advises Student in Course" could be reordered and rephrased as follows: "Student in Course is advised by Teacher." Note that there is no fundamental change in the fact's meaning. This revised form could be expressed as follows:

Student $^{in\,...\,is\,advised\,by}$ $\leftrightarrow$ Course, Teacher

The fact name for a fact involving more than two terms may be indicated on the *right* side of the bidirectional arrow, just as for facts with only two terms. Such facts must conform to the following conventions:

- Only one term is listed on the left side of the bidirectional arrow (as always).
- The fact name is given in left-to-right order (as always).
- The terms fit into the fact name in *reverse* order.

Here is an example:

Course $\leftrightarrow$ $^{advises\,...\,in}$ Student, Teacher

Inserting the terms in reverse order, this fact is read "Teacher advises Student in Course."

Facts Involving a Single Term

Most facts involve two or more terms. However, it is possible for a fact to have only a single term. An example, again starting with a sentence, illustrates:

Company pays slowly.

In this example, the fact, "... pays slowly," involves only a single term, Company. This example would be written in R-Notation for facts as follows:

Company $^{pays\,slowly}$ $\leftrightarrow$

This R-Notation fact type shows no terms on the right side since only a single term, Company, is involved.

As before, this fact implies a rule under the Existence Principle, as follows:

pays slowly $\rightarrow$ Company

APPENDIX L: SPECIAL BUILT-IN FACT TYPES IN R-NOTATION

Several useful predefined or built-in fact types are offered in R-Notation for facts. [1]

HASA

The first built-in fact type is HASA. The HASA fact type can be used to express closely held properties of a class term. An example using R-Notation for facts illustrates.

Customer $^{HASA} \leftrightarrow$ credit limit

This fact[2] can be read, "Customer has a credit limit."[3] This fact implies a rule under the Existence Principle, as follows:

HASA $\rightarrow$ Customer, credit limit

---

1. This discussion focuses primarily above the technical designer's perspective. Many more built-in predicates could be useful at the latter perspective. Common Prolog implementations, for example, usually feature several hundred. Many of these, however, are not relevant to business rules (Markus Schacher, private correspondence, September 5, 2001).
2. This example is a fact *type* because it includes class terms (Customer and credit limit).
3. A factbase could have literally hundreds or thousands of such HASA facts. Since all of them would have the same predicate name, "... has a ...", obviously some means for distinguishing them at the meta-level is required.

ISA

Another built-in fact type—a crucial one—is the ISA fact type. The ISA fact type, which means *is a category of,* can be used to express subsets or subtypes for a class term. An example using R-Notation for facts illustrates:[4]

Rush Order $^{\text{ISA}} \leftrightarrow$ Order

This fact type[5] can be read "Rush Order is a category of Order," or "Rush Order is a subset of Order." This fact implies a rule under the Existence Principle, as follows:

ISA → Rush Order, Order

INST

Another built-in fact type is the INST (*is instantiation of*) fact type. The INST fact type can be used to provide specific instance terms for a class term (or fact instances for a fact type). An example using R-Notation for facts illustrates. The INST fact type is especially useful in specifying *rules* that reference instance terms.[6]

"Acme Supply" $^{\text{INST}} \leftrightarrow$ Customer

This fact instance[7] can be read, "Acme Supply is an instance of Customer." This fact implies a rule under the Existence Principle, as follows.

INST → "Acme Supply," Customer

SEM

Another built-in fact type is the SEM fact type. This built-in fact type can be used to indicate that certain distinct fact names represent the very same fact

---

4. It is especially important here to remember that we are *not* examining these predefined fact types from the technical designer's perspective. How the ISA fact type should be viewed at that perspective might be quite different.

5. This example is a fact *type* because it includes variables (Rush Order and Order).

6. The INST predicate becomes *implicit* at the technical designer's perspective. Each row in a relvar, for example, is an "instantiation of" that relvar's predicate.

7. This example is a fact *instance* because it includes no class terms. "Acme Supply" is clearly not a class term. Customer is an instance term at the *meta*-level.

type—in other words, that they are *semantically equivalent.* The names might be aliases or they might be rephrased names (with reordered terms). An example of the latter using R-Notation for facts illustrates:

is placed by $^{\text{SEM}}\leftrightarrow$ places

This fact instance[8] can be read "'is placed by' is semantically equivalent to 'places'." This fact implies a rule under the Existence Principle, as follows:

SEM $\rightarrow$ is placed by, places

---

8. This example is a fact *instance* because it includes no variables. At the *meta*-level, both "is placed by" and "places" are instance terms rather than class terms.

Glossary

abnormal reuse (work): Using for abnormal circumstances a script that is already used for normal circumstances.

action (work): An activity, transform, transaction, or process that can be requested or used within a script to achieve a particular desired result. Upon execution, an action takes "input" and transforms it into "output." An action need not necessarily be automated.

actor (work): A real-world actor or a software actor that initiates events or performs work to respond to an event.

adaptability: The ability to make fit (as for a specific new use or situation), often by modification; that is, the ability to change quickly and easily.

anchor (Pattern-R rules): The left-hand expression of a Pattern-R rule.

antecedent (formal logic): In a specific rule, the left-hand expression.

architectural product: A deliverable necessary for prescribing the architecture of a functioning business or business capacity and/or for providing specifications essential to its construction. An architectural deliverable may be used to communicate such specifications to other project participants and/or to achieve a "sign-off" during a project, but the deliverable never exists *solely* for these latter purposes.

as-is data model: A data model for a database that has already been implemented.

as-is workflow model: A workflow model for a workflow that has already been implemented—that is, one that is currently operational. An as-is workflow model generally represents how a workflow is currently organized.

aspect: Any of the factors or requirements categories involved in building or operating a business or business capacity. These aspects are based (following the Zachman Architecture Framework where they are called abstractions[1]) on the six interrogatives, as follows:

- What (data)—what the business needs to know
- How (process)—transformations the business must be able to perform
- Where (location)—locations where work occurs and how they connect
- Who (people)—actors and how they interact
- When (time)—timing and precedence criteria for coordinating work
- Why (motivation)—appropriate guidance

assumption: Something believed to be true about the capability, knowledge, motivation, or tendencies of an actor or about the characteristics of the business environment in which the business or business capacity operates (for example, "Customers don't always know their needs or understand our products"). Such an assumption can be an internal influence that shapes rules.

atomic form (rule): A state of a rule in which it cannot be broken down or reduced into more granular rules without loss of meaning (across the entire set of more granular rules) significant to the business or business capacity. Formally, a rule is in atomic form only if both of the following are true:

- The rule has no ORs among its LHTs.
- The rule has no ANDs among it RHTs.

automated rule: An element of business logic that has been implemented in automated form. An automated rule is expressed in a form (syntax) recognizable by a rule engine, programming language, application generator, or similar technology. An automated rule is often the implementation counterpart to an operating rule.

---

1. For more information on the Zachman Architecture Framework, refer to the following references:

Zachman, John A. 2002. *The Zachman Framework: A Primer for Enterprise Engineering and Manufacturing* (electronic book). Available in November 2002 at *http://www.zachmaninternational.com*.

Collected articles by John Zachman published in the *Business Rules Journal*. Available at *http://www.BRCommunity.com*.

backward chaining: An algorithm for inference that starts from a consequent and works "backwards" (that is, through left-hand expressions of all relevant inference rules) toward known facts to see if that consequent can be proven (that is, proves true). This approach is sometimes also called *goal-driven reasoning.*

base fact: A fact that cannot be produced (computed or inferred) from other facts. Base facts reside in a factbase and are fundamental to expressing and evaluating rules. Base facts are also sometimes called *ground axioms.*

base term: A term that cannot be derived or computed (that is, produced) from other terms. Base terms are fundamental to understanding the business or business capacity since all knowledge (including facts and rules) starts with them.

Boolean: A truth value. *Boolean* as a noun is taken to mean a value of either true or false, in the same way that *integer* is usually taken to mean an integer value.

Boolean expression: See *logical expression.*

Boolean variable: See *truth-valued variable.*

bracket: Any specific value or range of values for an evaluation term.

BRS RuleSpeak: A set of practical guidelines to assist business workers and professionals with expressing rules in clear, unambiguous, well-structured business English.

business: See *enterprise.*

business analysis: Applying the skills and techniques needed to create a business model.

business analyst: A business professional responsible for the creation and revision of business capacities. A business analyst contributes to the development of business models for these business capacities by developing business requirements in a structured manner.

business capacity: Some functioning part of a business, often a business process. A business capacity provides the operational ability to support the business mission and to produce results that satisfy business goals.

Business Connectivity Map: An architectural product indicating which business locations or sites need to be interconnected and also which actors are connected at which sites. The focus of the Business Connectivity

Map is on optimization of the number and locations of sites for different purposes (for example, bank branches, factories, warehouses, distribution centers, and so on), transportation and communication between sites, communication requirements between actors at their different locations, and so on.

business event: See *event (business).*

business goal: See *goal.*

business initiative: A broad change effort set in motion by senior management to move the company (and its business systems) in a certain direction based on opportunities and/or risks. A business initiative normally takes a longer period of time than a project and may in fact involve many projects.

business logic: The basic knowledge and guidance appropriate for operating a business or business capacity—that is, business rules.

business logic server: Runtime system software that operates on the basis of business rules to automate the logic of a business process—especially the specific operational tasks, decision-making tasks, and/or creative tasks it includes. The business logic server is responsible for the logicbase, that is, for managing the factbase and executing the rules in the rulebase. A business logic server might also be called a *rule engine, rule-processing server,* or *decision management platform.*

business logic technology: Technology that aims toward managing and/or executing business logic.

business milestone: A particular stage in a Business Milestones analysis. The name of a business milestone is a term that is likely to be referenced by many rules. For example, business milestones for *order* might include *received, credit-checked, filled, shipped, invoiced,* and *completed.*

Business Milestones: An architectural product depicting all the stages (business milestones) in an organized regimen for coordinating some thing or concept (for example, *order*) from a business perspective. The emphasis in Business Milestones is on organizing the management of instances at an operational level, with special focus on standardizing the relevant vocabulary (that is, stage names such as *filled (order)*) and on identifying appropriate rules to govern transitions among the stages.

business mission: See *mission.*

business model: A collection of related architectural products for the business or business capacity aimed toward capturing (that is, describing and/or prescribing) its essential workings from a purely business perspective. The business model provides a comprehensive framework for developing requirements in a business-driven manner and for ensuring the completeness of requirements.

business process: A business capability that can take raw materials (as "input") in a certain state and transform it into some value-added form (as "output"). The inputs and outputs may be tangible (for example, physical resources or products) or intangible (for example, information).

business process owner: See *owner.*

business process rule: A rule that addresses workflow involved in operating the business or business capacity.

business rule (business definition): A directive intended to influence or guide business behavior.

business rule (business system definition): An atomic piece of reusable business logic, specified declaratively.

business rule (formal definition): A concept as represented by a term, a fact, or a rule.

business system: An automated system deployed to support the operation of a business or business capacity.

business tactics: The contents of the Policy Charter. The business tactics identify relevant ends and the means to achieve those ends.

cardinality: A data model construct that refers to the number of instances of some relationship type (usually a maximum number) that any individual instance of one of the two data objects directly related in the relationship type is permitted to possess. Cardinality usually is expressed simply as "one" or as "many." Cardinality is also called *multiplicity.*

categorization scheme: A group of two or more immediate categories in an organized scheme for categorizing instances of a concept. For example, the categorization scheme *gender* includes the categories *male* and *female* for the concept *person.* Categories included in a categorization scheme generally represent variations within a single perspective and/or different potential states for the instances of the given concept. A categorization scheme should be named (for example, *gender*).

category: A variation, kind, subset, or state of some other concept. A category should be named, such name being a term (for example, *retired employee, discontinued product,* and so on).

change effort: A formal, organized undertaking (that is, business initiative, project, or change request) that has a clear line of responsibility whose purpose is to create or change some area of the business, normally involving business systems in a significant manner. A change effort should have a well-defined beginning and end, with specific objectives to accomplish. A change effort may result in the creation of rules (and/or other parts of a business model) and/or in their modification, replacement, or discontinuation.

change request: A change effort requiring only limited resources and a relatively short duration of time whose purpose is relatively narrow.

chief policy officer (CPO): The corporate role with overall responsibility for coordinating the governance process of an enterprise, including rule management. The CPO is to business logic as the chief financial officer (CFO) is to finances.

clarification policy: An assertion made in a Policy Charter providing clarification or appropriate interpretation (that is, a definition) for some term used in the business tactics.

class (predicate calculus): A set of instances.

class term (predicate calculus): The name of a class.

computation rule: Any producer (rule or function) that computes a value following standard arithmetic operations (for example, sum, multiply, average, and so on) specified explicitly. A computation rule provides a precise formula for how a computed term is to be calculated. For example, a computation rule might be given to compute *the amount paid for an order.*

computed term: A term whose values are computed and therefore for which a computation rule could be given, for example, *The amount paid for an order must be computed as the sum of all payment amounts applied to the order.*

Concepts Catalog: A glossary of agreed-to (or proposed) terms used in the business or business capacity, along with their definitions in clear business English (or another natural language). A Concepts Catalog provides the basic vocabulary for specifying facts and rules and for developing other components of a business model.

conclusion (formal logic): In generalized reasoning about rules, the right-hand expression of a rule.

condition (Pattern-R rules): A logical implication used as a test or query in expressing higher-order rules.

conditional expression: See *logical expression.*

conflict (business tactics): A set of two or more tactics and/or core business rules recognized to be mutually antagonistic or counterproductive with respect to specified end(s). A conflict in business tactics should be resolved by means of one or more core business rule(s).

conflict (rule): A set of two or more rules recognized as being in disagreement or contradiction, indicating that at least one of the rules is impossible to satisfy if one or more of the other rules are satisfied. For example, the rule *A shipment must include at least three orders* is directly in conflict with the rule *An out-of-state shipment may include only one order.*

consequent (formal logic): In a specific rule, the right-hand expression.

consistency (logical): All relevant rules being satisfied by a set of terms and facts.

consolidated business logic: The collection of all decision criteria and their outcomes for a rule expressed in the array format of a decision table.

constraint (formal logic): See *rule (formal logic).*

constraint (Pattern-R rules): A logical implication used as a rejector or projector in expressing higher-order rules.

copier (rule): A projector (rule) that replicates (copies) actual values.

core business rule: A rule that addresses a significant risk to the business or business capacity. A core business rule also usually meets one or more of the following tests: (1) It has direct impact on customer service. (2) It relates to cost-effective use of corporate resources. (3) It has direct impact on the company's competitive standing.

corporate value: A principle or belief held to be intrinsically true (for example, "Veterans deserve special consideration," "Having more competent employees pays off in the long run, even if they cost more," and so on). Such a corporate value is part of the corporate culture and can act as an internal influence in shaping rules.

correspondent (Pattern-R rules): Any right-hand term or right-hand expression of a Pattern-R rule.

CPO: See chief policy officer

creative task: A task that always involves making a significant choice between alternatives, where neither the desired form nor the desired content of the result can be predicted in advance (except perhaps in general or "meta" terms). Creative tasks are highly knowledge-intensive, with many rules required for their correct or optimal performance (for example, design marketing logo, develop classification scheme, create architecture, and so on).

data-driven reasoning. See *forward chaining.*

data model: An architectural product focusing on delineating the required data (in appropriate format) to support system-level requirements. A data model often addresses the complexities of organizing historical data. The primary audience for a data model is system designers and database administrators (DBAs). A first-cut data model can be produced from a fact model.

data toggle (rule): An enabler (rule) that creates or deletes instances of actual data under appropriate circumstances. For example, a data toggle might be given to indicate that a juvenile's criminal record must be erased upon reaching 18 years of age.

decision crtieria: Any term, value, bracket, logical expression, or mathematical expression used as a label for one or more rows or columns of a decision table.

decision-making task: A task that always involves making a significant choice between alternatives, where the desired form of the result can be predicted in advance but not the desired content. Decision-making tasks are relatively knowledge-intensive, with rules required for their correct or optimal performance (for example, adjudicate claim, approve credit, evaluate applicant, and so on).

decision management platform: A business logic server aimed at supporting decision points. See also *business logic server.*

decision point: Any point in conducting work where a decision must be made that can influence the specific course of action to be taken in a significant way. Decision points are often reflected in decision-making tasks. Decision points also may reflect an exceptional, low-frequency, and/or ad hoc point for which no workflow task is specified. The decision to be made in a decision point may involve any of the following: classification, diagnosis, assessment, monitoring, prediction, design, assignment, planning, scheduling, modeling, and so on (for example, whether to declare an emergency situation, what on-the-spot discount should be given, what appropriate route to select, and so on).

decision table (rule): An array format effective for expressing suitable collections of rules in a consolidated form (that is, as a single rule). See also *consolidated business logic.*

declarative (specifications): Any set of discrete specifications (for example, rules) that result in exactly the same state for any sequence in which they are presented to a system. An application program (that is, lines of code) written in a traditional programming language is not declarative in this sense.

definition: A statement that expresses the meaning of a term.

deliverable: A specification, model, or document produced during some phase of a project to develop some portion of a functioning business or business capacity or to communicate and/or to achieve a necessary sign-off.

derivation rule: Any producer (rule or function) that derives a truth value (that is, true or false) based on logical operations (for example, AND, OR, NOT, EQUAL TO, and so on) specified explicitly. A derivation rule provides a precise definition for a *derived term.* For example, a derivation rule might be given to indicate whether a project is at risk depending on whether the project is over budget or understaffed.

derived fact: A fact that can be produced (computed or inferred) from other facts.

derived term: A truth-valued term whose value (true or false) is always established by specified logical operations and therefore for which a derivation rule could be given. For example, *at-risk project* means the project is over budget or understaffed.

directive: See *governing rule.*

disintermediation: Eliminating middlemen between customer and producer.

domain of discourse: The subject matter of a set of business rules.

enabler (rule): A projector (rule) that toggles (switches) something on or off.

end: A business purpose that an element of business tactics (the means) can serve or address. Ends are often goals but may also be risks. A tactic or core business rule may also be an end if there is any other lower-level tactic and/or core business rule that supports it.

enforcement level: A particular level or degree of enforcement for a rule (for example, strictly enforced, suggested, and so on).

enterprise: The entire business or organization, or some relatively self-contained line of business.

enterprise model: A business model covering the entire enterprise (that is, all business capacities).

evaluation term (rule): In the context of decision tables, any of the one or more other terms in a rule statement.

event (business): An occurrence that requires the business or business capacity to respond. Significant business events require a well-organized response, which can be developed by workflow models and/or coordinated by rules. Example of an event: Customer places an order.

event (business system): Any change in state, or any occurrence that needs to be noted or recorded. An event may cause one or more rules to fire (that is, to be tested). For example, customer places an order, which results in one or more system events to create data in a database, causing related rules to fire.

event (workflow): A business event or the completion of a task.

exception (rule): A rule that indicates another rule is *not* to be enforced under specified conditions. The former rule disables (stops the enforcement of) the latter rule under those specified circumstances. For example, in the rule *A library card must not be held by more than one borrower, unless one of the borrowers who holds the library card is Bill Gates*, the portion *unless one of the borrowers who holds the library card is Bill Gates* is an exception to the base rule, *A library card must not be held by more than one borrower.* See also *rule toggle (rule).*

executive (rule): A projector (rule) that causes an operation, process, or procedure to execute or a rule to fire.

existential quantifier (predicate calculus): EXISTS.

EXISTS (predicate calculus): See *logical quantifier.*

expert system: Runtime system software based primarily on inferencing rules, aimed toward automating decision-making tasks. Expert systems are typically interactive and generally attempt to mimic human decision-making activity.

explicit knowledge: See *explicit rule.*

explicit rule: A business rule that is formally recorded and/or encoded in a form that can be readily understood by business analysts. In contrast to tacit rules, if the person/people who know and understand an explicit rule are lost to the business or business capacity, the business rule itself is nonetheless retained.

external influence (rules): An influence arising outside the business or business capacity. Such an influence might be a law or regulation (for example, regarding taxes, fraud, personnel, government), a marketplace factor (for example, competition, customer, supplier, investor), an environmental factor (for example, nature, culture, economy, technology, experience), and so on.

fact: Something that is known or that can be known about one or more concepts or ideas. Facts structure basic business knowledge. Unlike rules, facts never place any constraints per se on this knowledge nor make any computation or inference based on it. A fact is asserted in a fact statement using an appropriate term for each concept or idea.

factbase: A store that holds base facts (loosely, persistent data) of the business or business capacity. The contents of the factbase are believed to be accurate and true.

fact instance: A fact whose fact statement(s) include(s) only instance terms. For example, "Acme Supply places a601" is a fact instance of the fact type "Customer places order."

fact model: An architectural product that structures basic knowledge about the business or business capacity in declarative form from a business perspective. Such knowledge is basic in the sense that it cannot be derived or computed from any other knowledge. In particular, a fact model provides a unified, graphic representation of fact statements. A fact model is a crucial starting point for developing more advanced forms of business knowledge, including measures and rules, and can be transformed into a first-cut data model.

fact name: The name given to a fact, often taken to be the verb or verb phrase of an associated fact statement. For example, in the fact "Customer places order" the verb "places" could be taken as the fact name.

fact statement: A declarative sentence that expresses a fact (for example, "Customer places order"). Such a sentence literally represents a "statement of fact"—something that can happen (or has happened) or that can be known (or is known).

fact type: A set of facts of the same kind. A fact statement for a fact type must include at least one class term. For example, "Customer places order."

factoring (requirements): Organizing architectural products by aspect.

FORALL (predicate calculus): See *logical quantifier.*

formal logic: A system of logic (such as Aristotelian logic or symbolic logic) that abstracts forms of thought from its content to establish abstract criteria of consistency. Also, the science of formal principles of reasoning or correct inference.[2]

forward chaining: An algorithm for inference that starts from known facts and works "forward" (that is, toward right-hand expressions) of all relevant inference rules to see if a consequent can be reached (that is, proves true). This approach is sometimes also called *data-driven reasoning.*

functional category (rule): The kind of a rule (that is, rejector, producer, or projector) based on its intrinsic operation or effect—in particular, how it responds to events.

goal: An effect (that is, a business result) that the business or business capacity wants to accomplish in performing the mission (for example, to be profitable, to keep customers satisfied, and so on). Goals can be achieved only indirectly; the business or business capacity must perform the mission in order to achieve the goals. Goals provide the ultimate motivation for core business rules.

goal-driven reasoning: See *backward chaining.*

governing rule: A legal statement (for example, law, act, statute), formal regulation, clause in a binding agreement (for example, contractual obligation), higher-level business policy or directive, and so on. Governing

---

2. From Simpson, Stephen G. 2000. "Logic and Mathematics," p. 2. Available at *http://www.math.psu.edu/simpson/.*

rules guide or constrain the business, regulating its interactions with external parties and/or limiting its exposure to risks or threats. Governing rules often must be interpreted into one or more operating rules to be applied in an actual business process or used for system design.

governance process: The business process that establishes, communicates, implements, evaluates, and retires policies and business rules for the business. The governance process addresses interpretation of governing rules to operating rules, and operating rules to implemented rules, and organizes all related review and sign-off activities.

ground axiom: See *base fact.*

has a (fact): A kind of fact relating two terms, wherein one of the terms possesses the other term as a property. For example, "Employee *has a* name."

higher-order rule: See *Pattern-R rule.*

IF-THEN connective (formal logic): See *rule (formal logic).*

IF-THEN syntax: The syntax used to express rule statements in the general form IF . . . THEN. . . . For example, *If a person is female and of age, then that person is a woman.*

implication connective: See *rule (formal logic).*

imprint rule: A copier (rule) that sets the value of something that persists (for example, something in a factbase or database). For example, an imprint rule might be used to initialize the tuition owed by a student in a given semester to the base tuition for that semester when the student enrolls.

inference: The process of inferring new facts—that is, knowledge—from existing facts by means of inference rules. Also called *logical deduction.*

inference engine: A kind of runtime business logic technology that uses an algorithm to systematically determine the truth of assertions (proposed facts), given a defined set of propositions (existing facts), in order to reason systematically about a problem of interest. Inference performed by a business logic server provides automated assistance and/or automation for making decisions.

inference rule: An enabler (rule) that infers a fact to be true under appropriate circumstances. For example, an inference rule might be given to indicate that a person must be considered a woman if criteria for that person's age and gender are satisfied. When the requested state of the logicbase is such that the left-hand expression of an inference rule is true but its right-hand expression is false, the business logic server infers that the right-hand expression has now become true. Since the right-hand expression of one rule may play a role in the left-hand expression of another inference rule, this process may cascade many times—an activity called *inference* or *logical deduction.*

influence (rules): Any factor that shapes a rule.

initiating event (workflow): The first event indicated by a workflow model.

instance (predicate calculus): Any specific member of a class.

instance model: A fact model or fact model extension that focuses on instance terms, often involving a rule-intensive product/service and/or reference data of the business or business capacity.

instance of (fact): A kind of fact relating two terms (or two other facts), wherein the first term or fact is an instance of the second term or fact. This second term or fact is the type of the first term or fact. For example, "ABC Supply, Inc." (the first term) is an *instance of* "customer" (the second term, and the type of the first term).

instance term (fact models): The name given to a member of a set wherein all members are perceived in like manner (that is, as having common characteristics). For example, Canada is an instance of the set of all countries.

instance term (predicate calculus): The name of an instance.

instantiation (predicate calculus): A substitution of instance terms for each of the class terms of a predicate.

integrity (data): Correctness.

integrity constraint: See *rejector (rule).*

internal influence (rules): An influence arising from inside the business or business capacity. Such internal influences include existing infrastructure, issues (irritants), assumptions, corporate values, and so on.

is a (fact): See *is a category of (fact).*

is a category of (fact): A kind of fact relating two terms, wherein one of the terms is a category of the other term. For example, "Employee *is a category of* Person."

issue: A problem or irritant that is cause for concern (for example, "We don't always know who our customers are"). Such an issue can be an internal influence that shapes rules.

jurisdiction (rules): Any organizational body within the business or business capacity itself (for example, an organizational unit as defined by the organizational chart), external political unit (for example, confederation of nations, nation, state, province), or geographical area (for example, North America). A jurisdiction is any organizational and/or geographical area within which a rule may be enforced.

knowledge retention: A business rule initiative to capture tacit business rules from subject matter experts and/or other business workers.

label (decision tables): The decision criteria used to identify one or more particular rows or columns of a decision table.

left-hand expression (formal logic): The complete logical expression on the left side of a rule expressed in the form $p \rightarrow q$.

left-hand term (formal logic): Any term on the left side of a rule expressed in the form $p \rightarrow q$.

LHE: See *left-hand expression.*

LHT: See *left-hand term.*

line of business: One or more products and/or services targeted to a particular marketplace or segment thereof.

location: Any place where any actor is located, and/or an event occurs, and/or a task takes place (for example, retail site, home office, and so on).

logic: See *formal logic.*

logical deduction: See *inference.*

logical expression: An expression that evaluates to a truth value. (In contrast, a *proposition* in formal logic is something that evaluates to either true or false, categorically.) For example, a logical expression might be formed by using the logical connectives OR and/or AND. Logical expressions are also known as *Boolean expressions, truth-valued expressions,* and *conditional expressions.*

logical implication: See *rule (formal logic).*

logical operator: A nonarithmetic operation that can be performed on truth-valued variables. The three basic operators are AND, OR, and NOT. All other logical operators can be expressed in terms of these three.

logical quantifier (predicate calculus): Taken to mean the fundamental tests EXISTS (the existential quantifier) and FORALL (the universal quantifier).

EXISTS provides a test for "at least one" or "there exists at least one." FORALL provides a test for "all" (or "for each" or "given any").

logicbase: A store that contains both a factbase and its associated rulebase. The current content of the logicbase comprehensively defines state for the targeted business or business capacity—or at least those parts of it that can be automated. A logicbase should be viewed as the authoritative and exclusive source of information describing the cumulative effect of business operations up to the current point in time.

logic trace: Support for auditing the results produced by a business logic server at any given point of operation. A logic trace makes it possible to work (or *trace*) backward from the result through the chain of rules (often inference rules) that produced it.

means: Any device used to achieve ends. In a Policy Charter, tactics and core business rules serve as means.

metadata: Data that defines other data.

mission: What the business or business capacity does directly, on a day-to-day basis, at the operational level. The business seeks to achieve its goals by performing the mission.

multiplicity: See *cardinality.*

objective: A specific target for a change effort. Objectives should always involve quantitative measures and end times. Objectives will be used to determine whether change efforts have satisfied their purpose.

operating rule: A declarative rule statement in well-structured business English (or another natural language), suitable for direct application to a business process and for consideration in a system design. An operating rule should be unambiguous and stated in a manner directly relevant to the internal workings of the business or business capacity. Operating rules may sometimes be derived or interpreted from governing rules or reverse-engineered from automated rules.

operational task: A task that does not involve making a significant choice between alternatives, or the creation of some new alternative(s), but rather aims at achieving a well-defined outcome whose desired form and desired content can both be predicted in advance (for example, register attendee for seminar, contact claimant for more information, report travel expenses, and so on).

optionality: A data model construct that refers to whether or not an instance of some relationship type is mandatory for a specific data object involved in that relationship type. If not, the relationship type is said to be *optional* for that data object.

organizational unit: Any body that exists internally to the business or business capacity (for example, department, team, and so on).

outcome (rule): A rule's definitive effect as expressed by one cell value in the array format of a decision table.

owner: The business-side persons(s), role(s), or organizational unit(s) who has (have) authority over setting the goals of the business or business capacity.

Pattern-R rule: An indivisible, two-part unit of business logic in the form of a rule (logical implication) of a known (Pattern-R) rule type. A Pattern-R rule has a higher level of expressive power that arises from a special "built-in" computation function, called the *yield-value function,* applied to an appropriate pattern of facts. Specification of a Pattern-R rule always includes a Pattern-R rule type, which effectively invokes the yield-value function desired for the indicated pattern.

Pattern-R rule type: The category of a rule based on the type of special computation a rule must perform. Commonplace examples of Pattern-R rule types include *mandatory, mutually exclusive, unique, cyclic, frozen, timed,* and so on. The type of a Pattern-R rule comprises both a logical function (that is, a truth-valued function) and a yield-value function (which is not truth-valued). The logical function produces a set of truth values that is based on evaluating the results of the yield-value function. This yield-value function is evaluated for each specific occurrence of a reference point (called the *anchor*) and the anchor's associated correspondents. The anchor and correspondent(s), collectively forming a pattern, can be terms, facts, and/or other Pattern-R rules, as appropriate for the given rule.

permission statement: A statement indicating the absence of any rule under a particular set of specified conditions. Such a statement indicates workers are not constrained by any rule in that situation and therefore may exercise judgment or discretion in taking relevant actions. For example, *Orders on credit for $1,000 or under may be accepted without a credit check.*

permission word: In RuleSpeak, a keyword (for example, *may* and *need not*) used to indicate that a statement represents a permission statement.

policy (Policy Charter): See *core business rule.*

Policy Charter: An architectural product that establishes the motivation for the core business rules of a business capacity. A Policy Charter identifies what tactics and core business rules are appropriate for achieving goals and other ends and what business risks are associated with them. The Policy Charter establishes an overall business approach or "battle plan" for a business process or problem, providing a basis for development of appropriate workflow models and other deliverables. The contents of the Policy Charter represent the business tactics.

predicate: A property, attribute, or mode of existence that a given subject may or may not possess.

predicate calculus: A general method or framework for reasoning about any subject matter whatsoever. Predicate calculus dates from the 1910s and 1920s and is basic for all subsequent logical research. It is a very general system of formal logic that accurately expresses a huge variety of assertions and modes of reasoning. [3]

premise (formal logic): In generalized reasoning about rules, the left-hand expression of a rule.

presentation rule: A copier (rule) that establishes a value or parameter related to how data is to be presented (for example, on a screen, in a report, and so on). For example, a presentation rule might be given to indicate that an order is to be displayed to the screen in red if the order is overdue.

procedural (specifications): Any specifications that are not declarative; that is, where a different sequence of presentation to the system can result in a different final state. An application program (that is, lines of code) written in a traditional programming language is usually procedural in this sense.

process (business): See *business process.*

process (business system): A capability for taking some input and transforming it into some desired output. A process operates according to an internal algorithm provided by its designer or programmer.

---

3. From Simpson, Stephen G. 2000. "Logic and Mathematics," pp. 2, 5. Available at *http://www.math.psu.edu/simpson/.*

process toggle (rule): An enabler (rule) that turns an action, process, or procedure on or off under appropriate circumstances, that is, makes it capable or incapable of executing. For example, a process toggle might be given to indicate that a sensitive process cannot be executed while a security breach is suspected.

process trigger (rule): A projector (rule) that causes an action, process, or procedure to execute. For example, when an order is shipped, a rule might be given to execute a process that automatically sends the intended recipient a notification.

producer (rule): Any rule that neither rejects nor projects events but rather simply computes or derives a value based on some mathematical function(s). Producers are categorized as either computation rules or derivation rules.

product: Something produced by human or mechanical effort or by a natural process that is deemed relevant to some marketplace.

product/service rule: A rule that addresses configuration, coordination, and/or constitution of a product or service of the business or business capacity.

product/service terminology model: An instance model for a particular product or service of the business or business capacity.

prohibited antecedent: A business milestone that an instance must never have achieved prior to the time that the instance achieves some other business milestone. Prohibited antecedents can be defined by means of a rule that thereby governs transition in state. For example, *A cancelled order must never have been shipped, invoiced, or terminated previously.*

project: A change effort requiring many resources and steps to accomplish but whose scope and purpose are sufficiently specific, and its duration short enough, such that the change effort can be well managed.

project manager: The person responsible for managing a project.

project objective: See *objective.*

project risk: A risk faced by a project in attempting to achieve its objectives, or a potential circumstance that may impact successful project completion.

projector (rule): Any rule that tends to take some action (other than rejection) when a relevant event occurs. A projector never rejects events (as rejectors do) but rather *projects* them—that is, causes some new event(s) to occur as a result. Projectors generally prescribe automatic system be-havior, providing a productivity boost for workers. For example, a pro-jector might be specified to reorder stock automatically if the quantity on hand drops below a certain point.

property (fact models): A description, characterization, or quantification es-tablished by a *has a* fact. For example, employee name could be specified as a property of employee using a *has a* fact.

proposition (formal logic): Something that evaluates to either true or false, unequivocally. For instance, "William Shakespeare wrote *Pride and Prej-udice*" is a proposition (a false one, as it happens).[4]

provisioning process: A process that provides essential business inputs (for ex-ample, product release information, customer information, and so on) for day-to-day operational processes. A provisioning process typically coordinates some resource of the business.

real-time compliance: The approach of applying business rules as early as possible in business processes, preferably at the original point where data is created, modified, or deleted, so that downstream error detection and resolution can be avoided.

real-world actor (workflow): An actor that has some physical manifestation. A real-world actor may include software but never is composed purely of software. Examples of an actor include person, role, organization, device (for example, robot, change dispenser), and so on.

reduction: The process of breaking down a rule into more granular form, possibly atomic.

reference data: The traditional name used in information technology for data typically produced by a provisioning process. Reference data often ap-pears in legacy systems as codes and/or in look-up tables. Typical kinds of reference data include product configurations, product families, cus-tomers, geographical areas, and so on.

reference source: Any existing material, normally textual, that provides the specific basis for a rule (for example, a law, regulation) or that provides background, context, or explanation (for example, memoranda, system

---

4. Example courtesy of Date, C. J. 2000. *An Introduction to Database Systems* (7th ed.). Boston, MA: Addison-Wesley, p. 13.

documentation). A reference source exists in published form (printed, electronic, and so on), and with proper authorization, may be reviewed to understand a rule more fully.

rejector (rule): Any rule that tends to disallow (reject) an event if a violation of the rule would result. Rejectors shield the business from inconsistent data (undesirable state). For example, a rejector might be specified to prevent a customer from placing an order on credit if the customer has a poor payment history. Rejectors are often called *integrity constraints* by IT professionals responsible for database systems.

resource: An available means, area of infrastructure, or logically organized set of constructs that is available to the business or business capacity to accomplish its mission and to achieve its goals (for example, personnel, customers, facilities, and so on).

RHE: See *right-hand expression.*

RHT: See *right-hand term.*

right-hand expression (formal logic): The complete logical expression on the right side of a rule expressed in the form $p \rightarrow q$.

right-hand term (formal logic): Any term on the right side of a rule expressed in the form $p \rightarrow q$.

risk: An exposure arising in some aspect of an endeavor undertaken by a business or business capacity that may prevent achievement of some desired end(s). Such exposure may arise either from inadequate internal support or from external factors beyond the control of the business or business capacity.

risk bracket (business tactics): A specific value or range of values established on the basis of quantitative measures (for example, specific amounts of money, a specific time frame) or other criteria (for example, category of customer) wherein a certain level of risk is perceived. A risk bracket should be addressed by a selective rule—often a core business rule.

R-Notation: A scheme based on conventional notation for rules in formal logic extended for certain special needs, particularly for representing facts and higher-order (Pattern-R) rules.

rule (business rule): An atomic piece of business logic, specified declaratively, whose intent is to control, guide, or enhance behavior. A rule may be established in order to ensure that one or more business goals are achieved, to enhance productivity in performing day-to-day work, to assist the business in making decisions, and/or to regulate or guide external activities. A rule is always based on one or more facts.

rule (formal logic): A logical expression of the form OR ((NOT p), q), where p (the premise) and q (the conclusion) must be Boolean expressions. Such a rule may also be expressed as IF p THEN q or as p → q, which can be read "p implies q." For example, it-is-raining implies streets-are-wet. In specific rules such as this example, the "p" (it-is-raining) is called the *antecedent,* and the "q" (streets-are-wet) is called the *consequent.* Rules in formal logic are also known as the *IF-THEN connective, implication connective,* or *logical implication.*

rulebase: A store that contains the business rules for a factbase. This store roughly contains metadata but with emphasis on rules and their current operational status and evaluation. These rules will have been specified in a declarative manner.

Rule Book: A compilation of business rules, preferably automated, that categorizes rules, records properties of the rules, and traces relevant links. These links may be to other rules, to information about other aspects of the business, and/or to the implementation environment supporting the rules. An automated Rule Book provides the foundation for rule management.

rule engine: See *business logic server.*

Rule Independence: The principle of specifying and managing rules apart from processes, procedures, or applications such that business logic can be accessed, analyzed, and changed directly.

rule management: The use of expertise, techniques, and tools aimed toward providing business workers and/or business analysts with the ability to manage and access business logic directly.

rule mining: Reverse-engineering the program code of legacy systems to recover the embedded business rules.

rule-processing server: See *business logic server.*

rule sentence template: A basic sentence structure or pattern in RuleSpeak for expressing a rule in a consistent, well-organized rule statement.

RuleSpeak: See *BRS RuleSpeak.*

rule statement: An assertion of a rule, usually in the form of a sentence.

rule toggle (rule): An enabler (rule) that turns another rule on or off under appropriate circumstances, that is, makes the rule capable or incapable of firing. For example, a rule toggle might be given to indicate that some normal operating rule is to be suspended under emergency circumstances. Rule toggles that turn other rules off are called *exception-type rules.*

rule trigger (rule): A projector (rule) that causes a rule to fire. For example, when data about a shipment is displayed to the screen, a rule might be given that fires another rule to predict the shipment's arrival date.

rule type: The name for a specific kind of rule based on the nature of the test it performs (for example, mandatory, mutually exclusive, mutually inclusive, mutually prohibited, unique, ascending, descending, frozen, and so on). See also *Pattern-R rule type.*

rule word: In RuleSpeak, a keyword (that is, *must, should, only*) used to indicate that a statement represents a rule.

scope: The extent of business operations to be considered by a project. See also *universe of discourse.*

script (work): A procedure with no embedded rules, consisting of a prescribed series of requests for action that workers can follow to perform work.

semantic equivalence: A circumstance in which a set of two or more rule statements, each expressed differently, are recognized to have the exact same effect as each of the others. Semantic equivalence often occurs when subjects are reversed. For example, the rule *An auditor must not audit any manager in the same city* is semantically equivalent to *A manager must not be audited by any auditor in the same city.*

service: Work done for others as an occupation or a business.

session (work): One execution of a script.

sign-off document: A deliverable that requires explicit, formal approval ("sign-off") by a project sponsor, project manager, or other project person with oversight responsibility. A sign-off document is often compiled specifically for that purpose.

single-sourcing: Originating all copies from a single source.

software actor (workflow): A logical grouping of software that appears as a discrete unit. A software actor has well-defined interfaces that can be requested to perform known services. By this means, a software actor (for example, component, Web site, inference engine, legacy system, and so on) can participate intelligently in work.

sponsor: The person responsible for providing the highest-level business view for a project, including strategic business opportunities and challenges. The sponsor is responsible for clarifying the business goals and for giving ongoing approval as to whether the project is on target with respect to supporting these goals. The sponsor also controls scope.

state: The condition in which a complex system, or any part thereof, finds itself at any given point in time.

subject (predicate): A term representing a concept about which something is affirmed or denied.

subject (rule): The first term (or fact) included in a rule statement, indicating what the rule is about.

subsetting scheme: See *categorization scheme*.

subsumation: In a set of two (or more) rules, the situation where either of the following conditions hold: (a) One rule covers a set of circumstances that represents a strict subset of the set of circumstances covered by the other(s), or (b) one rule covers the exact same set of circumstances as the other rule(s) but in a less restrictive manner. In either case, the former rule is said to be *subsumed* by the latter rule(s), the implication being that the former rule is not really necessary. For example, the rule *A rush order must have a destination* is subsumed by the rule *An order must have a destination.*

subsumption: See *subsumation*.

suggestor: A rule that fires and can detect a "violation" but takes no enforcement action. A suggestor might simply send a message reporting any violation to a worker's screen, providing guidance about a preferred course of action or outcome.

suspense criteria: The interval of time that an instance is allowed to remain in some business milestone without achieving some other business milestone. Suspense criteria are often expressed by use of a rule, which indicates what to do when the given interval of time is exceeded. For example, *An expeditor must be assigned to an order that has been shipped but not invoiced for more than a week.*

tacit knowledge: See *tacit rule*.

tacit rule: A business rule that is not formally recorded and/or encoded in a form that can be readily understood by business analysts. In contrast to explicit rules, if the person/people who know and understand a tacit rule are lost to the business, then the business rule itself is effectively lost too.

tactic: A course of action the business or business capacity might adopt to support the mission, to achieve goals, or to address risks. A tactic indicates that some capability (or a particular characteristic or feature of a capability) will provide a means to achieve the desired end(s).

task: A specific type of work or value-adding activity that must be performed, normally in response to some event, as viewed from a business perspective. A task involves one or more of the following: an activity, an approach for making a decision or producing some desired result, and/or an organized collaboration between actors. A task represents a transformation at the business level that accepts materials and/or information in one state (the "input") and aims toward producing one or more desired results and/or materials in a new state (the "output"). The performance of a task is guided by rules. Examples of tasks include receive order, adjudicate claim, and so on.

template (rule statement): See *rule sentence template.*

term (business rules): A word or expression that has a precisely limited meaning in some uses or is peculiar to a science, art, profession, trade, or special subject. Terms are used in fact statements and rule statements to refer to some concept of the business or business capacity or of the context in which the business or business capacity operates. These concepts may be about people, places, things, and so on.

term (predicate logic): A name given to one of the following: (1) An individual thing. The thing so named might be a particular person, place, item, concept, and so on, for example, Mary, Memphis, gold, true, and so on. (2) A variable capable of holding a value. For example, variables defined to hold the values above might be named person, city, metal, and of-age, respectively. (3) A function capable of producing a value.

terminator: See *terminologist.*

terminologist: A specialist in defining, coordinating, and applying terms and definitions for the business or business capacity; that is, in developing its business vocabulary.

thin process: A process or procedure that only prescribes the necessary series of steps to accomplish the desired work result and that excludes rules and all the error handling when violations of rules occur.

time shock. Disorientation and loss of productivity as workers are constantly thrust into new roles and responsibilities due to the accelerating rate of change.

time word: In RuleSpeak, a keyword (for example, *before, on or before, during, by, after*) used to indicate a temporal qualification for a rule.

to-be data model: A data model developed to support a reengineered or revised view of the business or business capacity.

to-be workflow model: A workflow model that specifies a reengineered or revised view of a workflow.

toggle (rule): See *enabler (rule)*.

traceability: The ability to explore relationships between rules, especially interpretations from governing rules to operating rules to automated rules, as well as the reverse.

trigger (rule): See *executive (rule)*.

truth value: A value of either true or false.

truth-valued expression: See *logical expression*.

truth-valued variable: A variable capable of holding a Boolean, that is, a variable of type Boolean. Truth-valued variables are also known as *Boolean variables*.

type code: A special kind of attribute in a data model for distinguishing the type of instances (for example, F = female, M = male).

universal AND: An assumption in rule theory that since all rules must be satisfied, an implicit AND must therefore be considered to exist for all rules within the universe of discourse.

universal quantifier (predicate calculus): FORALL.

universe of discourse: The complete set of ideas (that is, all basic knowledge) to be entertained by a business rule system, as evidenced by terms, facts, and rules (business rules). See also *scope*.

UoD: See *universe of discourse*.

update event: An event in a business system involving the creation, modification, or deletion of data.

vision: Something the business aspires to. A vision always expresses something the business would like to be or achieve.

work: The actual collaborations between actors that occur in the business in response to some event. Work always results when actors follow a workflow model or script. Business rules provide the basic knowledge (via terms and facts) and guidance (via rules) for performing work. Work changes the state of the business and therefore the state of its knowledge.

worker: Any staff member involved in managing or operating the business or business capacity.

workflow: The sequence in which work is conducted. Workflow can be prescribed by use of a workflow model or script and managed by means of a workflow engine.

workflow engine: Runtime system software that manages workflows and/or scripts.

workflow model: An architectural product that depicts a series of organized collaborations between actors involving two or more tasks in response to some initiating event. A workflow model indicates how the end results appropriate from a business perspective are to be achieved.

work product: Anything produced under an organizational relationship between actors.

work session: See *session (work)*.

yield value (Pattern-R rules): The result computed by the yield-value function associated with a Pattern-R rule type for a Pattern-R rule applied to a given set of facts.

yield-value function (Pattern-R rules): The computation function associated with a Pattern-R rule type.

Bibliography

Appleton, Daniel S. 1984. "Business Rules: The Missing Link." *Datamation,* October 15, pp. 145–150.

Burlton, Roger T. 2001. *Business Process Management: Profiting from Success.* Indianapolis, IN: Sams Publishing.

Business Rules Group (Ronald G. Ross and Keri Anderson Healy, eds.). 2000. "Organizing Business Strategy: The Standard Model for Business Rule Motivation." Version 1, November 2000. Available at *http://www. BusinessRulesGroup.org.*

Charniak, Eugene, and Drew McDermott. 1985. *Introduction to Artificial Intelligence.* Reading, MA: Addison-Wesley.

Chisholm, Malcolm. 2001. *Managing Reference Data in Enterprise Databases.* San Francisco, CA: Morgan Kaufmann.

Crevier, Daniel. 1993. *AI: The Tumultuous History of the Search for Artificial Intelligence.* New York: BasicBooks.

Date, C. J. 2001. "Constraints and Predicates: A Brief Tutorial (Parts 1, 2, and 3)." *Business Rules Journal,* July, September, and December (respectively). Available in November 2002 at *http://www.BRCommunity.com/a2001/b065b.html.*

————. 2000. *An Introduction to Database Systems* (7th ed.). Boston, MA: Addison-Wesley.

————. 2000. *What Not How: The Business Rule Approach to Application Development.* Boston, MA: Addison-Wesley.

Date, C. J., and Hugh Darwen. 2000. *Foundation for Future Database Systems: The Third Manifesto* (2nd ed.). Boston, MA: Addison-Wesley.

Elmasri, Ramez, and Shamkant B. Navathe. 1994. *Fundamentals of Database Systems* (2nd ed.). Redwood City, CA: Benjamin/Cummings.

GUIDE Business Rules Project Report. 1995. Third edition available in November 2002 as "Defining Business Rules—What Are They Really?", edited by David C. Hay and Keri Anderson Healy, Business Rules Group, July 2000, at *http://www.BusinessRulesGroup.org.*

Halpin, Terry. 2001. *Information Modeling and Relational Databases.* San Francisco, CA: Morgan Kaufmann.

Halpin, Terry, and Roderic Girle. 1981. Deductive Logic (2nd ed.). Brisbane, Australia: Logiqpress.

Hofstadter, Douglas R. 1980. *Godel, Escher and Bach: An Eternal Golden Braid.* New York: Vintage Books.

Lam, Gladys S. W. 1998. "Business Knowledge—Packaged in a Policy Charter." *DataToKnowledge Newsletter* (formerly *Data Base Newsletter*), May/June. Available at *http://www.BRCommunity.com.*

Morgan, Tony. 2002. *Business Rules and Information Systems.* Boston, MA: Addison-Wesley.

Nilsson, Nils J. 1998. *Artificial Intelligence: A New Synthesis.* San Francisco, CA: Morgan Kaufmann.

Ross, Ronald G. 1997. *The Business Rule Book* (2nd ed.). Houston, TX: Business Rule Solutions, LLC. Available at *http://www.BRSolutions.com.*

———. 1994. *The Business Rule Book* (1st ed.). Boston, MA: Database Research Group.

———. 1987. *Entity Modeling: Techniques and Application.* Boston, MA: Database Research Group.

———. 1978. *Data Base Systems: Design, Implementation and Management.* New York: AMACOM.

Ross, Ronald G., and Gladys S. W. Lam. 2000. *The BRS Core Business Rule Practitioner's Guide: Using Business Rules in Developing Business Strategy.* Houston, TX: Business Rule Solutions, LLC. Available at *http://www.BRSolutions.com.*

———. 2000. *The BRS Fact Modeling Practitioner's Guide: Developing the Business Basis for Data Models.* Houston, TX: Business Rule Solutions, LLC. Available at *http://www.BRSolutions.com.*

———. 2000. *Capturing Business Rules.* Workbook for public seminar, presented in Boston, MA, June 19–21.

Seer, Kristen. 2002. "How to Develop Effective Business Analysts," Parts 1, 2, and 3. *Business Rules Journal*, May, July, and September (respectively). Available at *http://www.BRCommunity.com*.

Simpson, Stephen G. 2000. "Logic and Mathematics." Available in November 2002 at *http://www.math.psu.edu/simpson/*.

Tarski, Alfred. 1995. *Introduction to Logic and to the Methodology of Deductive Sciences* (2nd ed.). New York: Dover Publications. (Originally published in 1946 by Oxford University Press, New York.)

von Halle, Barbara. 2002. *Business Rules Applied: Building Better Systems Using the Business Rule Approach*. New York: Wiley Computer Publishing.

Widom, Jennifer, and Stefano Ceri (eds). 1996. *Active Database Systems: Triggers and Rules for Advanced Database Procession*. San Francisco, CA: Morgan Kaufmann.

Zachman, John A. 2002. *The Zachman Framework: A Primer for Enterprise Engineering and Manufacturing* (electronic book). Available at *http://www.zachmaninternational.com*.

Index

Note: Page numbers followed by *f, t,* and *n* represent figures, tables, and notes, respectively.